Why Mission?

To Rick & Cindy,
dear friends.

Dean Flem

June 2?, 2017

Reframing New Testament Theology
Edited by Joel B. Green

Why Mission?

DEAN FLEMMING

Abingdon Press

Nashville

WHY MISSION?

Copyright © 2015 by Abingdon Press

All rights reserved.

This book is printed on acid-free paper.

Library of Congress Cataloging-in-Publication Data

Flemming, Dean E., 1953-
    Why mission? / Dean Flemming; edited by Joel B. Green.—First [edition].
        pages cm.—(Reframing New Testament theology; 4)
        Includes bibliographical references and index.
        ISBN 978-1-4267-5936-9 (binding : soft back) 1. Bible. New Testament—Criticism, interpretation, etc. 2. Mission of the church. 3. Missions—Theory. I. Green, Joel B., 1956- editor.
II. Title.
        BS2361.3.F54 2015
        266—dc23
                                                                                    2015027716

15 16 17 18 19 20 21 22 23 24—10 9 8 7 6 5 4 3 2 1
MANUFACTURED IN THE UNITED STATES OF AMERICA

In grateful memory of my father, Floyd O. Flemming (1926–2014)

Contents

Foreword

At first glance, the phrase "New Testament theology" seems clear enough. However, attempts to explain it immediately expose some speed bumps. Do we want to describe the theology we find in the New Testament? Construct a theology on a New Testament foundation? Or perhaps sketch an account of early Christian beliefs and practices from the New Testament era? This series of books frames the question in a different way: How do we take seriously that, together with the Old Testament, the New Testament has in the past and ought in the present inform, form, and transform the church's faith and life?

Almost everyone will agree that the New Testament books concern themselves with *theology*. This truism is supported on almost every page as New Testament writers speak of God, the significance of Jesus of Nazareth for God's agenda for the world, the character of God's people, faithful life before God, and God's coming to set the world right.

How does the New Testament witness relate to the church's life today? This is less clear and therefore more controversial. The church affirms its allegiance to the God of whom scripture speaks and, therefore, ties itself, its faith and witness, to the Old and New Testaments. How the church's affirmations work themselves out in terms of engagement with the New Testament materials—this is the question.

Reframing New Testament Theology gets at this question by encouraging active, theological engagement with the New Testament itself. Readers will find among the books in this series an awareness of the obstacles we face—obstacles like the following:

- New Testament texts were written in another time and another place. In what sense, then, can we say that they were written *to* us or *for* us? After all, those first readers of Matthew's Gospel or the Letter of James would be dumbstruck by the idea of streaming video in a church service, just as most of us lack any firsthand experience with anything analogous to the challenges of peasant farmers and fisherfolk in ancient Galilee.

- What of the sheer variety of voices we hear among the New Testament books? If we want the New Testament to help orient our thinking about mission or salvation, how do we make sense of the different perspectives we sometimes encounter? Do we accord privilege to some voices over others? Do we try to synthesize various viewpoints?

- New Testament writers raise issues that may seem foreign to us today and overlook some of our contemporary concerns. Our educational systems, political structures, immigration policies, knowledge of the universe, modes of transportation, and the countless other day-to-day realities that we take for granted separate us from the equally countless assumptions, beliefs, and behaviors that characterized people living in the ancient Mediterranean world. Faced with these differences, how do we work with scripture?

Additionally, our readers will find an awareness of a range of questions about how best to think about "New Testament theology"—questions like these:

- Since the "new" in "New Testament" presumes an "Old Testament," what status should our New Testament theological explorations assign to the Old Testament? How do we understand the theological witness of the New Testament in relation to the Old?

- Are we concerned primarily with what the New Testament writers *taught* (past tense) their first readers theologically, or do we want to know what the New Testament *teaches* (present tense) us? Is "New Testament theology" a descriptive task or a prescriptive one?

- Do we learn from the New Testament writers the "stuff" of Christian theology, or do we apprentice ourselves to them so that we might learn how to engage in the theological task ourselves? Does the New

Testament provide the raw material for contemporary theology, or does it invite us into ongoing reflection with it about God and God's ways?

If contributions to this series demonstrate an awareness of obstacles and issues like these, this does not mean that they address them in a uniform manner. Nor are these books concerned primarily with showing how to navigate or resolve conundrums like these. What holds this series together is not a particular set of methodological commitments but a keen sense that scripture has in the past and should in the present instruct and shape the church's faith and life. What does it mean to engage the New Testament from within the church and for the church?

One further consideration: The church turns to the scriptures believing that the Bible is authoritative for what we believe and what we do, but it does so while recognizing that the church's theology is shaped in other ways, too—by God's self-disclosure in God's "book of nature," for example—and in relation to the ecumenical creeds with which the church has identified itself: the Apostles' Creed, the Nicene Creed, and the Athanasian Creed. Not surprisingly, New Testament "theology" invites reflecting on, interacting with, learning from, and sometimes struggling with the scriptures, and doing so in relation to human understanding more generally as well as in the context of our common Christian confessions.

Intended for people interested in studying the New Testament and the nature of the Christian message and the Christian life, for classrooms, group interaction, and personal study, these volumes invite readers into a conversation with New Testament theology.

Joel B. Green
General Editor

Acknowledgments

Book writing is never a solitary process, and many individuals have helped make this book possible. Special appreciation goes to Joel B. Green, editor of this series, for giving me the opportunity to reflect on what a missional reading of the New Testament might entail and for his sound guidance along the way. I am also grateful to a number of faithful friends who read and commented on portions of the manuscript, including Tim Isbell, Andy Johnson, Jason Veach, and Lynn Nichols. In particular, I am indebted to Michael Gorman and Steven Merki for carefully reading an earlier version of this book. I deeply appreciate their encouragement and valuable insights. Furthermore, I want to thank Kathy Armistead and David Teel of Abingdon Press for their capable help and direction in this project.

I am thankful, as well, for the support of my colleagues at MidAmerica Nazarene University during the writing of this book. Special mention goes to my teaching assistant, Michael Reynolds, for his many hours of research and editorial support.

I also want to express my appreciation to the following journals and editors: the *Journal of Theological Interpretation* (*JTI*) and editor Joel Green for permission to publish a revised version of the Revelation chapter, which originally appeared in the Fall 2012 issue of *JTI*; and the *Wesleyan Theological Journal* (*WTJ*) and editor Jason Vickers for permission to include in the 1 Peter chapter a revised form of an article that originally appeared in the Spring 2014 issue of *WTJ*. In addition, I want to thank *Evangelical Quarterly* (*EQ*) and Paternoster Periodicals for permission to use revised material from the article, "Exploring a Missional Reading of Scripture: Philippians as a Case Study," which was originally published in the January 2011 issue of *EQ*, in the introduction and the chapter on Philippians.

Finally, I am deeply grateful to my father, Dr. Floyd O. Flemming, for his consistent encouragement throughout the years of my teaching and writing. He read some of the chapters of this book. However, afflicted with cancer in 2014, he did not live to see its completion. Throughout my life, he served as my mentor and example. This book is gratefully dedicated to his memory and his joyful participation in the mission of God.

Introduction

The New Testament and the Mission of God

T his book is about reading the New Testament in light of the mission of God. We will explore what that might look like, shortly. But first, we need to consider a prior question. What is the relationship between *the Bible* and *mission* in the first place? Like many relationships, this one has often been strained.

The problem is rooted in how we *read* the Bible. Biblical interpreters—particularly Bible scholars—sometimes try to read biblical texts in a dispassionate way. They set their sights on what the Bible *meant* in its original context. Often, they emphasize the historical conditioning of the text and the great gap between the world of the Bible and the world in which we live. As a result, they don't give much thought to "mission," which seems to concern the practical ministry of the church today.

At the same time, Christians engaged in the missionary enterprise of the church often approach scripture in search of a "biblical foundation for mission." David J. Bosch observes that many sincere Christians turn to the Bible in order to mine "missionary texts," which support the kinds of mission activities they are already engaged in.[1] I recall hearing certain favorite texts preached again and again at the missionary conferences I attended growing

1. David J. Bosch, "Reflections on Biblical Models of Mission," in *Toward the Twenty-First Century in Christians Mission: Essays in Honor of Gerald H. Anderson,* ed. James M. Phillips and Robert T. Coote (Grand Rapids: Eerdmans, 1993), 175–76.

up: "Go and make disciples of all nations" (Matt 28:19); "You will be my witnesses... to the end of the earth" (Acts 1:8); "How can they hear without a preacher?" (Rom 10:14); "Here am I. Send me!" (Isa 6:8 NIV). Such appeals to scripture sought to undergird a mission that was primarily about *going* across a body of salt water—from the West to the rest of the world. The goal was to win converts and plant churches among unevangelized peoples. I do not intend in the least to disparage such missionary efforts. I am simply describing a way of using the Bible in order to provide a basis for a specific understanding of what the "missionary work" of the church entails.

Neither of these approaches does justice to the connection between the Bible and mission. The former fails to take that relationship seriously enough, acting as if "the Bible" and "mission" live in parallel worlds. The latter shrinks the Bible's interest in mission to a limited number of texts and a particular view of mission. But in recent decades, a more promising way of relating mission and the Bible has begun to emerge. It seeks to engage in an intentional, self-involved, *missional* reading of scripture as a whole. Several factors have coalesced to spark this fresh interest in missional interpretation.[2]

First, there has been a growing recognition that "mission" involves more than simply the church's cross-cultural missionary activity; it is anchored in the comprehensive mission of God.

Second, biblical interpretation has seen a substantial movement away from detached, purely historical readings of the Bible in favor of strategies that are more open to the missional dimensions of scripture. A prime example is *theological interpretation*—an approach that brings scripture and theology into conversation, with the goal of shaping Christian communities in their love for God and others.[3] Indeed missional readings of scripture can be viewed as a form of theological interpretation, or perhaps an extension of it.[4]

Third, the center of gravity in global Christianity has experienced a seismic shift from the North and West to the South and East.[5] As a result, Western theologians and biblical scholars increasingly are discovering conversation partners in the majority world.[6] Bible interpreters in the majority world tend

---

2. See Michael W. Goheen, "Continuing Steps Towards a Missional Hermeneutic," *Fideles* 3 (2008): 57–61. The following paragraphs rely on material adapted from Dean Flemming, "Exploring a Missional Reading of Scripture: Philippians as a Case Study," *Evangelical Quarterly* 83 (2011): 3–9.

3. See, e.g., Joel B. Green, *Practicing Theological Interpretation: Engaging Biblical Texts for Faith and Formation* (Grand Rapids: Baker, 2012), and the *Journal of Theological Interpretation*, which Green edits.

4. Michael J. Gorman, *Becoming the Gospel: Paul, Participation, and Mission* (Grand Rapids: Eerdmans, 2015), 51.

5. See Philip Jenkins, *The Next Christendom: The Coming of Global Christianity* (Oxford: Oxford University Press, 2002).

6. See, e.g., Craig Ott and Harold A. Netland, eds., *Globalizing Theology: Belief and Practice in an*

be more sensitive to the missional dimensions of scripture and their implications for the church. Listening to their voices may help expose some of the blind spots of Western biblical scholarship regarding missional concerns.

Fourth, biblical scholars, missiologists, and church leaders have begun to seriously reflect on a missional reading of scripture. For example, the Gospel and Our Culture Network in North America has sponsored a series of annual meetings on the meaning and implications of missional *hermeneutics* (how we interpret scripture) for over a decade.[7] Along with that, a variety of influential writings have emerged, which argue for the importance of reading the whole of scripture in view of the mission of God.[8]

This book attempts to dive into the stream of this fresh, missiological reading of scripture. I am grateful for the work that has been done and want to build upon it. At the same time, I hope to extend the conversation by taking seriously the contributions of diverse New Testament voices to the church's understanding of mission. As far as I know, no other study engages in a missional reading of a range of New Testament books within one volume. The reflections that follow, then, seek to apply a missional hermeneutic to a variety of representative New Testament texts.

What Is a Missional Reading of the New Testament?

What does a "missional reading" of scripture look like? To answer that question, I first need to clarify some terms.[9] I use the word *missional*, not in

Era of World Christianity (Grand Rapids: Baker, 2006); Timothy C. Tennent, *Theology in the Context of World Christianity: How the Global Church Is Influencing How We Think About and Discuss Theology* (Grand Rapids: Zondervan, 2007).

7. See the Gospel and Our Culture Network website for resources connected with these meetings, which began in 2002 (http://www.gocn.org). Since 2005, a Forum on Missional Hermeneutics has met annually at the same time as the Society of Biblical Literature. In addition, a noteworthy conference on "A Missional Reading of Scripture" convened at Calvin Seminary, Grand Rapids, in November 2013 (http://www.calvinseminary.edu/ministry-connections/media-archive/missional-reading-of-scripture/).

8. See, especially, David J. Bosch, *Transforming Mission: Paradigm Shifts in Theology of Mission* (Maryknoll, NY: Orbis, 1991); Richard Bauckham, *The Bible and Mission: Christian Witness in a Postmodern World* (Grand Rapids: Baker, 2003); Christopher J. H. Wright, *The Mission of God: Unlocking the Bible's Grand Narrative* (Downers Grove, IL: IVP Academic, 2006); Michael W. Goheen, *A Light to the Nations: The Missional Church and the Biblical Story* (Grand Rapids: Baker Academic, 2011); Gorman, *Becoming the Gospel.*

9. Since words derive their meaning from the larger context in which they are used, precise "definitions" are not always helpful. See the comments of C. Kavin Rowe, *World Upside Down: Reading Acts in the Graeco-Roman Age* (Oxford: Oxford University Press, 2009), 12–13. Nevertheless, because of the variety of ways that some key terms are used, I need to explain what I generally mean when I use them.

a narrow, technical sense (e.g., the "missional church"), but simply as an adjective denoting something having to do with or participating in the mission of God.[10] And *mission*, from a broad perspective, is anchored in God's sweeping project to bring about salvation in every dimension. This includes God's purpose to redeem all human beings and to restore the whole of creation, as well as all that God has called and sent the church to do in connection with his mission. This understanding stands in contrast to narrower notions of mission, which primarily focus on the cross-cultural missionary activity of the church. That is *part* of mission, but not the *whole* of mission. Rather, the mission of God's people is no less than a participation in the mission of the triune God (the *missio Dei*), a mission that is as wide as creation itself. *Missional interpretation*, then, tries to read scripture in light of God's comprehensive mission.

But can we be more specific regarding how to go about that? Although there has been a good deal of interest of late in a missional reading of scripture, there's still no consensus about what this entails. George R. Hunsberger helpfully maps four different "streams" or understandings of a missional hermeneutic, which arose out of a series of meetings sponsored by the Gospel and Our Culture Network.[11] Each represents a somewhat different emphasis. Stream one spotlights the missional direction of the biblical narrative, which tells the story of God's mission and the people who are sent to participate in God's mission. The second stream accents the missional *purpose* of scripture—how the biblical writings equip and energize God's people to engage in the mission of God.[12] The focus of these two streams lies on the message and function of the biblical text.

In contrast, the latter two streams place more weight on the reader and the context. Accordingly, the third stream highlights the missional location of the Christian communities that are reading scripture and the questions they bring to the text.[13] And the final stream features the missional engagement with different cultures and social contexts; the canonical biblical tradition must critically engage our various human contexts in light of the Christ-

---

10. Wright, *Mission of God*, 24. Wright argues convincingly that the term *missional* is more appropriate language for a reading of the whole of scripture than the terms *missionary* or *missiological*, which tend to have a narrower focus (23–25).

11. George R. Hunsberger, "Proposals for a Missional Hermeneutic: Mapping the Conversation," *Missiology* 39 (2011): 309–21.

12. See Darrell L. Guder, "Missional Hermeneutics: The Missional Authority of Scripture—Interpreting Scripture as Missional Formation," *Mission Focus: Annual Review* 15 (2007): 106–24.

13. See Michael Barram, "The Bible, Mission, and Social Location: Toward a Missional Hermeneutic," *Interpretation* 61 (2007): 58.

centered gospel.[14] All four of these streams are relevant to missional inter-pretation, and they frequently overlap. Nevertheless, the primary focus of this book, as the series intends, lies with the witness of the biblical text itself (streams one and two), rather than with how that message is contextualized in specific situations. Indeed, the first two streams seem to be foundational to a mission reading of scripture. Perhaps we can speak of two essential dimensions of a missional hermeneutic. One has to do with what the Bible is *about*. The other concerns what the Bible *does*. The former sees the Bible as a *witness*, the latter as an *instrument*. What do these two claims mean with respect to the New Testament?

The New Testament as a Witness to God's Mission

In the first place, missional interpretation consciously reads scripture as a *witness* to the gracious mission of the triune God, that is, the *missio Dei*. As Christopher Wright puts it, a missional hermeneutic "proceeds from the assumption that the whole Bible renders to us the story of God's mission through God's people in their engagement with God's world for the sake of the whole of God's creation."[15] In other words, a missional reading of the Bible "works" because the mission of God is more than simply one biblical theme standing alongside others (e.g., justification, sanctification, the church). "Mission," in its comprehensive sense, is central to the entire biblical story.[16]

Put simply, the God who created all things is on a mission to redeem and reclaim a rebellious and sinful world—to set right a world that has gone wrong and ultimately to restore all of creation. To that end, God calls the people of Abraham to be an instrument of blessing for all the peoples of the earth. God's mission through Israel climaxes when God the Father sends the Son into the world, in the power of the Holy Spirit, to bring about God's salvation at every level. What's more, the church, the saved and sent community, is caught up in and defined by this loving mission of God. God's restoring purpose for his creation, then, offers a coherent framework for the story scripture tells. Instead of talking about "biblical basis for mission," Wright argues, we ought to think in terms of a "missional basis of the Bible."[17]

14. See James V. Brownson, *Speaking the Truth in Love: New Testament Resources for a Missional Hermeneutic* (Harrisburg, PA: Trinity Press International, 1998), 78–82.

15. Wright, *Mission of God*, 51 (italics deleted).

16. Richard Bauckham, "Mission as Hermeneutic for Scriptural Interpretation," (lecture, Cambridge), 1, http://richardbauckham.co.uk/uploads/Accessible/Mission%20as%20Hermeneutic.pdf.

17. Wright, *Mission of God*, 29, 62.

This book affirms that we read scripture—in our case, the New Testament—more faithfully if we read it with our ears attuned to the music of God's mission. That doesn't mean that a missional hermeneutic will explain *everything* we need to know about scripture. Nor is a missional reading exclusive of other ways of approaching biblical texts. For example, we can talk about a *christological* reading that sees Christ as an interpretive key for our understanding of both Testaments.[18] Yet the work of Christ has meaning precisely within the context of the all-encompassing mission of God to reconcile all people and ultimately all things through him.[19]

Recognizing that scripture as a whole bears witness to God's mission enables us to listen with more sensitivity for how individual books or passages may evidence that framework. Wright shows convincingly how such an interpretive perspective works in relation to the Old Testament.[20] When we consider the New Testament—the focus of this study—a missional emphasis is even clearer. Reflecting on the overarching focus of the New Testament writings, I. Howard Marshall concludes, "New Testament theology is essentially missionary theology."[21] He goes on to clarify that the New Testament documents came into being precisely as a result of the kingdom mission of Jesus and the mission of his followers to call people to faith and continued commitment to Jesus Christ. The ancient authors themselves were engaged in God's mission. They carried out their missional calling in the writing of these materials.[22] The New Testament writings are therefore the *product* of the early Christian mission and express the concerns of that mission. From Matthew to Revelation, they bear witness to God's purpose to redeem and restore all things in Christ. Mission is woven into the very fabric of the New Testament.

The New Testament as an Instrument of God's Mission

Second, a missional reading of the New Testament is not only concerned with what scripture *says*, but also what it *does* in the life of God's people. In other words, scripture not only tells the story of God's loving mission. It also

---

18. Ibid., 30–31.

19. As George Hunsberger recognizes, there is a certain circularity to this way of approaching a missional hermeneutic, which must be acknowledged: "From the scriptures is discerned the core narrative that becomes the key or clue for understanding the scriptures" ("Proposals for a Missional Hermeneutic," 312).

20. Wright, *Mission of God.*

21. I. Howard Marshall, *New Testament Theology: Many Witnesses, One Gospel* (Downers Grove, IL: IVP Academic, 2004), 34.

22. Ibid., 34–35.

plays an active role in accomplishing the ongoing purpose of God.[23] From the beginning, the New Testament writings addressed Christian communities that were engaged in God's mission. The Gospels, letters, and other New Testament writings unpacked the apostolic gospel and its significance for missional communities. These texts intentionally formed and energized God's people so that they might faithfully share in the divine mission throughout the Mediterranean world. Biblical texts, then, don't have to focus on evangelizing unbelievers (e.g., Paul's missionary preaching in Acts) in order to reflect God's mission. Christian nurture and formation are also missional, not least because they enable and equip Christian communities to engage in the restoring mission of God.

But can we be content with *simply* discovering how, say, Matthew or Paul wanted the first-century Christian communities to which they wrote to engage in God's mission? After all, *we* read scripture as missional communities, as well. To read the church's scripture *missionally* cannot remain a detached, purely descriptive reading. Scripture continues to call us into fellowship with God, as active participants in the mission of God.[24] Reading the scriptures in that light will help us to understand their present role in the life of the church. We must continually ask, "How do these texts form and renew a missional people for participation in the ongoing story of God's mission in the world? How do they shape Christian communities today to embody the gospel in their local settings?"

Critical Questions

To summarize, our two primary concerns in this book rest with the following: (1) how the various New Testament writings bear witness to God's mission; and (2) how those writings call and equip Christian communities to participate in that mission. This second issue involves both how the text shaped missional communities in the first century, as well as how it continues to do so today. And although the issue of what it looks like for contemporary Christian communities to embody God's mission will remain largely implicit in the course of this book, it will never drift far from view.

With these aims in mind, a missional reading of scripture will lead us to ask certain questions of New Testament texts. These include the following:[25]

23. Goheen, "Continuing Steps," 90.

24. J. Ross Wagner, "*Missio Dei*: Envisioning an Apostolic Reading of Scripture," *Missiology* 37 (2009): 24.

25. This list is adapted from series of questions stated in Gorman, *Becoming the Gospel*, 56; and Christopher J. H. Wright, "Reading the Old Testament Missionally," in *A Missional Reading of Scripture:*

- What do these texts contribute to our understanding of the missional character of God and God's missional purpose for world?

- How do these texts relate to the whole biblical story of God's mission, as witnessed in both Testaments? How are these texts affected by the wider story? What distinctive contributions do they make to that story?

- What do these texts tell us about the character and mission of God's people, specifically about the church as the agent of God's mission in the world?

- What do these texts contribute to our understanding of the good news of Jesus Christ, and how God's people proclaim, enact, and embody the gospel? How do these texts reflect the contextualization of the gospel in their biblical setting, and how do they inform our practice of contextualizing the gospel today?

- How do these texts function as an instrument of God's mission in the world? How do they invite God's people to participate in the *missio Dei*, both in the first century and the twenty-first century?

- What questions do these texts ask of us as readers regarding our missional engagement in the world? How do they critique and correct us within our specific ecclesial and social contexts?

This is not an exhaustive list, but such questions will inform the missional reading of New Testament texts in this book. Perhaps all of these issues point back to two foundational questions: "What is God up to in the world?" and "What is the church's role in what God is doing?"

The Journey before Us

It's one thing to discuss missional interpretation in theory. It's quite another to actually *engage* in such a reading. An attempt to read the entire New Testament missionally would run well beyond the size and scope of this series. Instead, I will focus on representative writings in the New Testament. In each case, I will ask our two key questions: How does this New Testament book

Hermeneutics, Preaching, and Theological Education, ed. Michael W. Goheen (Grand Rapids: Eerdmans, forthcoming).

bear witness to the *missio Dei*? And, how does it function as an instrument of the mission of God? Not all of the answers will be the same. Consequently, this study will not only look for the common pageant of God's mission that runs through the New Testament. It will also listen attentively to the diverse voices of the New Testament writings, and how each one contributes to our understanding of the mission of God and of his people.

Chapter 1, then, seeks to read the Gospel of Matthew missionally in light of the entire biblical narrative. Jesus's kingdom ministry stands as the climax of Israel's story and the fulfillment of Israel's mission. At the same time, I ask what role Matthew's celebrated "Great Commission" passage at the end of his Gospel (Matt 28:16-20) plays in helping us understand how the *whole* Gospel equips God's people to participate in the *missio Dei*.

The second chapter surveys the sweeping story of God's saving mission, as narrated in Luke and Acts. It looks at both the Third Gospel's portrait of Jesus's holistic, boundary-breaking mission and how Jesus's followers continue and extend his mission in Acts. We need to take note of how Luke and Acts are similar, but also how they differ in their mission focus. The chapter concludes with a summary of the various ways in which Luke invites his readers, by the power of the Spirit, to enter the unfinished story of God's mission that he tells.

The final chapter on the Gospels, chapter 3, reads the Gospel of John in view of God's mission of seeking, sending love. John's Gospel holds surprises in the richness and depth of its theology of mission. This chapter explores the trinitarian mission of the Father, Son, and Spirit, as well as how John's deeply relational understanding of mission shapes the mission of God's people in the world.

Chapter 4 explores Paul's mission theology. Instead of surveying Paul's understanding of mission as a whole, this chapter focuses on one letter, his epistle to the Philippians, as a kind of "case study" for a missional reading of Paul. In Philippians, the critical missional text is Philippians 2:6-11, the story of God's self-giving activity in Christ on behalf of the whole of creation. I ask how this narrative snapshot of the *missio Dei* not only articulates the *content* of God's cruciform mission, but also invites God's people to *embody* the story of Jesus in their world. Along the way, I tackle the thorny question of whether or not Paul expected his converts to actively evangelize unbelievers or simply to "be the church" where they live.

In chapter 5, I attempt to uncover 1 Peter's many-faceted witness to God's saving mission, expressed above all in the suffering, death, and resurrection of Jesus Christ. But Peter especially spotlights what mission means for Christians who find themselves pushed to the margins of their own culture. This chapter, then, weighs in on what it means to speak and live the gospel as "misfits," who are nonetheless fully engaged in the public life and the relationships of their social world. First Peter fashions a missional identity that carries no small importance for Christian communities in many global contexts today.

Chapter 6 begins by asking "Why Revelation?" in a book about the New Testament understanding of mission. As it turns out, the book of Revelation has a great deal more to say about the mission of God and the church's participation in it than many Christians imagine. This chapter probes Revelation's witness to God's sweeping mission to redeem all people and restore all of creation through the slain Lamb. And it especially explores Revelation's clarion call for Christian communities to reimagine their present identity and mission in light of John's visions of God's future. Revelation, we will see, invites the church to become an instrument of God's healing the nations in anticipation of God's final triumph.

This study concludes with an attempt to take stock of where the interpretations found in these six chapters cohere and where they contrast. I also ask the "So what?" question. How does reading biblical texts through the eyes of God's mission lead us both toward a richer understanding of the New Testament message and toward a more faithful embodiment of the mission of God in our various circumstances?

No interpretation of biblical texts is neutral, including my own. I read scripture from the vantage point of one who is part of the Wesleyan theological tradition and the broader evangelical movement. I write as a North American male, who has lived and ministered in Asia and Europe for most of my adult life. Others will need to supplement and, no doubt, correct my understandings, particularly Christians from other cultures, social locations, and life experiences.

The title of this book is *Why Mission?* My sincere hope is that the missional readings from the New Testament that follow will help to give us a clearer vision of *why* it is the church's calling to get caught up in the robust mission of God. Let us, then, commence that journey of discovery.

Chapter One

Reading from the Back: Mission in Matthew

A missional reading of Matthew is, in some ways, like reading a detective novel. David C. Steinmetz makes a fascinating comparison between Christian scripture and classic mystery stories.[1] Steinmetz notes that mysteries often have *two* narratives: first, the sprawling, sometimes disjointed narrative of characters, clues, false leads, and seemingly unconnected events that make up the main plot of the novel; and second, the narrative that is recited by the principal investigator in the book's final chapter. In this second narrative, the investigator lays out in detail what was *really* happening while the larger narrative was unfolding. Suddenly, casual conversations between characters or actions that seemed to carry little importance take on great meaning. By reading the last chapter at the beginning, the reader recognizes a complex and coherent story that is carefully guided to its intended end by the author.[2]

Steinmetz draws an analogy to how the first Christians read scripture. The event of Jesus's life, death, and resurrection was so radically transforming that it caused them to re-read Israel's story. Consequently, "the long, ramshackle narrative of Israel, with its promising starts and unexpected twists... is

1. David C. Steinmetz, "Uncovering a Second Narrative: Detective Fiction and the Construction of the Historical Method," in *The Art of Reading Scripture*, ed. Elaine F. David and Richard B. Hays (Grand Rapids: Eerdmans, 2003), 54–65.

2. Ibid., 54–56.

retold and reevaluated in the light of what early Christians regarded as the concluding chapter God had written in Jesus Christ."[3] "Reading from the back" or "reading backwards,"[4] is an activity in which the New Testament writers regularly engage, as they retell the Old Testament story and reinterpret texts in light of what God has done in Christ (see, e.g., Acts 7; 13:16-47; 1 Pet 2:4-10).

In particular, reading the last chapter first suggests a rich reading strategy for the Gospel of Matthew. This is true in two senses, both of which contribute to a missional interpretation of Matthew. First, how does Matthew make sense of what a redeeming God has been doing all along in light of the ministry, death, and resurrection of Jesus? We will explore this issue in connection with Matthew's *witness* to the mission of God.

There is a second sense, however, in which we can read Matthew *from the back*. It relates to the structure of the First Gospel itself, with the well-known "Great Commission" passage (Matt 28:16-20) coming at the very end. How does reading Matthew in light of this final commission enable us to understand the missional character of the Gospel as a whole? In particular, in what ways does such a reading shape *the church's participation* in the mission of God, then and now?

Although a missional reading of Matthew won't tell us *everything* about its message, it seems to be faithful to the core concerns of the First Gospel. How, then, does Matthew contribute to both our understanding and our practice of the mission of God?

Matthew's Witness to the *Missio Dei*

The Mission of God and Israel

How the New Testament Gospels begin tells us much about their focus. Matthew, for example, raises the curtain on his Gospel with a Jewish genealogy (Matt 1:1-17). The opening line of Matthew trumpets that Jesus is "the Messiah, a descendant of David and Abraham" (Matt 1:1 NLT). This summary then launches Matthew's forty-two generation record of Jesus's earthly ancestry (Matt 1:2-17). As perplexing as Matthew's opening tactics may seem for modern Western readers, this Jewish genealogy offers striking evidence

---

3. Ibid., 56.

4. See Richard B. Hays, *Reading Backwards: Figural Christology and the Fourfold Gospel Witness* (Waco, TX: Baylor University Press, 2014).

that Matthew is contextualizing his Gospel for his audience. In all likelihood, Matthew writes as a Jewish Christian primarily to Jewish Christians. And this reality profoundly shapes how Matthew articulates the *missio Dei*.

Matthew's opening genealogy strikes up a theme that plays out, in different variations, throughout the Gospel: *what God has done in Jesus of Nazareth is the climax of Israel's story and the fulfillment of Israel's scriptures.*[5] Matthew reads the Old Testament through what Michael Goheen calls a "Messianic and missional lens."[6] Put differently, Matthew reads the Old Testament story "from the back," in light of the kingdom mission of Jesus Messiah. Jesus, the son of Abraham, the son of David (Matt 1:1), fulfills God's covenant promises to restore Abraham's people and to bring them a Messiah from David's royal line. Indeed, Matthew's whole Gospel represents what N. T. Wright describes as "the story of Jesus *told as the history of Israel in miniature*."[7]

Yet Jesus also recapitulates Israel's mission to be a "light to the nations" (Isa 42:6; 49:6). As the son of Abraham, Jesus embodies the calling of God's people to be a blessing to all peoples (see Gen 12:1-3). As David's descendant, he fulfills God's promises of future rule over the whole world.[8] Matthew underscores this universal mission by including the names of four women in the lineage of Jesus—Tamar, Rahab, Ruth, and Bathsheba—all Gentiles. Matthew is "preaching," even by means of a Jewish genealogy, that God's mission embraces non-Jews, as well as Israel.

We find the same messianic and missional hermeneutic at work in Matthew's well-known "fulfillment" statements, which read something like, "This happened to fulfill what the prophet said." What readers of the First Gospel sometimes miss is that not only do these fulfillment texts support Matthew's Christology, but a number of them also carry a *missional* thrust. For example, Matthew interprets the movements of Jesus's family into Egypt and back again as a fulfillment of Hosea's prophecy, "I have called my son out of Egypt" (Matt 2:15; cf. Hos 11:1). Matthew discerns a correspondence between God's deliverance of his son Israel in the exodus and his rescue of his Son Jesus out of Egypt.[9] Through this connection, Matthew shows that Jesus is the

5. Matthew's appeal to Israel's scriptures is impressive. His Gospel contains no fewer than sixty Old Testament quotations and many more allusions and echoes of scripture.

6. Michael W. Goheen, "A Missional Approach to Scripture for the Theological Task," in *The End of Theology: Shaping Theology for the Sake of Mission*, ed. Jason S. Sexton and Paul Weston (Minneapolis: Augsburg Fortress, forthcoming).

7. N. T. Wright, *The New Testament and the People of God* (Minneapolis: Fortress, 1996), 402.

8. See N. T. Wright, *Matthew for Everyone, Part 1: Chapters 1–15* (London: SPCK, 2002), 3.

9. Hays, *Reading Backwards*, 41.

3

embodiment of the new exodus, God's new act of redemption. Jesus himself fulfills Israel's destiny and mission.[10]

In particular, Matthew turns to the Servant Songs in Isaiah to show how Jesus fulfills Israel's mission. For the Jews of Jesus's day, the story of Yahweh's servant was *Israel's* story. But for Matthew, Jesus embodies Israel's role; he is the true servant that Isaiah foretold. Consequently, Matthew announces that Jesus's healing ministry fulfills Isaiah's prophecy of "the one who took our illnesses and carried away our diseases" (Matt 8:16-17; Isa 53:4). Although the immediate concern is physical restoration, N. T. Wright hits the nail on the head when he claims that "for Matthew there is no sharp line between the healing Jesus offered during his life and the healing for sin and death which he offered through his own suffering."[11]

Later, Matthew quotes another fulfillment passage, Isaiah 42:1-4, to show the *manner* in which Jesus performs his role as God's servant (Matt 12:15-21). Jesus is not the kind of messiah who rules by political or military force. Rather—and here is the surprise for Matthew's audience—he comes humbly and gently as Isaiah's servant, as the one who "will not crush the weakest reed" (Matt 12:20 NLT). What's more, Jesus fulfills Israel's unrealized mission; he himself becomes the servant in whom "the Gentiles will put their hope" (Matt 12:21).

Jesus's kingdom mission, then, fulfills and completes what God has been doing all along in Israel's story. In the Sermon on the Mount, Jesus puts it in plain language: "Don't even begin to think that I have come to do away with the Law and the Prophets. I haven't come to do away with them, but to fulfill them" (Matt 5:17). The Gospel of Matthew sits in precisely the right place in the Christian canon, serving as a bridge between the Old Testament and the New. For Matthew, God's restoring mission begins not in a stable in Bethlehem nor even on a mountain in Galilee as Jesus commissions his future followers (Matt 28:18-20). It is a much older story; a story of God's faithfulness to Israel; a story that only makes sense when read "from the back," through the lens of its fulfillment in the mission of God's Messiah; a story that will continue until the end of the age (Matt 24:14; 28:20).

The Mission of God in Jesus

Restoring Israel. It is only in light of God's faithfulness to Israel that we can rightly understand the story of Jesus and his kingdom mission that Mat-

---

10. Craig S. Keener, *A Commentary on the Gospel of Matthew* (Grand Rapids: Eerdmans, 1999), 108–9.

11. Wright, *Matthew for Everyone*, 1:87.

thew tells. How, for example, do we make sense out of Jesus's reply to a Canaanite woman who came begging for his help: "I've been sent only to the lost sheep, the people of Israel" (Matt 15:24; cf. Matt 10:5-6)? Didn't Jesus also promise that a multitude of Gentiles would stream in from all points of the compass to join Abraham and Isaac and Jacob in the kingdom of heaven (Matt 8:11)? Doesn't this Gospel reach its climax with Jesus's sending of his disciples to reproduce themselves in "all nations" (Matt 28:18-20)?

Once again, Jesus's earthly mission needs to be displayed on an Old Testament wallpaper. Prophetic voices like Isaiah, Jeremiah, and Ezekiel foretold that in the last days Israel would be gathered and restored as a prelude to the influx of the nations into the people of God (e.g., Ezek 37:15-28; cf. Isa 2:2-3). The pattern of sacred history runs: *first* Israel, *then* the Gentiles (cf. Rom 1:16). Israel was God's chosen instrument through which all nations would ultimately come to see God's salvation. This helps to explain why Matthew, more than the other Gospels, spotlights Jesus's intentional mission to Israel during his earthly ministry (Matt 10:5-6; 15:24). For Matthew, Jesus's lordship over the nations is only possible because of his mission to Israel.[12]

But Jesus's mission to restore Israel has a flip side: those who reject his kingdom message will face God's judgment. Hard on the heels of Jesus's promise that Gentiles will flood to the banquet table of the Jewish patriarchs from all directions, he states, "But the children of the kingdom will be thrown outside into the darkness" (Matt 8:11-12). In the parable of the wicked tenant farmers who kill the landowner's son, Jesus solemnly warns, "I tell you that God's kingdom will be taken away from you and will be given to a people who produce its fruit" (Matt 21:43). Those who refuse God's Son exclude themselves from the gathered and renewed Israel of the last days. Matthew's Gospel chronicles an intensifying pattern of rejection by Jesus's own people, in particular their religious leaders. It is striking that, in this most Jewish of Gospels, we encounter some of scripture's harshest critique of Israel's hardhearted and hypocritical officials (see Matt 23:1-36). The current of rejection in Matthew's Gospel swells until it reaches its climax in the cross. Matthew alone records the bone-chilling scene in which Pilate washes his hands before the crowd:

"I'm innocent of this man's blood," he said. "It's your problem."
All the people replied, "Let his blood be on us and on our children."
(Matt 27:24-25)

---

12. Eckhard J. Schnabel, *Early Christian Mission*, vol. 2, *Paul and the Early Church* (Downers Grove, IL: IVP Academic, 2004), 1495.

Up to this point, Matthew's passion story distinguishes between the "crowds" and the "leaders" of the Jews. But now the masses and the religious officials are lumped together in "the people" (*laos*). With one voice, they use an Old Testament formula to declare responsibility (cf. Jer 26:15), accepting Jesus's blood on themselves and their descendants.[13] For Matthew, Jesus's death is the ultimate evidence of unbelieving Israel's decision to say "no" to the purposes of God.

In contrast, Jesus's ministry in Galilee and Judea focuses on creating a *renewed* and *restored* Israel. To this end, Jesus appoints twelve disciples, who represent the reconstituted twelve tribes of Israel. As Michael Goheen observes, "The twelve symbolize that the gathering of Israel for the sake of the nations has begun."[14] In Matthew, Jesus describes the role of this restored Israel in language that evokes Israel's original mission.[15] In particular, Jesus speaks of his followers as the "light of the world" and a city on a hill that can't be hidden. They are to let their light shine so that others will see their good deeds and bring glory to God (Matt 5:14-16). This echoes passages that prophesy the nations' pilgrimage to Jerusalem, such as Isaiah 60:2-3:

> Though darkness covers the earth
> and gloom the nations,
> The LORD will shine upon you;
> God's glory will appear over you.
> Nations will come to your light
> and kings to your dawning radiance.

In Jesus's kingdom mission, "Israel is being restored to be a light to the nations" (Isa 42:6; 49:6).[16]

This mission of *attraction* seems to be the primary mode of operation on the few occasions that Jesus encounters Gentiles in Matthew's Gospel. The Magi, for example, make a pilgrimage to Judea in order to worship the infant

13. Donald Senior and Carroll Stuhlmueller, *The Biblical Foundations for Mission* (Maryknoll, NY: Orbis, 1983), 245. For a response to the charge that Matthew is "anti-Semitic," see Grant R. Osborne, *Matthew* (Grand Rapids: Zondervan, 2010), 1095. See also Timothy B. Cargal's suggestion that Matthew 27:25 may have a second, ironic sense: Matthew holds open the possibility that Jesus's blood might be poured out on the Jewish people for "the forgiveness of sins" (Matt 26:28 NIV; cf. 1:21); Cargal, "'His Blood Be on Us and Our Children': A Matthean Double Entendre?" *New Testament Studies* 37 (1991): 101–12.

14. Michael W. Goheen, *A Light to the Nations: The Missional Church and the Biblical Story* (Grand Rapids: Baker Academic, 2011), 84.

15. Ibid.

16. Michael W. Goheen, *Introducing Christian Mission Today: Scripture, History, and Issues* (Downers Grove, IL: IVP Academic, 2014), 55.

king (Matt 2:1-12). During Jesus's earthly ministry, Gentiles like a Roman centurion and a Canaanite come *to him*, drawn by his miracle-working power (Matt 8:5-13; 15:21-28). Only after Jesus's resurrection does his mission turn intentionally *toward* the nations, and only then through the community of his disciples (Matt 28:16-20).

Comprehensive Mission

What is the shape of Jesus's mission in the First Gospel? Matthew offers two nearly identical summaries of Jesus's earthly ministry: "Jesus traveled among all the cities and villages, teaching in their synagogues, announcing the good news of the kingdom, and healing every disease and every sickness" (9:35; cf. 4:23). It's noteworthy that Matthew mentions Jesus's teaching ministry first. Throughout his Gospel, Matthew spotlights Jesus's role as the *teacher of Israel*. He is the supreme teacher, whose authority enables him both to fulfill and reinterpret the Torah (Matt 5:17, 21-48; 7:28-29). "Don't be called teacher (*kathēgētēs*)," Jesus warns his followers, "because Christ is your one teacher" (Matt 23:10; cf. 23:7-11). Even the structure of the Gospel accents Jesus's teaching ministry. Matthew features five teaching discourses of Jesus that, for his Jewish audience, would surely recall the five books of Moses.

Jesus instructs his intimate band of disciples, but he also teaches the wider crowds (Matt 5:1-2; 13:1-3). His "classroom" might be found in a synagogue (Matt 4:23; 13:54), the temple (Matt 21:23; 26:55), a city or village (Matt 9:35; 11:1), on a mountainside or lakeshore (Matt 5:1-2; 13:1-3), or along the road (Matt 20:17-28). In other words, anywhere and everywhere. But Jesus's teaching ministry is not limited to his original hearers. Matthew's Gospel assumes a "church" (Matt 18:17; cf. 16:18), which needs ongoing instruction for its common life and its mission in the world. Jesus continues to teach the church of Matthew's day and beyond as its living Lord.

In addition to teaching, Jesus *proclaims* "the good news of the kingdom" (Matt 4:23; 9:35).[17] In concert with John the Baptist, who preceded him (Matt 3:2), Jesus launches his Galilean mission by announcing, "Change your hearts and lives! Here comes the kingdom of heaven!" (Matt 4:17). Jesus's preaching declares that God's powerful reign is even now breaking into the world in his own life and mission. By its very nature, that announcement

---

17. Matthew makes more of a distinction between "teaching" and "preaching" than the other Synoptic Gospels, although there is considerable overlap. "Proclamation" seems to emphasize the initial announcement (e.g., Matt 4:17; 10:7, 27), while "teaching" often has more focus on ongoing instruction (e.g., Matt 21:23; 28:20).

makes claims on people. In spite of all the First Gospel's emphasis on Jesus's teaching, Matthew does not picture Jesus as a Galilean guru who travels about the land dispensing little nuggets of wisdom about how to live a better life. Rather, Jesus acts more like a Hebrew prophet, proclaiming the arrival of God's gracious rule in human history and calling people to repent, believe, and obey (Matt 4:17-23).

As Matthew's summaries of Jesus's mission make clear, however, kingdom ministry involves more than just words. Jesus also demonstrates the good news through his actions. On one occasion, John the Baptist sends his disciples on a "reconnaissance mission" to find out if Jesus was truly the awaited Messiah. Jesus's answer is telling:

> Go, report to John what you hear and see. Those who were blind are able to see. Those who were crippled are walking. People with skin diseases are cleansed. Those who were deaf now hear. Those who were dead are raised up. The poor have good news proclaimed to them. (Matt 11:4-5)

Jesus's reply recalls a number of passages from Isaiah, which envision God's end-time salvation of his people Israel. The point is this: the healing and restoration that characterize God's future kingdom have broken into the world in the powerful actions of God's anointed king. When Jesus brings wholeness to a leper (Matt 8:1-4) or sight to blinded eyes (Matt 9:27-31; 20:29-33), his actions announce that God's coming deliverance from pain, suffering, and death is present among them. Jesus's power over winds and waves on the Sea of Galilee (Matt 8:23-27) broadcasts God's glorious purpose to one day restore all of creation. What's more, the phrase "the poor have good news proclaimed to them" (Matt 11:5) refers to more than preaching alone. Coming at the climax of Jesus's response, it sums up everything that John's disciples "hear and see" (Matt 11:4); in other words, Jesus's entire mission of word and deed.

Jesus's acts of compassion and healing, then, are part and parcel of the "gospel of the kingdom" that his ministry proclaims. They form the hands and feet of the good news. Matthew drives home the point by the way he organizes the material recorded in chapters 5–9. Jesus's Sermon on the Mount in Matthew 5–7 represents his kingdom teaching. Following that comes a section dominated by Jesus's miraculous deeds (Matt 8–9). And all of this is bracketed by twin summaries of Jesus's word and deed ministry (Matt 4:23; 9:35). It's as if Matthew is saying, "This is a snapshot of Jesus's kingdom mission; he is *both* the Teacher of Israel *and* the powerful Son of God."

Jesus's kingdom mission also demonstrates God's reign by confronting evil at every turn.[18] As in the other Synoptic Gospels, Jesus's activity of driving out demons gets particular attention. Matthew describes both the story of Jesus's ministry of exorcism (Matt 8:16, 28-34; 12:22-23; 17:14-21), as well as his teaching on the subject (Matt 7:22; 12:24-30, 43-45). The Spirit's power, evidenced in Jesus's confrontations with the powers of darkness, signals the arrival of God's kingdom among people. "If I throw out demons by the power of God's Spirit," Jesus declares, "then the kingdom has already overtaken you" (Matt 12:28). Jesus's ministry demonstrates that God's reign *already* is triumphing over evil in all of its forms—demonic activity, disease, sin, and death, among them.

The presence of the kingdom in Jesus's ministry, then, "launches an all-out attack on evil in all its manifestations."[19] This involves not only confronting personal evil, but also the sin that weaves its destructive web in human relationships, societies, and cultures. This is a dimension of God's liberating power that Christians in the West too often miss. Matthew, however, has no such problem. He pictures Jesus challenging the unjust structures and self-serving cultural norms of both Jewish and Roman societies. In chapter 21, for example, Matthew narrates two symbolic actions of Jesus back to back. First, Jesus rides into Jerusalem, not in a royal chariot, but on a lowly donkey, as the prophet foretold (Matt 21:1-5; cf. Zech 9:9). In that act of humility, he subverts the prevailing Roman practices of power and domination. No sooner has he dismounted, than Jesus enters the temple and upends the tables of the money changers and the dove sellers (Matt 21:12-13). Jesus's shocking act symbolizes that God's kingdom confronts the systems of economic exploitation of the Jewish religious leaders, who have virtually "turned the temple into a mafia-like stronghold"[20]—a "hideout for crooks" (Matt 21:13).

It is important to recognize, however, that when Jesus's kingdom mission overcomes the power of evil, it does not use human strong-arm tactics. Jesus refuses to follow the script for popular Jewish expectations of a Messiah who would defeat Israel's enemies by force. Even as he is being arrested, Jesus rebukes a disciple who tries to defend him with the sharp edge of a sword. Jesus tells him plainly, "Put the sword back into its place. All those who use the sword will die by the sword" (Matt 26:52).

---

18. For the following section, see the similar arguments in Dean Flemming, *Recovering the Full Mission of God: A Biblical Perspective on Being, Doing and Telling* (Downers Grove, IL: IVP Academic, 2013), 76–77.

19. David J. Bosch, *Transforming Mission: Paradigm Shifts in Theology of Mission* (Maryknoll, NY: Orbis, 1991), 32.

20. Osborne, *Matthew*, 763.

Jesus likewise rejects that posture of Gentile officials, who wield their authority like a billy club. Instead, he acts in humility, as a servant who comes "to give his life to liberate many people" (Matt 20:25-28). He dies the victim of a Roman political system and a Jewish religious establishment. But Jesus is a *voluntary* victim. Only by means of his death could "what the prophets said in the scriptures . . . be fulfilled" and God's redemptive purpose realized (Matt 26:56; cf. 26:54). And only in what appeared to be utter defeat—a crucified criminal, powerless to save himself (Matt 27:39-42)—could God's triumph over the powers of evil be accomplished.[21] This is the paradox that lies at the heart of the *missio Dei*.

The Mission of God in the Twelve

From the beginning of his ministry, Jesus formed a missional community. Jesus's initial call to discipleship was a call to mission:

> As Jesus walked alongside the Galilee Sea, he saw two brothers, Simon, who is called Peter, and Andrew, throwing fishing nets into the sea, because they were fishermen. "Come, follow me," he said, "and I'll show you how to fish for people." Right away, they left their nets and followed him. (Matt 4:18-19)

It's significant that the personal call to follow *Jesus* precedes the commission to fish for people. As I have written elsewhere, "'Follow me' is an invitation to walk, talk and eat with Jesus; to experience his authority, to live like he lives, to share his way to the cross. The disciples' mission is grounded in a relationship of intimacy and companionship with Jesus."[22] But "fishing for people"—an image exquisitely tailored to fishermen—also means sharing in Jesus's saving and healing mission, first to the people of Israel, and ultimately to all nations (Matt 28:19). Discipleship and mission are inseparable.

In chapter 10, we see what fishing for people looks like, as Jesus sends out the Twelve on an itinerant mission. Matthew highlights this discourse, expanding Mark's six-verse narrative to a full forty-two verses (Matt 10:1-42; cf. Mark 6:7-12). In particular, Matthew goes to great pains to show us the marriage between Jesus's mission and that of his disciples. An assortment of features bring out that connection, including the following:

21. Howard Peskett and Vinoth Ramachandra, *The Message of Mission: The Glory of Christ in All Time and Space* (Downers Grove, IL: InterVarsity Press, 2003), 196.

22. Flemming, *Recovering the Full Mission of God*, 80.

- Matthew introduces the discourse by describing Jesus's own compassion for the crowds and the need for workers in God's harvest (9:36-38). Furthermore, Matthew brackets the whole sending narrative with summaries of Jesus's ministry of preaching, teaching, and healing (Matt 9:35; 11:1).

- Jesus sends out the Twelve as *apostles* (Matt 10:2), bearing his own authority to act and speak in his name (Matt 10:1).

- The disciples' mission looks like that of Jesus; they are to proclaim the message of the kingdom, heal the sick, and drive out demons (Matt 10:1, 7-8).

- The scope of the two missions is the same; the Twelve are sent to "the lost sheep, the people of Israel" (Matt 10:5-6; cf. 15:24).

- Like Jesus, they must expect harassment and rejection (Matt 10:16-25). "Disciples aren't greater than their teacher," Jesus assures them, "and slaves aren't greater than their master" (Matt 10:24).

- Jesus makes the identification between the Sender and the sent ones explicit in his saying on hospitality: "Those who receive you are also receiving me, and those who receive me are receiving the one who sent me" (Matt 10:40).

- Even as Jesus's mission is anchored in the Spirit's empowering (Matt 3:16; 4:1) and the Father's loving care (Matt 3:17), so it is with his disciples (Matt 10:19-20, 29-31). Therefore, they should proclaim the good news without fear (Matt 10:26-28).[23]

The horizon of the disciples' mission, however, is not confined to the immediate travels of the Twelve in Galilee. Matthew describes disciples who are beaten "in their synagogues" and hauled before governors and kings, as a "testimony to them and to the Gentiles" (Matt 10:17-18). Here Matthew fast-forwards to the ministry of the Twelve and the later church, following Jesus's resurrection. Matthew's mission discourse therefore prefigures the missional church to come—its holistic ministry, its suffering witness, and its dependence on the Spirit's power (Matt 10:19-20), the Father's protection (Matt 10:26-31), and the risen Lord's presence (Matt 10:40-42). But Matthew 10 is

---

23. Senior and Stuhlmueller, *Biblical Foundations for Mission*, 251.

incomplete without Jesus's post-Easter commission of his disciples to extend his mission to all corners of the earth (Matt 28:19-20). We turn to that now.

Matthew's Great Commission and the Church's Mission

Last words matter. A person's final words are often remembered and continue to influence those who remain behind. Sometimes they endure. John Wesley's life ended, for example, with the memorable testimony, "Best of all, God is with us!," echoing Matthew 1:21. And Jesus's final words at the conclusion of Matthew, his "Great Commission" (Matt 28:18-20), carry exceptional, ongoing significance for his followers.

Unfortunately, the very importance of this passage for the church has meant that too often it is plucked out of the whole narrative of Matthew and read by Christians as a freestanding text. As a result, both the church's understanding of its mission and its reading of Matthew's Gospel suffer. On the one hand, Christians sometimes treat the "Great Commission" as if it is the sum of what the Bible has to say about the church's mission in the world. On the other hand, readers of Matthew's Gospel often miss how this post-resurrection text connects with Matthew's whole narrative and with the entire biblical story.

A far better strategy, however, is to read Matthew "from the back"; that is, Jesus's postresurrection commission serves as a necessary culmination to the entire Gospel. Why read Matthew in this way? In the first place, Matthew 28:16-20 itself is steeped in language and themes that appear throughout the First Gospel.[24] This passage recapitulates and brings together various emphases in Matthew's narrative of God's saving purpose in Jesus (e.g., Jesus's authority and presence, making disciples, teaching, obeying Jesus's commands). Second, Matthew writes largely for Christian communities who already were familiar with the story. They *knew* the ending—that Jesus is raised from the dead and that he gives the church a mandate for its mission in the world. It was only natural that they should allow the story's goal to shape how they read and understood what came before. Third, reading from the back, with an eye to Jesus's mission commission, helps us to grasp how Matthew's Gospel as a whole equips God's people to participate in the *missio Dei*.

Matthew 28:16-20, then, remains a key to the message of the entire Gospel. It demonstrates that part of Matthew's goal is to form the missional iden-

---

24. Bosch, *Transforming Mission*, 57.

tity of the churches to which he writes. How, then, does reading Matthew in light of its final words show us how the First Gospel becomes an instrument of mission for its audience?

The Basis of Mission

All authority. It is crucial that we notice the structure of Matthew 28:16-20. For contemporary readers, Jesus's commission to "go and make disciples of the nations" in verse 19 normally gets most of the headlines. But if the commission itself is the capstone of the passage, verses 18 and 20 are the columns that support it. Jesus's last words begin with a declaration of his authority and end with a promise of his presence.

First, Jesus affirms, "I've received all authority in heaven and on earth" (Matt 28:18). Matthew has shined a floodlight on Jesus's authority throughout the narrative. In the temptation, Satan offered Jesus a similar place of honor, but without the humiliation of the cross (Matt 4:8-9). Later, Jesus claimed authority as the true interpreter of the law—"You have heard that it was said . . . but *I* say to you" (Matt 5:21, 27, 33, 38, 43). Little wonder that his hearers were astonished at his authority (Matt 7:28-29; cf. 9:6; 11:27). And he gave his disciples the authority to continue his mission (Matt 10:1).

But now, in the wake of his resurrection, Jesus announces that the Father has granted him *all* authority in heaven and earth. This is no less than a claim to cosmic and sovereign lordship, fulfilling Daniel's prophecy about the exalted Son of Man (Dan 7:13-14). The same Jesus who has been slandered and rejected, humiliated and crucified, now takes his rightful place as ruler over all the powers that oppose him, whether spiritual, cosmic, social, or political. And it is on the basis of this supreme authority ("therefore," Matt 28:19) that Jesus sends the church on its mission in the world. It's an authority that empowers the church to "bind" and "loose" in Jesus's name (Matt 16:19; 18:18).

Always present. The second supporting column for Jesus's commission is the promise, "I am with you always" (Matt 28:20 NRSV). Matthew brackets his Gospel with two magnificent promises of God's presence in Jesus: the angel's words to Joseph, "And they will call him Immanuel [which means 'God with us']" (Matt 1:23 NIV) and the final promise of Jesus's presence with his followers to "the end of this present age" (Matt 28:20). In between, Jesus assures the community that when they gather in his name, he is there among them (Matt 18:20). Jesus's permanent presence in the church means that God's saving purpose will continue into the present age. The presence of the risen Lord is the context for the church's mission to the world.

13

Churches, then and now, need to recognize how Matthew frames Jesus's mission charge, for several reasons. First, it makes a difference in *why* we engage in the mission of God. For Matthew, the motivation for the church's mission involves more than simply a command to do certain tasks. Above all, the church's mission arises out of the lordship and abiding presence of Jesus. As Goheen puts it, "On the basis of [his] global dominion, he charges his disciples to invite all humankind to submit to his lordship."[25] Second, verse 20 provides encouragement to Christian communities facing opposition and difficulties. Jesus's intimate, abiding presence sustains the church in mission, whatever the cost. And third, Jesus's promised presence stands as an assurance that those he commissions, he will enable to obey.[26]

The Agents of Mission

Matthew emphasizes that it is the eleven (now minus Judas) who hear Jesus's commission (28:16). Like the Twelve, prior to Jesus's death, the eleven disciples represent the restored Israel, the new people of God. They are the embryos of the church to come, which will embrace Israel's mission to be a light to the nations. It's worth noting that Jesus gathers and commissions a *community*, not just an assortment of specially called individuals. Matthew alone among the Evangelists uses the term *church* (16:18; 18:17). When he does so, he speaks directly to his own postresurrection community (cf. Matt 10:17-18).[27] Matthew broadcasts that Jesus wants to form a missional community.

When the eleven, the gathered community, meet the risen Jesus on a mountain, they offer the only appropriate response: worship. Even as the disciples worshipped Jesus after he stilled a storm (Matt 14:33) and the women worshipped him following his resurrection (Matt 28:9) so now the eleven worship the one who has supreme authority over heaven and earth, the one who remains "God with us" (Matt 1:23). The church's worship and its mission go hand in hand.

It is all the more surprising, then, that Matthew quickly adds, "but some doubted," or perhaps, "some hesitated" (*edistasan*). Throughout the Gospel, Matthew has highlighted the disciples' "little faith" (Matt 6:30; 8:26; 14:31;

---

25. Goheen, *Light to the Nations*, 117.

26. David J. Bosch, "The Structure of Mission: An Exposition of Matthew 28:16-20," in *The Study of Evangelism: Exploring a Missional Practice of the Church*, ed. Paul W. Chilcote and Laceye C. Warner (Grand Rapids: Eerdmans, 2008), 91.

27. Jeannine K. Brown, "Matthew, Gospel of," in *Dictionary of Jesus and the Gospels*, ed. Joel B. Green, Jeannine K. Brown, and Nicholas Perrin, 2nd ed. (Downers Grove, IL: IVP Academic, 2013), 582.

16:8; 17:20). Perhaps he wants to offer courage to a church in the midst of its own struggles between hesitation and worship (see Matt 14:31, 33).[28]

The Focus of Mission

This brings us to Jesus's actual commission in Matthew 28:19.[29] The word *therefore* is vital. Only on the basis of Jesus's universal authority (28:18) is a universal mission possible. As for Jesus's commission itself, it is important to follow Matthew's lead as to where the focus lies. Christians today sometimes place far too much weight on the word *go*, with the result that mission becomes primarily the task of missionaries who cross geographical boundaries. Matthew, however, puts the weight on the command to "make disciples," which is the main verb in the passage. The other verbs around it, "go," "baptizing," and "teaching," explain *how* disciples are made.

"Making disciples" is a task that Jesus has engaged in throughout Matthew's Gospel. We see him calling people to follow (Matt 4:18-22; cf. 9:9), teaching them, modeling grace and compassion, and involving them in his ministry (Matt 10:1-42; 14:16-21). Now Jesus urges his original cadre of followers to make others into what they are themselves: disciples.[30] One needs to *be* a disciple in order to *make* a disciple.

Both the terms *disciple* and *follow* command special attention in Matthew.[31] Discipleship begins with the call to follow Jesus himself. Jesus invites his followers to take his yoke upon themselves and learn from him (Matt 11:29). But disciples are not called to follow Jesus individually; they learn and grow as part of a disciple community, which can be a collection of very different people.[32] Although Jesus's disciples are frequently guilty of "little faith" (Matt 8:26; 14:31; 16:8), Matthew casts them in a more positive light than we find in Mark (see e.g., Mark 6:51-52; 9:32). In Matthew, the disciples <u>understand</u> Jesus's teaching (Matt 13:51; 16:12; 17:13); and, despite their

---

28. Peskett and Ramachandra, *Message of Mission*, 174.

29. For the following two paragraphs, see Flemming, *Recovering the Full Mission of God*, 96.

30. Bosch, *Transforming Mission*, 74.

31. The word "disciple" (*mathētēs*) occurs more frequently in Matthew (73x), in comparison to the other Synoptic Gospels, Mark (46x) and Luke (37x). The verb "to follow" (*akolouthein*) appears 25x in Matthew, compared to 18x in Mark and 17x in Luke. Donald A. Hagner, "Holiness and Ecclesiology: The Church in Matthew," in *Holiness and Ecclesiology in the New Testament*, ed. Kent E. Brower and Andy Johnson (Grand Rapids: Eerdmans, 2007), 47. In addition, Matthew has three of the four NT occurrences of the verb "make disciples" (13:52; 27:57; 28:19).

32. Richard A. Burridge, *Imitating Jesus: An Inclusive Approach to New Testament Ethics* (Grand Rapids: Eerdmans, 2007), 220.

somewhat wobbly faith, they do believe and worship him (Matt 13:31, 33; 28:17).[33]

What's more, the call to discipleship is a call to mission, not only in Matthew 28 but also throughout the Gospel. As we have seen, Jesus's disciples follow their master by engaging in his multidimensional ministry: preaching, healing, confronting the power of Satan, and enduring persecution (Matt 10:1, 7-8, 16-25). The commission to "go and make disciples," then, comes as no surprise. It simply reinforces and expands what Matthew's Gospel has been saying all along.

The Scope of Mission

If Jesus is lord over the whole world (Matt 28:18), then it surely follows that his disciples must enable others to acknowledge and submit to that universal lordship. They must make disciples in *all nations*. Frederick Dale Bruner speaks of "the breathtaking scope of the 'alls'" in this passage.[34] The one who owns *all* authority and is *always* present sends his followers to disciple *all* nations, by teaching them *all* things!

In Matthew's world, both Jewish and Greek traditions could praise teachers who raised up many disciples. But the notion of discipling *nations* would have sounded quite revolutionary.[35] "Nations" (*ethnē*) does not refer to modern constructs like "nation states" or ethno-linguistic "people groups," but more broadly, to all peoples.[36] Discipling the nations fulfills God's ancient promise to Abraham that his descendants would become an instrument of blessing for all the earth's peoples (Gen 12:3; 18:18). Matthew, it seems, gives his Gospel missional bookends: the opening announcement that Jesus is the son of Abraham (Matt 1:1) and the concluding mission mandate that embraces all nations. Reading Matthew "from the back," the mention of Abraham in Matthew 1:1 implies Israel's calling to be a people for the sake of the world, which is explicitly laid out in the Great Commission. Christopher Wright observes that Matthew 28:18-20 "could be seen as a christological mutation of the original Abrahamic commission—'Go...and be a blessing...and all nations on earth will be blessed through you.'"[37]

33. Ibid., 219.

34. Frederick Dale Bruner, *Matthew: A Commentary*, vol. 2, *The Churchbook: Matthew 13–28* (Dallas: Word, 1990), 1084.

35. Keener, *Gospel of Matthew*, 719.

36. Bosch, "The Structure of Mission," 85. "All nations" in Matthew 28:19 therefore functions similarly to "the end of the earth" in Jesus's promises of the church's universal witness in Acts 1:8.

37. Christopher J. H. Wright, *The Mission of God: Unlocking the Bible's Grand Narrative* (Downers

The charge to make disciples of *all nations* is a striking reversal of Jesus's marching orders for his disciples in the mission discourse in chapter 10. There he explicitly tells them, "Don't go!" to the Gentiles and Samaritans and "Go!" to the lost sheep of Israel (Matt 10:5-6). Furthermore, the prophets foretold that all nations would stream *to* Jerusalem in the last days (e.g., Isa 2:2-3).

Jesus's resurrection, however, makes all the difference. In its wake, mission propels outward. Jesus's followers are to "go" and make disciples in all nations. For Matthew's audience, this is not a *replacement* of the Jewish mission in chapter 10, but an *extension* of it.[38] "All nations" doesn't mean *other* nations; it includes Jews, as well. But, as an expansion of Jesus's earthly ministry, the emphasis in Matthew 28 falls firmly on the Gentiles. Craig Keener suggests that it may be precisely this mission to Gentile peoples that Matthew's mainly Jewish Christian audience needs encouragement to engage in.[39] Going to all nations, then, may involve crossing geographical and cultural barriers, but it also includes mission in one's own setting.

This extension of Jesus's mission should not take careful readers of Matthew by surprise. The evangelist drops a series of rather visible "bread crumbs" along the way, foreshadowing the Gentile mission. These include the following:

- The names of four Gentile women in the genealogy that begins the Gospel (Matt 1:3, 5-6)

- The appearance of Persian magi, who seek out the infant Jesus to worship him (Matt 2:1-12)

- The statement that Jesus's ministry in "Galilee of the Gentiles" fulfills Isaiah's prophecy, bringing light to the Gentiles living in darkness (Matt 4:14-16; cf. 12:17-21)

- Jesus's encounters with Gentiles with exemplary faith, such as a Roman centurion from Capernaum (Matt 8:5-13) and a Canaanite woman (Matt 15:21-28)

- Jesus's warning to unbelieving Israel and its leaders "that God's kingdom will be taken away from you and given to a people who produce its fruit" (Matt 21:43)

Grove, IL: IVP Academic, 2006), 213.

38. See Keener, *Gospel of Matthew*, 719.

39. Ibid., 719–20.

• Jesus's promise that before the end comes the gospel would be proclaimed throughout the world as a testimony to all nations (Matt
24:14)

After Jesus's resurrection, the restrictions of his earthly ministry are utterly stripped away. What Matthew has foreshadowed throughout now strides
to center stage; mission in all nations becomes the mandate of the church.

The Means of Mission

Making disciples of all nations entails more than initial evangelism and
preaching the gospel, although this is surely assumed. The phrases that follow
the controlling verb "make disciples" (Matt 28:19-20) unpack more specifically the *means* by which the church goes about its disciple-making task.[40]

"Baptizing" converts in the name of the Father, Son, and Holy Spirit
implies personal faith in and allegiance to Jesus. But it also suggests incor-
poration into a community of believers. Moreover, those who are baptized
need to be taught. "Teaching" is essential to creating mature communities
of disciples among the nations. Here Matthew picks up a signature theme
of the First Gospel. For Matthew, to teach means no less than patterning
oneself after Jesus, the true and authoritative teacher of the law. Even as the
disciples have learned under the "master teacher" (Matt 10:24-25), they are
now charged with teaching others. Above all, teaching involves instruction in
what it means to follow Jesus—to obey everything he has commanded (Matt
28:20).

That "everything" to be obeyed surely includes the whole body of Jesus's teaching in the First Gospel (including the Great Commission itself). In
particular, Matthew spotlights Jesus's five teaching discourses, headlined by
the Sermon on the Mount in Matthew 5–7. Matthew's emphasis on Jesus's
instruction signals that his Gospel was intended to be a teaching resource for
early Christian communities, and it retains that function today.

But teaching is not simply a matter of head knowledge. Matthew shares
the Jewish understanding that true religion is a way of life, not just a pattern
of belief.[41] Especially in the Sermon on the Mount, Jesus urges his followers
to do good deeds, which bring praise to their Father in heaven (Matt 5:16).
Disciples don't just "hear" (Matt 7:24-27) or "teach" (Matt 5:19) Jesus's commands; they put them into practice. Matthew repeatedly emphasizes that

40. For this section, see Flemming, *Recovering the Full Mission of God*, 96–97.
41. John Nolland, *The Gospel of Matthew* (Grand Rapids: Eerdmans, 2005), 1270.

words and actions are woven together, like threads in a tapestry (Matt 6:1-18; 7:21; 23:1-12). Jesus warns his disciples not to be like the legal experts and the Pharisees, "for they don't practice what they teach" (Matt 23:3 NLT). On the contrary, those who are a part of God's kingdom bear its fruit (Matt 21:43; cf. 7:15-20), do the Father's will (Matt 7:21), and practice righteousness (Matt 5:20; 6:33). "Righteousness" (*dikaiosynē* in Greek) is a key term for Matthew. Unfortunately, it is difficult to translate, since no single English word captures its meaning. In Matthew's Gospel, it embraces *both* a righteous character—a radical, inward obedience that surpasses that of the Pharisees (Matt 5:20)—*and* the practice of justice, which seeks God's will to be done "on earth as in heaven" (Matt 6:10).

Above all, obeying Jesus's commands is summed up in his call to love God unreservedly and to love our neighbor as ourselves (Matt 22:34-40). The love command interprets all of the Law and the Prophets (Matt 22:40; cf. 7:12). Consequently, it is at the heart of what Jesus wants his followers to communicate and model as they form new disciples in the nations. Matthew extends the love command beyond the normal networks of family and friends to embrace enemies, as well (Matt 5:43-48). Loving others involves a radical forgiveness toward those who don't deserve it (Matt 18:21-33). And only Matthew's Gospel paints a vivid portrait of the love command in action in Jesus's parable of the sheep and the goats (Matt 25:31-46).[42] In the parable, love is embodied in concrete acts of compassion and justice—providing food for the hungry, hospitality for the stranger, and care for the sick and imprisoned. And precisely because the practice of discipling others presupposes that disciples practice what they teach, the mission itself must be characterized by love, servanthood, and justice, in the footsteps of Jesus. The "Great Commission" without the "Great Commandment" is like a body without a heart.

What's more, in the Sermon on the Mount, Jesus forges a link between practicing Jesus's commands and mission. Jesus affirms that the identity of his followers is to *be* the salt of the earth and the light of the world (Matt 5:13-14). The phrases "of the earth" and "of the world" give this saying a missional thrust. Being salt and light has to do with how the church lives out its visible, public life in the world. Furthermore, Jesus's language recalls Israel's missional calling to be a "light to the nations" (Isa 42:6; 49:6). For the Christian community to be salt and light includes having a transforming effect on the surrounding culture, even as salt and light positively affect whatever they touch, without compromising their own character.

---

42. Victor Paul Furnish, *The Love Command in the New Testament* (Nashville: Abingdon, 1972), 79.

19

In Matthew 5:16, Jesus explicitly relates being salt and light to a missional lifestyle: "Let your lights shine before people, so they can see the good things you do and praise your Father who is in heaven." The good deeds practiced by Jesus's followers in this context correspond to obeying all that he commands in the Great Commission passage (Matt 28:20). Such good deeds likely include everything that God's people do to witness to the kingdom in their everyday lives, through their words and deeds, their interpersonal relationships and their acts of love, justice, and compassion. And this happens in the public square. Jesus wants the ordinary practices of his followers to so reflect his own character and lifestyle, that those who "see" them will be attracted to worship the one true God. Surely this kind of lifestyle, evangelistic witness is a crucial aspect of "making disciples of all nations."

The Horizon of Mission

The Great Commission closes with Jesus's personal promise to be present with his disciples in mission "until the end of this present age" (Matt 28:20). Appropriately, the last words in Matthew give mission an end-time horizon. The phrase "the end of the age" is unique to this Gospel. Earlier it draws attention to Jesus's second coming and the final judgment (see Matt 13:39-40, 49; 24:3). For Matthew, the church's mission is bounded by the resurrection and the end. The end-time kingdom of God has already broken into the world in the person and mission of Jesus (see Matt 12:28). That's the "already" of the kingdom. But the "not yet" of the kingdom means that "the gospel of the kingdom will be proclaimed throughout the world as a testimony to all the nations" before the end comes (Matt 24:14). It is this eschatological perspective that encourages communities of disciples who feel the scorpion's sting of persecution to faithfully endure to the end (Matt 10:16-31; 24:13).

The climax of Jesus's mission mandate, then, blends ecclesiology and eschatology.[43] Jesus's promise to be present until the end of the age expands the horizon of mission from a mountain in Galilee to Matthew's church and beyond. This passage gives the church a magnificent calling in the time between Jesus's first and second comings. It is a call to participate in God's purpose to create communities of mature and obedient disciples among all the peoples of the earth.

Conclusion

Both mystery novels and biblical writings are often best understood by reading the last chapter first. This is certainly true of Matthew's Gospel. In

43. Osborne, *Matthew*, 1083.

one sense, the strategy of "reading from the back" allows Matthew to read the Old Testament through the lens of the fulfillment of God's saving purpose for the world in Jesus Christ. But in another sense, that strategy enables readers of Matthew—ancient and modern—to view the entire Gospel in light of Jesus's climactic commission to the church in Matthew 28:16-20. I close this chapter by noting some implications of this second "backwards" reading of Matthew for the church in mission today:

- The whole Gospel of Matthew, not just the celebrated "Great Commission" passage, becomes a *mission text*, intended to equip a missional people.

- Mission has a *communal* character. As the restored Israel, the new people of God, we must embrace Israel's calling to be a light to the nations, to *be* salt and light in the world, to live out our common life in a way that attracts outsiders to the kingdom (Matt 5:14-16). Mission is not the sole provenance of a specialized cadre of cross-cultural missionaries. It is the identity of the whole people of God.

- The church extends Jesus's integrated mission. We are caught up in Jesus's kingdom ministry of proclaiming the good news, teaching the Jesus way, healing the whole person, and confronting the powers that oppose God at every level.

- Like Jesus, the church in mission can expect opposition. But Jesus assures us that the Holy Spirit will empower his people for witness in the crucible of suffering.

- Our fundamental missional task is to make disciples (Matt 28:19). The mission of disciple making assumes initial evangelism, but its goal is no less than to form communities of disciples that look and act like Jesus.

- Matthew's Gospel affirms the vital teaching ministry of the church. Instructing God's people in a life of inward and outward righteousness, obedience to Jesus's commands, and love for God and others is essential to the church's missional calling.

- We participate in God's mission not simply to fulfill a command. Mission is anchored in Christ's authority over the whole world and his enduring presence among his people.

- The mission of the risen Lord projects outward. "All nations" (Matt 28:19) means that there is no place, no people, no culture, no religious community, no political persuasion, that is "beyond the pale" of the mission of God's people, beginning with our near neighbors who are not like us.

- Mission leans into God's future. Jesus's charge to make disciples "until the end of the age" (Matt 28:20) means that *we*, the church in mission, are drawn into Matthew's story. *We* are the disciples who are sent, with the abiding presence of the authoritative Lord, to form communities of disciples who embody the life of Jesus, even as we await the day when God's kingdom comes in its fullness, on earth as it is in heaven!

Chapter Two

A Mission of Divine Embrace: Luke and Acts

Towering high above the city of Rio de Janeiro, Brazil, stands perhaps the most iconic statue of Jesus on earth—the mammoth ninety-eight-foot-high (thirty meter) figure of Christ the Redeemer. What stuns me the most about the statue is not its sheer height, but the wide open arms of Jesus, arms that seem to embrace the entire city, its financial high-rises and its crowded hovels, its glittering mansions and its crime-riddled slums. Those welcoming, extended arms could serve as a metaphor for Luke's picture of Christian mission. In both the Third Gospel and the book of Acts, Luke tells the story of a mission, empowered by the Spirit, which embraces outsiders, shatters boundaries, and encompasses the whole world and the whole of human need.

This chapter is, by necessity, somewhat longer than the others in this book. After all, Luke and Acts together make up almost 30 percent of the New Testament. But there is still far more to say about mission in Luke-Acts than can be addressed in a single chapter, so I won't try to cover it all. Rather, in this missional reading, I begin with an overview of how Luke and Acts bear witness to God's saving purpose for the world. The chapter then traces three missional trajectories that course their way through Luke's two volumes, like a river flowing through a canyon, sometimes in broad pools, sometimes in barely visible, but living streams. First, mission in these books is all-embracing. The whole gospel addresses the whole person. Second, the missions of Jesus and the church consistently shatter boundaries and reach out to all kinds of people. Third, mission is the work of the Holy Spirit, from beginning to end. Finally, I reflect more specifically on how Luke's understanding of Christian mission equips and empowers the church to get caught up in the story of God's saving purpose for the world—the mission of God.

Luke and the Mission of God

Among the Gospel writers, Luke alone gives the church a *two*-volume work—Luke-Acts. *Why* this is the case raises the question of Luke's purpose in writing these narratives. I agree with Joel B. Green that Luke's agenda is not simply to tell the story of Jesus, followed by the story of the early church.[1] Rather, Luke sets his eyes on something much more comprehensive—the entire saving purpose of God. As one scholar puts it, Luke's two-volume work seeks to "confirm that God's great plan of salvation, inaugurated through Israel in the Old Testament, has come to its climax in the life, death, resurrection and exaltation of Jesus the Messiah and continues to unfold in the growth and expansion of the early church."[2]

Luke, then, wants us to know that we are part of something very big indeed. And that "something" is no less than God's saving project for the world and the people he has made—the *missio Dei*. This means that the Gospel of Luke is not in the first place *christological*, although it is surely about Jesus. Nor is Acts primarily *ecclesiological*, although it tells the story of the church. First and foremost, Luke-Acts is *theological* in its focus.[3] These books offer a narrative of God's saving mission, which is unfolded in Israel's scriptures, the life and mission of Jesus, and the Spirit-propelled Christian community. At the same time, Luke's portrayal of God's mission functions as a call for God's people to enter the same story. Part of Luke's purpose for Luke-Acts is to invite Christian communities to faithfully bear witness to the saving purpose of God by who they are, how they live, and what they say.

1. Joel B. Green, *The Theology of the Gospel of Luke* (Cambridge: Cambridge University Press, 1995), 47.

2. Mark L. Strauss, "The Purpose of Luke-Acts: Reaching a Consensus," in *New Testament Theology in Light of the Church's Mission: Essays in Honor of I. Howard Marshall,* ed. Jon C. Laansma, Grant Osborne, and Ray Van Neste (Eugene, OR: Cascade, 2011), 143.

3. See Joel B. Green, "Luke, Gospel of," in *Dictionary of Jesus and the Gospels,* ed. Joel B. Green, Jeannine K. Brown, and Nicholas Perrin, 2nd ed. (Downers Grove, IL: IVP Academic, 2013), 542.

This theme of God's missional purpose for the world runs like a golden thread throughout Luke and Acts. Luke's Gospel begins with a reference to "the events that have been fulfilled among us" (Luke 1:1). In other words, the "events" Luke describes in the story of Jesus are the fulfillment of what God has been doing all along on behalf of his people.[4] This becomes clear in the opening chapters, as a parade of Spirit-inspired persons testify to God's ancient plan (see Luke 1:32-33, 54-55, 67-79; 2:29-32, 38). The priest Zechariah, for example, rejoices that the God of Israel has come to rescue his people (1:68). God has raised up a Savior in David's line, in fulfillment of the words of the prophets and his covenant promise to Abraham (Luke 1:69-72). When Jesus announces the launch of his public mission in his hometown of Nazareth, he describes it as the "fulfillment" of Isaiah's prophecy (Luke 4:18-21).

In particular, Jesus interprets his death and resurrection as events that "must" happen for God's salvation to be realized (9:22; 17:25; 22:37; 24:27). It comes as no surprise, then, that after his resurrection, Jesus reminds his frightened followers that "everything written about me in the Law of Moses, the Prophets, and the Psalms must be fulfilled" (Luke 24:44). Jesus goes on to explain, "This is what is written: The Messiah will suffer and rise from the dead on the third day, and repentance for the forgiveness of sins will be preached in his name to all nations, beginning at Jerusalem" (Luke 24:46-47 NIV). In other words, God's climactic act in Jesus, the Messiah, *and* the mission of the church that follows, are the fulfillment of Israel's scriptures and, as such, of God's whole saving plan.

In Acts, the speeches of Peter and Paul loudly echo this fulfillment theme. In sending Jesus onto the stage of human history, God has made good on his promise to Abraham that through his descendants all peoples on earth would be blessed (Acts 3:25-26). Jesus suffered and died on a cross "in accordance with God's established plan and foreknowledge" (Acts 2:23; see 3:18; 13:27-29; 17:3), and he was raised from the dead in fulfillment of the scriptures (Acts 2:25-32; 13:32-37). God's missional purpose, however, extends beyond Jesus's own ministry to the mission of the church, the restored Israel (see Acts 1:6-8; 28:20). Paul, for example, audaciously reads the words of Isaiah 49:6 as a personal commission from God: his mission will become "a light for the Gentiles," so that God's salvation could truly reach the ends of the earth (Acts 13:46-47; cf. 26:23). The Gospel of Luke, then, "is incomplete in itself."[5] It is only in Acts that we witness the fulfillment of God's ancient plan that all people everywhere might be saved (Acts 10:35, 43; 28:28).

4. Green, *Theology of the Gospel of Luke*, 29–30.
5. Joel B. Green, *The Gospel of Luke* (Grand Rapids: Eerdmans, 1997), 10.

Chapter Two

An All-Embracing Mission

If Luke and Acts tell the story of God's restoring mission, then what is the shape of that mission? And how does Luke envision the church participating in the mission of God? To answer these questions, we need to consider three dimensions of Luke's portrayal of the mission of God. First, Luke spotlights the *all-embracing* nature of God's mission. Luke has no interest in a narrow, squinty vision of God's restoration. On the contrary, God's purpose is to bring people salvation in all of its *fullness*.

Jesus's "Mission Statement"

In Luke's Gospel, Jesus is the supreme agent of God's sweeping mission. Nowhere do we see this more clearly than in what could be called Jesus's personal "mission statement" in Luke 4:18-21.[6] In his hometown synagogue in Nazareth, Jesus takes the scroll of Isaiah and reads,

> *The Spirit of the Lord is upon me,*
> *because the Lord has anointed me.*
> *He has sent me to preach good news to the poor,*
> *to proclaim release to the prisoners*
> *and recovery of sight to the blind,*
> *to liberate the oppressed,*
> *and to proclaim the year of the Lord's favor.* (Luke 4:18)

Like an inauguration speech, this sermon launches Jesus's entire public ministry. It sets the tone for how Jesus carries out God's saving purpose in the Gospel. What, then, does it tell us about the nature of Jesus's mission? That is a much debated question. Some interpreters take the various images of the passage (e.g., the poor, release to the captives, sight to the blind) primarily as metaphors for the *spiritual* salvation that Jesus proclaims.[7] Others read this text in a literal and concrete sense; it describes the *political* and *socioeconomic* liberation Jesus brings to the poor and the oppressed.[8]

6. See Christopher J. H. Wright, *The Mission of God: Unlocking the Bible's Grand Narrative* (Downers Grove, IL: IVP Academic, 2006), 301. For the following section, see the similar arguments in Dean Flemming, *Recovering the Full Mission of God: A Biblical Perspective on Being, Doing and Telling* (Downers Grove, IL: IVP Academic, 2013), 101–5.

7. See, e.g., Graham H. Twelftree, *People of the Spirit: Exploring Luke's View of the Church* (Grand Rapids: Baker Academic, 2009), 184–87.

8. See, e.g., E. H. Scheffler, "Reading Luke from the Perspective of Liberation Theology," in *Text and Interpretation: New Approaches in the Criticism of the New Testament*, ed. P. J. Hartin and J. H. Petzer

To ask, however, whether this is passage is about *either* spiritual *or* socio-political restoration is like asking farmers whether their crops need sunshine *or* rain. Jesus's mission is comprehensive. On the one hand, Jesus receives a divine commission to proclaim the good news of the kingdom. Three times in the passage we see words for preaching. Jesus has been sent to "preach good news [*euangelizomai*] to the poor," to "proclaim [*kēryssō*] release to the prisoners, and to "proclaim [*kēryssō*] the year of the Lord's favor." In Luke's Gospel, announcing the good news of God's reign is indispensable to Jesus's calling (see Luke 4:43-44; 7:22; 8:1). What's more, the language of "release" (literally, "to proclaim *release* to the captives... to send forth the oppressed in *release*," Luke 4:18) often refers to Jesus's ministry of forgiving people's sins (see Luke 3:3; 5:20-24; 7:47-49; 24:47). In other cases, "release" means rescue from the power of Satan (Luke 4:33-37; 13:16). The good news of release through Jesus carries a profound spiritual dimension.

On the other hand, the *content* of Jesus's preaching assures us that Jesus's ministry goes beyond verbal witness and "spiritual" salvation alone. Here Jesus's preaching of the good news is mainly directed toward the poor—the disposable and the downtrodden of society. The headline statement in the sermon provides a key to the passage: proclaiming "good news to the poor" is the fundamental mission for which Jesus is sent (see Luke 7:22). The phrases that follow in Luke 4:18-19 unfold what it means to bring good news to the poor.

Who are the "poor"? In the context of Isaiah 61, which Jesus quotes in Luke 4, the poor and the oppressed are those in exile, people who have lost their rights and their land.[9] More broadly in the Old Testament, the poor "were in one sense the victims of the unjust structures of society—powerless, vulnerable, insignificant, exploited, economically deprived, and oppressed; in another sense they were the spiritually pious who were humbly and utterly dependent on God."[10] It follows that we cannot restrict "the poor" to *either* the materially *or* the spiritually destitute.

Furthermore, being "poor" in Luke's Gospel is not simply about one's economic state. "The poor" include all those who are on the periphery of society in the ancient Mediterranean world, for whatever physical, cultural, social, economic, or religious reasons.[11] "Good news to the poor," then, is a word of grace and embrace that addresses the whole person.

(Leiden: Brill, 1991), 284–96.

9.   R. Geoffrey Harris, *Mission in the Gospels* (London: Epworth, 2004), 119.

10.   Paul Hertig, "The Jubilee Mission of Jesus in the Gospel of Luke: Reversal of Fortunes." *Missiology* 26 (1998): 173.

11.   Green, *Gospel of Luke*, 211.

It follows, then, that the other activities in Jesus's sermon define his ministry holistically. "Recovery of sight to the blind," for example, can refer to actual physical healing (Luke 7:21-22; 18:35-43), but it can also signify the light of revelation and salvation that Jesus brings (1:77-79; 2:29-32; 10:23-24; cf. Acts 26:18, 23).

The Isaiah quotation also bristles with the language of the Jubilee from Leviticus 25. The phrases "release to the prisoners," "to liberate the oppressed," and, particularly, "the year of the Lord's favor" envision a time when debts would be cancelled, land restored to its original owners, and those enslaved due to poverty would be liberated. Isaiah 61 draws on Jubilee imagery to give the returned exiles a vision of Israel's eschatological restoration and release. Following Isaiah's lead, Jesus declares that God's end-time purpose to bring liberation to the poor and the marginal had erupted into the arena of human history in his own mission.[12] Jesus announces, "Today, this scripture has been fulfilled, just as you heard it" (Luke 4:21).

At the same time, the phrase "to liberate the oppressed," which has been inserted into the quotation, comes from Isaiah 58. That context powerfully announces God's demand for justice and compassion for the poor and the misused. The Jubilee imagery, then, in Jesus's mission manifesto, "serves both as a *symbol of future hope* and also as an *ethical demand in the present*."[13] If Jesus embodies the mission of a God who loves justice (Isa 61:8), then it seems unthinkable that Jesus is *only* concerned that the oppressed be freed in a strictly *spiritual* sense. Jesus's Spirit-anointed ministry means the reversal of the structures that victimize people.[14] Perhaps more than any other passage in Luke and Acts, Luke 4:18-19 display the *integrated, all-encompassing* character of Jesus's mission.

Holistic Mission in Practice

What Jesus announces in Luke 4, he practices in the rest of the Gospel. Luke takes great pains to show that Jesus comes to bring God's salvation in every dimension. Chapter 13 includes a vignette about a nameless woman who had suffered from a disabling illness for eighteen years (Luke 13:10-17). Her "bent over" physical posture symbolizes her low social state. It is likely that her disease brought exclusion from the normal social and religious life of her village. Defying his Jewish religious critics, Jesus addresses the fullness of

12. Howard Peskett and Vinoth Ramachandra, *The Message of Mission: The Glory of Christ in All Time and Space* (Downers Grove, IL: InterVarsity Press, 2003), 162.

13. Wright, *Mission of God*, 302 (italics original).

14. David E. Garland, *Luke* (Grand Rapids: Zondervan, 2011), 198.

her need. He heals her crippled body (Luke 13:12), liberates her from Satan's bondage (Luke 13:16), and so restores her to the community of God's people. He dignifies this nameless woman as a true "daughter of Abraham" (Luke 13:16). She becomes a signpost for Jesus's mission of forgiveness, freedom, and wholeness. No wonder the crowd of onlookers rejoices over what he has done (Luke 13:17)!

"Saving" the lost. Elsewhere, Luke summarizes Jesus's mission as coming "to seek and save the lost" (Luke 19:10). In its Gospel setting, this statement concludes Luke's poignant account of Jesus's encounter with the toll collector Zacchaeus (Luke 19:1-10). As a tax collector, Zacchaeus straddles social categories. On the one hand, he is a wealthy oppressor, who's made his fortune by cheating ordinary Jewish people (Luke 19:8). On the other hand, he's a hated chief tax collector, a social pariah, one of the "lost" Jesus came to save. So what does it mean for "salvation" to come to Zacchaeus's house (Luke 19:9)? More than simply getting his soul ready for heaven. God's robust salvation brings Zacchaeus forgiveness of his sins, restoration into God's people as a true "son of Abraham," and a transformed life, evidenced by his economic repentance—he gives half his possessions to those in need (Luke 19:8-9). And this is not merely the conversion of an individual. Zacchaeus's entire household is caught up in Jesus's saving work (Luke 19:9).

Jesus's kingdom mission, then, is about restoration at every level—spiritual, physical, psychological, social, and economic.

Reversal of fortunes. The Third Gospel shines a bright spotlight on the economic consequences of Jesus's mission, as we saw in the case of Zacchaeus. Jesus's message of good news for the poor and the lost regularly translates into "bad news" for the powerful and the rich. Salvation in Luke's Gospel often comes in the form of eschatological reversal, in which the tables are turned on the current state of affairs. Those who are poor and hungry *now* will one day have plenty, while the rich, who currently "have it made," are in danger of God's coming judgment (Luke 6:20-21, 24-25; cf. 13:30). Only Luke includes two parables about rich people who thumb their noses at the needs of others: the parable of the rich fool (12:16-21) and the rich man and Lazarus (16:19-31). In the latter, the beggar Lazarus suffers at the gate of a wealthy man, who enjoys a sumptuous and extravagant lifestyle. But at death, lowly Lazarus is lifted up to Abraham's bosom, while it's the *rich man's* turn to suffer in Hades.

Such overturning of economic realities is not *only* a future hope. The breaking in of God's kingdom in the mission of Jesus signals that the end-time reversal of fortunes has *already* begun. As Mary sings early on in the Gospel:

> He has pulled the powerful down from their thrones
> and lifted up the lowly.
> He has filled the hungry with good things,
> and sent the rich away empty-handed. (Luke 1:52-53)

Jesus's mission, throughout Luke's Gospel, is about lifting up the lowly.

In summary, then, Jesus's many-faceted mission results in a comprehensive salvation. Jesus proclaims good news to sinners, restores the sick to health, delivers people from Satan's bondage, offers freedom to the oppressed, confronts the rich and the proud, and turns social realities upside down.

Holistic Mission in Acts

Continuing Jesus's mission. Alone among the Gospel writers, Luke offers a sequel to the story of Jesus. At the beginning of Acts, Luke portrays the narrative of the Third Gospel as "all that Jesus began to do and to teach" (Acts 1:1 NIV). This surely implies that Acts is about to unfold what Jesus *continues* to do and teach, now as the resurrected Lord, through his Spirit-empowered community. And Luke's story bears this out. Luke draws many lines of continuity between Jesus's ministry of word and deed and the faithful witness of the church. For example, before his resurrection, Jesus appoints the twelve "apostles" and sends them out with his authority to proclaim the kingdom and perform acts of power (Luke 6:13; 9:1-2). And after Easter, the Twelve initially take the lead in preaching the word of the risen Lord and doing "signs and wonders" in Jesus's name (Acts 2:42-43; 3:1-10; 5:12-16).[15]

Just as Jesus, then, embodied the all-encompassing mission of God, so does the church in Acts. The mission of God's people is portrayed as a logical extension of the mission of Jesus. In Acts, we find the church and its representatives doing the same kinds of saving work that Jesus did:

• Proclaiming the good news (see Acts 2:14-41; 5:42; 8:4-5, 12; 10:42; 11:19-21; 13:16-41)

---

15. For other parallels between the ministries of Jesus and that of the church in Acts, see Harris, *Mission in the Gospels*, 112–14.

- Teaching believers and unbelievers (see Acts 2:42; 5:21, 42; 11:26; 13:1; 15:35; 18:25-26)

- Healing the sick (see Acts 3:1-10; 5:12, 15-16; 8:6-8; 9:32-43; 19:11-20; cf. 10:36-38)

- Confronting the powers of evil (see Acts 5:16; 8:7-24; 13:6-12; 19:12-20)

Yet, in other ways, Acts extends and refocuses Jesus's mission. In particular, Acts understands the church's mission in terms of witnessing to the risen Lord.

Mission as witness. Even as Jesus gives his own ministry a "mission statement" in Luke 4:18-19, he provides one for his followers in Acts 1:8: "You will receive power when the Holy Spirit has come upon you, and you will be my witnesses in Jerusalem, in all Judea and Samaria, and to the end of the earth." The phrase "you will be my witnesses" sets the tone for the church's participation in the mission of God in Acts. Luke highlights the disciples' role as witnesses throughout his narrative.[16] This should come as no surprise to attentive readers, since Jesus's postresurrection commission at the end of Luke anticipates the theme ("You are witnesses of these things," Luke 24:48).

But what does it mean to be Christ's witnesses? In Acts, *witnessing* is a comprehensive notion. In the first place, being a witness means giving reliable testimony to what God has done in Jesus, particularly his resurrection from the dead. Apostles like Peter (Acts 2:32; 3:15; 5:32; 10:39, 41) and Paul (Acts 22:15; 23:11; 26:16) repeatedly make reference to this witnessing role.[17] Early on, at Pentecost, Peter declares, "This Jesus God raised up. We are all witnesses to that fact" (Acts 2:32). Beyond the mere facts of what happened, however, God's witnesses testify to the saving meaning of Jesus's life, death, and resurrection. Paul summarizes his ministry as witnessing "to both Jews and Greeks that they must change their hearts and lives as they turn to God and have faith in their Lord Jesus" (Acts 20:21). God's witnesses, then, tell the saving story—the good news. They speak the truth about what God has done to redeem humanity in Jesus.

What is the consequence of repenting and turning to God? In Acts, the blessings of salvation focus especially on forgiveness of sins (Acts 2:38; 5:31;

16. "Witness" (*martys*) appears thirteen times in Acts, "to bear witness" (*martyreō*) eleven times, and "to testify" (*diamartyresthai*) nine times.

17. Although the role of "witness" begins with the apostles, Luke extends it more broadly (Acts 10:43; 22:20). This suggests that the apostles represent the wider church in their witnessing function.

31

10:43; 13:38; 26:18) and receiving the gift of the Holy Spirit (Acts 2:38; 10:47; 11:14-15; 19:5-6), although the gospel message is tailored for different groups of people.[18] Salvation, however, involves not just a change in belief but also a change in behavior, the need to "demonstrate their repentance by their deeds" (Acts 26:20 NIV). Gospel preaching in Acts also retains a darker side, the warning of a coming judgment for those who refuse the gift of salvation (Acts 10:42; 13:40-41; 17:31; 24:25).

Luke underlines this verbal testimony by peppering his story with a whole series of speeches and sermons, which unpack the content of the apostles' witness. And beyond the specific language of "witnessing," Luke pictures apostles and missionaries "preaching" (*kēryssō*) and "announcing the good news" (*euangelizomai*) in an assortment of settings—from local synagogues to lecture halls, before great gatherings (Acts 2:5-41) and within an African's private chariot (Acts 8:26-40). In addition, Luke highlights the progress of the word. God is powerfully present in the church's witness, and so Luke can report that "the word of the Lord grew mightily and prevailed" (Acts 19:20; cf. 6:7; 12:24).

But although Acts gives special attention to verbal testimony, God's servants bear witness through *deeds*, as well as words. "Signs and wonders" in the form of healings and exorcisms attest to God's miraculous power (see Acts 2:43; 5:12-16; 9:32-35, 36-42; 19:11-20). At times, miracles play an important role in leading people to faith in God (see Acts 9:33-35, 41-42; 13:12; 19:17). In one case, when Peter raises a compassionate woman named Tabitha from the dead, Luke immediately inserts, "The news spread throughout Joppa, and many put their faith in the Lord" (Acts 9:42). Miraculous deeds are vital to the church's mission in Acts.

Like Jesus and his disciples, the church also confronts the powers that oppose the purposes of God. Luke extends Jesus's defeat of Satan and the demonic powers to the arena of magic, which was woven into the fabric of popular Greco-Roman religion. Luke spotlights this theme by narrating three different occasions when God's agents face off with the power of magic and those who practice it (Acts 8:9-24; 13:6-12; 19:13-20).

In addition to signs and wonders, witness also occurs through the shared life of the Christian community. In the early chapters of Acts, the common life and practices of the new community of the Spirit confirms the word that the apostles proclaim. In addition, the church's common life becomes an em-

---

18. Contrast, for example, the scripture-based appeal to Jews and God-fearers in the sermons in chs. 2, 10, and 13 with the emphasis on God's activity in creation and human history in chs. 14 and 17. For more on how the gospel is "contextualized" in Acts, see Dean Flemming, *Contextualization in the New Testament: Patterns for Theology and Mission* (Downers Grove, IL: IVP Academic, 2005), 25–88.

bodiment of the gospel in its own right.[19] Luke paints a striking portrait of the community's life together in Acts 2:42-47:

> The believers devoted themselves to the apostles' teaching, to the community, to their shared meals, and to their prayers. A sense of awe came over everyone. God performed many wonders and signs through the apostles. All the believers were united and shared everything. They would sell pieces of property and possessions and distribute the proceeds to everyone who needed them. Every day, they met together in the temple and ate in their homes. They shared food with gladness and simplicity. They praised God and demonstrated God's goodness to everyone. The Lord added daily to the community those who were being saved.

Here Luke describes the regular practices of the newly formed Jerusalem community, which include instruction of believers and evangelistic proclamation (both are implied by "the apostles' teaching," 2:42), united and joyful fellowship, common meals, prayer, acts of power, praise and worship, and sharing possessions with those in need. This final practice evidences a radical generosity, which, by chapter 4, has progressed from selling goods to selling lands and houses to care for the poor. The result is that "there were no needy persons among them" (Acts 4:34). By redistributing their resources to serve the poor and the marginalized, the Jerusalem community gives fresh expression to the Old Testament Jubilee principle (see Lev 25), which Jesus announced in his own mission manifesto in Nazareth (Luke 4:19; see 12:33-34).

Acts 2:42-47 carries three further missional implications. First, the practices of the Jerusalem community are visible to the outside world. Jesus's followers continue to teach, pray, and worship publicly, at the temple. And surely others were well aware of their generosity, hospitality, and joy. Second, their community life is contagious. Luke tells us they enjoy "the goodwill of all the people" (Acts 2:47 NRSV). As a result, "the Lord added daily to the community those who were being saved" (Acts 2:47; see 5:14). Outsiders are attracted to the church's winsome lifestyle, like bees to a flower. Third, being "saved" is more than simply an individual decision. Salvation involves being incorporated into a community with certain practices and "whose life is a testimony to the identity of the resurrected Lord of all."[20]

19. For a fuller discussion of this theme, see Flemming, *Recovering the Full Mission of God*, 149–53.

20. C. Kavin Rowe, *World Upside Down: Reading Acts in the Graeco-Roman Age* (Oxford: Oxford University Press, 2009), 124.

Given the prominent role Luke gives this passage near the beginning of Acts and the detail of his description, it seems likely that he sees the Jerusalem congregation as a model for other churches.[21] Surely this carries implications for how local Christian communities share in the mission of God today.

Witness in Acts, however, is not simply a matter of words and practices. It also defines the very character and identity of the church. Jesus gives his followers a missional identity in his postresurrection promise: "You will *be* my witnesses" (Acts 1:8, italics added). In other words, Jesus's disciples will not only *proclaim* the good news of Christ's life, death, and resurrection. They will give it bones and blood. In Acts, the church doesn't just *have* a mission; "it is to *be* missional and *is* a mission."[22]

That missional identity comes into focus in Luke's portrayal of missionaries who live and act in ways that resemble Jesus. For example, Stephen, in the jaws of impending death, forgives his enemies and commends his spirit to the "Lord Jesus" (Acts 7:59-60), recalling Jesus's own attitude on the cross. C. Kavin Rowe is surely correct that "witness" in Acts involves not only proclaiming Jesus's resurrection, but also "living out the pattern of life that culminates in resurrection." Rowe continues, "The main characters in Acts, to put it plainly, look like Jesus—and precisely in this way embody his life and carry it forth in the wider Graeco-Roman world."[23] In Acts, missional practices flow from a missional identity.

What about social justice? If Jesus's mission of restoration included justice for the poor and oppressed (see Luke 4:18-19), do we also find this in Acts? Does mission in Acts carry any implications for the unjust structures of society? The answer to this question has often been a resounding no. According to one recent interpreter, "From Luke's perspective... mission = evangelism = proclaiming forgiveness or demonstrating the gospel in healing or exorcism, no less and no more."[24] But is mission in Acts simply about *personal* redemption and healing?

This is too narrow an understanding of what mission means in Acts, for at least three reasons. First, Acts is the second volume of a two-volume work. As a continuation of what Jesus began to do and teach (Acts 1:1), Acts assumes

21. See Eckhard J. Schnabel, *Acts* (Grand Rapids: Zondervan, 2012), 1094.

22. Darrell L. Bock, *A Theology of Luke and Acts: God's Revised Program, Realized for All Nations* (Grand Rapids: Zondervan, 2012), 139.

23. Rowe, *World Upside Down*, 153.

24. Twelftree, *People of the Spirit*, 197. See also the influential reading of Acts by Hans Conzelmann and others, who explain that a significant part of Luke's purpose for Acts is to show that the early Christian movement was no political or social threat to the Roman Empire. For a convincing critique of this view, see Rowe, *World Upside Down*.

Jesus's comprehensive kingdom message. In Acts, Luke puts into the limelight the progress of the *word* from Jerusalem to Rome. It shouldn't astound us, then, that there would be less focus on meeting human social needs.

Second, we have already seen that Luke *does* care about justice for the poor and the marginalized—within the early Christian community (Acts 2:45-56; 4:32-35; cf. 6:1-7). The lifestyle of economic justice within the Spirit-formed community serves as a symbol, or, as Richard Hays puts it, "the first fruits" of Jesus's mission to create a community in which "good news is proclaimed and enacted for the poor and oppressed."[25] The just actions of the Christian community are not separate from, but part of Jesus's broader purpose of loving the fragile and needy of society through his people.

Third, more broadly, the Acts narrative has a good deal more to say about social and political transformation than is usually recognized. C. Kavin Rowe argues convincingly that the universal Lordship of God in Jesus constructs an alternative pattern of thinking and living, which, by its very nature, threatens the political, social, and economic stability of the Roman world.[26] In Acts 19, for example, Paul's preaching against idolatry in Ephesus turns the city upside down (Acts 19:23-41). Local silversmiths panic when their business of selling idols of the goddess Artemis comes under threat. What's more, undermining the worship of the "great" Artemis puts at risk the political honor of Ephesus itself (Acts 19:27). Here the gospel not only brings personal transformation. It also subverts the systems of politics and economics that oppose the lordship of Christ.

Rowe is on target that the book of Acts shows no interest in reforming society through a government takeover or by political protest. Rather, Luke focuses on a Spirit-filled community that embodies an alternative way of living. It models a life of compassion, justice, and forgiveness, which, despite its political powerlessness, ultimately disrupts the way things operate in the Roman world.[27]

In Acts, then, the apostolic witness to the resurrection of Jesus is actualized in sins being forgiven, bodies healed, Satan and magic defeated, communities of Christlike compassion and justice established, and seeds of societal transformation planted. A robust mission indeed.

---

25. Richard B. Hays, *The Moral Vision of the New Testament: Community, Cross, New Creation; A Contemporary Introduction to New Testament Ethics* (San Francisco: HarperSanFrancisco, 1996), 124.

26. Rowe, *World Upside Down*, 140.

27. Rowe summarizes the tension created by the Christian mission's engagement with the Gentile world: "New culture, yes—coup, no" (ibid., 5, 91).

A Boundary-Breaking Mission

Jesus's Inclusive Ministry

A second aspect of the mission of God in Luke-Acts is its propensity to cross barriers and shatter boundaries. But that poses a question. If God's project is to bring salvation to all nations and to include Gentiles in the people of God (Luke 24:47; Acts 1:8; 10:34-35), then why don't we see more evidence of this universal mission in the Gospel of Luke? After all, Jesus's own mission was confined essentially to a Jewish sphere of influence.

Here we need to consider Luke's entire narrative. We find a distinct line of continuity between Jesus's ministry to the poor and the outcasts of Jewish society in Luke and the universal mission to the Gentiles in Acts. In each case, the mission of God dissolves boundaries and draws in outsiders. In a richer and more intentional way than the other Gospels, Luke shows that Jesus's mission to bring "good news to the poor" (Luke 4:18; 7:22) draws him out of the safe center of respectability into the messy periphery of human existence. As Darío López Rodriguez frames it, "Luke repeatedly highlights God's special love for the poor and the rejected, the 'scum' of society, and those on the other bank of history and the high tide of exclusion."[28] The groups of peripheral people Jesus relates to in Luke include lepers, tax collectors, sinners, Samaritans, Gentiles, women, children, the sick, and the disabled. Using Miroslav Volf's memorable language, whereas Palestinian society leaned toward *exclusion*, we can say that Jesus practiced a mission of *embrace*.[29]

Two practices, in particular, spotlight the boundary-crossing character of Jesus's mission in Luke.[30] First, he *embraces the untouchable*. Like lepers. In first-century Jewish society, lepers were excluded from interaction with others because of their disease and their unclean status before God. But Jesus risks ceremonial uncleanness by reaching out his hand to touch a leper who begs to be made whole (Luke 5:12-16). Instead of Jesus becoming *unclean*, the needy man becomes *clean*. Physical, social, and religious fences collapse in that single touch.

What's more, only Luke tells the story of Jesus healing ten lepers as a group (Luke 17:11-19). When they approach Jesus, the diseased men adhere

---

28. Darío López Rodriguez, *The Liberating Mission of Jesus: The Message of the Gospel of Luke*, trans. Stephanie E. Israel and Richard E. Waldrop (Eugene, OR: Pickwick, 2012), 28.

29. See Miroslav Volf, *Exclusion and Embrace: A Theological Exploration of Identity, Otherness, and Reconciliation* (Nashville: Abingdon, 1996).

30. For the following, see Flemming, *Recovering the Full Mission of God*, 74–76.

36

to society's boundaries, shouting from a distance. Not until one of them re-turns, on his own, does the social barrier come down. Entering Jesus's space, he falls at the healer's feet in praise and gratitude. Only now we learn that this man bears a double burden of exclusion. He is not only a leper but also a "foreigner," a Samaritan (Luke 17:16, 18)—part of the sewage of society, in Jewish eyes. To such a person, reviled and avoided, Jesus pronounces a word of grace and acceptance that runs deeper than physical healing alone: "Your faith has *made you whole*" (Luke 17:19 AT; literally, "*saved* [*sōzō*] you").

Second, Jesus *eats with the unworthy*. In Jesus's social world, *meals mattered*. Sharing the table with people signaled a relationship of acceptance and intimacy. In effect, it meant treating them like they were part of one's ex-tended family. At the same time, the table could also become a place of exclu-sion. To refuse to eat with others because they were considered unworthy or unclean was to treat them as outcasts.[31]

Luke, then, goes out of his way to picture Jesus eating with the wrong kinds of people. Much of Jesus's ministry revolves around meals in the Third Gospel. Jesus's practice of stunningly inclusive table fellowship becomes a deliberate mission strategy. His willingness to wine and dine with tax collec-tors and sinners at Levi's home shocked the Pharisees (Luke 5:29-32). Tax collectors were well known for collaborating with the Roman oppressors and "sinners" were people the Pharisees considered to be ritually impure and transgressors of the law. By sharing food with sinners and tax collectors like Levi and Zacchaeus (19:1-10), Jesus "proclaims" God's love and grace for outsiders. Jesus's teaching in Luke reinforces the point. He urges a high status Pharisee, in effect, "When you throw a party, don't invite the rich or those who can afford to return the favor. Rather, fill your banquet table with fragile and marginalized people—'the poor, crippled, lame and blind'" (Luke 14:12-14; cf. 4:15-24). In Luke, Jesus's "table manners" announce the inclusive, boundary-shattering character of the kingdom of God.

"To the End of the Earth"

Jesus's mission of embrace continues in the book of Acts, but it veers in a new direction.[32] The torch is passed, in effect, from Jesus and his disciples to the apostolic church. Jesus's resurrection and the pouring out of the Spirit on all flesh signal that the mission of God is about to cross new barriers. The mission of Jesus, which is largely restricted to Palestine and to the Jewish

31. See Green, *Gospel of Luke*, 87.
32. Harris, *Mission in the Gospels*, 115.

people, becomes a universal force that radiates "to the end of the earth" (Acts 1:8).[33]

Not that we haven't seen it coming. Luke's Gospel repeatedly foreshadows this universal mission. For example:

• At Jesus's birth, Simeon announces that the child will fulfill Isaiah's prophecy to be a "light of revelation to the Gentiles" (Luke 2:30-32; cf. 2:14; 3:6).

• Jesus interprets his Nazareth sermon in Luke 4 to mean that he has come to minister to people like the widow from Zarephath in Sidon and the enemy general Naaman from Syria (Luke 4:23-27). God has shown interest in such Gentile outsiders in the past, and this becomes the trajectory of Jesus's own ministry (cf. Luke 10:12-16; 11:30-32).

• On occasion, Jesus ministers to non-Jews, like the Roman centurion, who has faith like no one in Israel (Luke 7:1-10; cf. 8:26-39; 17:11-19).

• People come from all points of the compass to eat at the end-time banquet (Luke 13:29).

• Luke alone tells us that Jesus sends out a larger group of seventy-two disciples into mission (Luke 10:1-12). It is likely that the number seventy-two carries symbolic significance that prefigures the mission to the nations to come.[34]

In particular, Jesus's "mission commission" at the end of Luke (Luke 24:44-49) acts like a hinge between the Gospel and the book of Acts. It recalls themes from Luke, including the fulfillment of scripture, the story of Jesus's suffering and resurrection, and the preaching of repentance and forgiveness of sins. But it also points forward to a mission to the nations and the role of Jesus's followers as witnesses in the power of the Spirit. What is incomplete in the Gospel will be fulfilled in Acts.

A programmatic promise. The structure of Luke's narrative in Acts "demonstrates that the theology of Acts is a mission theology."[35] Early on, Jesus

33. Ibid.
34. For example, in the LXX (Greek OT), Genesis 10:2-31 lists seventy-two nations. Some manuscripts read "seventy" rather than "seventy-two," but the latter, as the harder reading, is preferable.
35. Schnabel, *Acts*, 1084.

promises his followers that they will be his witnesses in Jerusalem, in Judea and Samaria, and to the end of the earth (Acts 1:8). Even as Jesus's mission in Luke's Gospel moves geographically from Galilee *toward* Jerusalem, the church's mission radiates out *from* Jerusalem to the end of the earth in Acts. And as it does, it crosses boundaries, reaching both new locales and new groups of people.[36] Just as "outsiders" like Samaritans and tax collectors become "insiders" in the Third Gospel, so people on the margins like Samaritans and pagan Gentiles are embraced by the loving mission of God in the book of Acts.

What motivates the church's mission to the end of the earth in Acts? It's noteworthy that Acts 1:8 is not a command ("Go out and testify!"), but a *promise*: this is what the church, empowered by the Spirit, *will* do. According to Acts, Christian mission is not based on any external command to obedience. Nor does it originate in the idea of mission, as such. Rather, as Rowe insists, "mission is the necessary response to the universal Lordship of God in Jesus Christ.... The ultimate origin of the Christian mission lies in the act of God."[37] Because God has raised Jesus from the grave, because the Holy Spirit has descended on "all flesh" (Acts 2:17), because Jesus is "Lord of all" (Acts 10:36), the church is defined by a mission that extends to all people everywhere. The impetus to cross cultural, ethnic, religious, and geographical boundaries, then, flows out of the reality of the universal Lordship of Christ.

Baby steps. But it doesn't happen all at once. Instead, Acts narrates an incremental journey of apostolic witness to various groups of people. The early chapters of Acts portray a mission to Jewish people in Jerusalem, the point of departure for the church's universal witness in Acts. Yet, the pivotal moment of the Spirit's outpouring at Pentecost signals a broader mission. The miracle of languages enables Jews and proselytes from all corners of the Mediterranean world to hear the word of the Lord in their own languages (Acts 2:4-11). This symbolizes that the good news of what God has done in Jesus is not confined to any nation or to the Hebrew tongue. From the beginning, the gospel bridges barriers of language and communication.

Following Stephen's martyrdom, persecution scatters the Jerusalem disciples. These unexpected circumstances serve as a catalyst for mission. Philip the evangelist takes the lead and brings the good news to a group of social, religious, and political rivals of the Jews, the Samaritans (Acts 8:4-25). The Samaritan mission builds on Jesus's ministry to Samaritans in Luke's Gospel

---

36. After discussing the background and meaning of the phrase "the end of the earth" (Acts 1:8), Darrell L. Bock concludes that it is both "geographic and ethnic in scope" (*A Theology of Luke and Acts*, 138).

37. Rowe, *World Upside Down*, 116, 123.

(Luke 9:51-56; 10:25-37; 17:15-19) and in part fulfills Jesus's promise of Spirit-empowered witness in "Judea and Samaria" (Acts 1:8). For Luke, the Samaritans, although not Jews in the strict sense, remain on the margins of Judaism. They stand "as a halfway house between Jewish and Gentile worlds leading to a transition to the Gentile mission."[38]

Philip's divinely orchestrated meeting with an Ethiopian official on a chariot ride enables the Christian mission to cross additional boundaries (Acts 8:26-39). Luke's narrative sculpts an intriguing figure. In some ways, the official is an "insider." A pious sympathizer with Judaism, he is making a return trip from worshipping the God of Israel at the Jerusalem temple. What's more, Philip finds him poring over the text of Isaiah the prophet. But from a Jewish perspective, he is also clearly an "outsider." He's a dark-skinned African, a castrated male (see Deut 23:1), and probably a Gentile.[39] Furthermore, he hails from a place that is widely considered to be at the "end of the earth." For the Ethiopian to come to faith in Jesus as Messiah, the gospel must cross religious, racial, cultural, physical, and geographical barriers and upend human power structures. The eunuch is baptized on the spot, and the Christian mission takes another step in its embrace of marginal people.

A tale of two conversions. This brief interlude on the road to Gaza anticipates what, for Luke, is a Himalayan peak in his narrative of the widening Christian mission—Peter's encounter with Cornelius (Acts 10:1–11:18). The sheer amount of attention Luke gives to this story, telling it twice (Acts 10 and 11) and referencing it a third time (Acts 15:7-11), testifies to its importance in the Acts narrative. This crucial test case lays the groundwork for the universal mission of the church.

Acts 10 and 11 tell the story of *two* complementary conversions. The first and most obvious one is that of the Roman centurion Cornelius, who represents the inclusion of Gentiles into the people of God (Acts 11:1, 18). But although Cornelius is a *representative* Gentile, he's far from a *typical* Gentile. Luke goes out of his way to depict Cornelius as a pious worshipper of Israel's God, someone whose prayers, faith, and almsgiving demonstrate his openness to divine grace (Acts 10:2-4). Cornelius and his household, then, represent a kind of "bridge group" for the gospel's advance into the Gentile world.

The second conversion in this story is that of Peter, the representative of the apostles and the Jewish Christian community. His is not a conversion to faith, but it is no less significant a transformation. With painstaking detail,

38. P. U. Maynard-Reid, "Samaria," in *Dictionary of the Later New Testament and Its Developments*, ed. Ralph P. Martin and Peter H. Davids (Downers Grove, IL: InterVarsity Press, 1997), 1076.

39. See C. K. Barrett, *A Critical and Exegetical Commentary on the Acts of the Apostles*, vol. 1, *Preliminary Introduction and Commentary on Acts I–XIV* (Edinburgh: T&T Clark, 1994), 420–21.

Luke describes Peter's difficult journey to a new vision of the people of God, one that embraces "unclean" Gentiles, as well as Jews. Peter's "conversion" requires his overcoming two barriers. The first is *theological*. Peter must grasp that God accepts Gentiles *as Gentiles* into the community of faith. "I really am learning," Peter testifies, "that God doesn't show partiality to one group of people over another. Rather, in every nation, whoever worships him and does what is right is acceptable to him" (Acts 10:34-35). In the end, not only Peter, but the once-skeptical Jewish Christian church understand that God has given new life even to the Gentiles (Acts 11:18), apart from observing the demands of the Jewish law.

The second, equally significant, obstacle to a mission to the Gentiles is the *social* barricade of table fellowship. Jewish revulsion toward eating with Gentiles was deeply entrenched.[40] Indeed, law-abiding Jewish Christians would have considered it nonnegotiable. Food laws guarded Jews from ritual impurity and served as crucial boundary markers, setting them apart as God's holy people. When God gives Peter a vision of a "non-kosher picnic"[41] and commands him to "Eat!" it's little wonder the apostle recoils in horror (Acts 10:9-14). For Peter to offer hospitality to Gentiles (Acts 10:23) and then receive it from Cornelius (Acts 10: 27-28, 48) meant, on the one hand, that the barriers of impurity and distinctiveness no longer applied. On the other hand, table fellowship with Gentiles signaled friendship, acceptance, and a life shared in common.[42] Just as Jesus shared the table with social outcasts in Luke's Gospel, so now table fellowship with Gentiles represents their inclusion into the people of God in Acts. Peter's "conversion," in effect, translates into a new missional identity for the church.

A decision for inclusion. The so-called Jerusalem Council in chapter 15 marks another critical step in the church's mission of crossing new frontiers in Acts. The need for the Council is triggered by the progress of the Gentile mission. Luke chronicles how some Greek-speaking Jews evangelize Gentile "Greeks" in Antioch and plant the first truly multicultural congregation (Acts 11:19-26). Antioch's missional vision generates the Christian movement's first intentional "overseas" mission to Gentiles as well as Jews (Acts 13:3). In the course of their missionary travels, Paul and Barnabas respond to Jewish rejection by shifting the focus of their mission to the Gentiles (Acts 13:46-

---

40. See Philip F. Esler, *Community and Gospel in Luke-Acts: The Social and Political Motivations of Lucan Theology* (Cambridge: Cambridge University Press, 1987), for a study of first-century Jewish food regulations and attitudes toward table fellowship with Gentiles, in light of Luke-Acts.

41. David A. deSilva, *Honor, Patronage, Kinship, and Purity: Unlocking New Testament Culture* (Downers Grove, IL: InterVarsity Press, 2000), 285.

42. Harris, *Mission in the Gospels*, 126.

47). This momentous decision spawns an influx of Gentile disciples into the church (Acts 13:48, 14:1, 21). What began with the conversion of a God-fearing Roman centurion and his household has snowballed into the establishing of multiple new communities of Jews and uncircumcised Gentiles worshipping the Lord Jesus together.

What prompts the Jerusalem Council is not the *fact* of Gentiles entering the church, but rather the *conditions* of their membership in the people of God.[43] The issue centers on whether Gentile converts need to be circumcised and keep the Torah, just as Gentile proselytes have always done, in order to experience full acceptance by God (Acts 15:1, 5). In other words, do Gentile believers need to become "naturalized Jews" in order to be saved? Luke shows no embarrassment in airing the sharp disagreement among believers over two competing interpretations of the gospel. This is a high-stakes dispute. If the Pharisees' position wins out, the journey toward a universal Christian mission could be potentially derailed. Not only would it place a massive obstacle in the way of the gospel's progress to non-Jewish people, but it also would effectively strip uncircumcised Gentile believers of their citizenship in the kingdom of God.[44]

On the basis of a series of testimonies to what God has been doing among the Gentiles (Acts 15:7-12), as well as James's reading of Amos 9:11-12 to support the Gentile mission (Acts 15:13-18), the gathered church and its leaders reach a decision. No "burden" of circumcision or keeping the law of Moses should be placed on Gentile converts (Acts 15:28; cf. 15:19). Salvation comes to all by God's grace through faith, without preconditions (Acts 15:9, 11). At the same time, Gentile believers are asked to abstain from certain practices found in the Jewish Holiness Code (Lev 17 and 18). In all likelihood, this is an "essential" (Acts 15:28) compromise on the part of Gentile Christians, so that Jews and Gentiles might continue to eat together at one table. In this way, the Council preserves both a united fellowship and a robust Gentile mission.

The Jerusalem Council, then, serves as a fascinating case of the church doing theology in the service of mission. In the Acts narrative, the Council settles the question once and for all that Gentiles can be converted without prior conditions and within their cultural identity. The missional impact is immediate, as missionaries broadcast the good news in Antioch (Acts 15:35). Beyond that, the decision "clears the path for Paul's ever widening horizon

---

43. A similar issue seems to be at stake in Paul's letter to the Galatians (see, e.g., Gal 2:11-14; 5:2-12; 6:12-13).

44. David Seccombe, "The New People of God," in *Witness to the Gospel: The Theology of Acts*, ed. I. Howard Marshall and David Peterson (Grand Rapids: Eerdmans, 1998), 365.

of mission that becomes Luke's dominant focus in the second half of Acts."[45] As David Seccombe observes, the basis for the Christian mission's ongoing ability to cross cultural barriers and adapt to new situations is "hammered out" in Acts 15.[46]

At the same time, what happens in the Jerusalem Council is not just a means to an end. Breaking down barriers between divided communities is not simply a catalyst for mission. It is an integral part of the mission itself. Earlier, Luke summarizes the gospel as God "proclaiming *peace* through Jesus Christ" (Acts 10:36 AT, italics added), a *shalom* that, in the context, includes peace between Jews and Gentiles (see Acts 10:34-35). Mission that is anchored in the gospel of Jesus Christ brings reconciliation to divided peoples.

Into the pagan world.[47] It is in the missionary work of Paul and his associates that the universal mission to "the end of the earth" begins to take its shape. It's hard not to be astounded by the sheer sweep of Paul's missionary activity in Acts. He bears witness to Jews, God-fearers, proselytes, and pagans. He seeks to establish and strengthen Spirit-led congregations among Cypriots, Asians, Macedonians, and Achaeans, among others. The lame and the possessed, magistrates and magicians, simple townsfolk and Stoic philosophers, Roman governors and Jewish kings—in Paul's words, "the lowly and the great" (Acts 26:22)—all encounter the good news of God's salvation through the Pauline mission.[48]

Paul's ministry enables the gospel to cross further boundaries during its journey from Jerusalem to the end of the earth. In chapters 14 and 17, Paul encounters groups of pagan Gentiles who are worlds apart from pious Gentile God-fearers like Cornelius, or those attached to the synagogue in Pisidian Antioch (see Acts 13:16, 26). The crowds Paul meets at Lystra (Acts 14:8-20) are simple townspeople who worship the deities of Greek popular religion. Paul's offer of "good news" (Acts 14:15-17) to the Lycaonians speaks with a very different accent than previous sermons to Jewish crowds in Acts. Rather than talking about Jesus the Messiah as the fulfillment of scriptural prophecy, he centers on the one, living God who created all things and cares for human needs by giving rain and fruitful harvests, things his audience understands. At the same time, Paul confronts their idolatry head on. They must "turn *to* the

---

45. Flemming, *Contextualization in the New Testament*, 52.

46. Seccombe, "New People," 366.

47. I use the term *pagan*, not in any derogatory sense, but as a simple and commonly used way of designating people in the ancient world who were not Jewish or Christian. See Rowe, *World Upside Down*, 14.

48. See Rowe, who asserts that the Christian mission in Acts "actively envisioned its target audience as anyone or everyone" (ibid., 125). For the following discussion, see Flemming, *Recovering the Full Mission of God*, 140–42.

living God and *away* from such worthless things" (Acts 14:15, italics added; cf. 1 Thess 1:9-10). Here the gospel and Greco-Roman religion collide. If the gods and the practices that maintain their worship are "worthless," then the whole infrastructure of pagan piety collapses.[49]

In Athens, Paul's mission encounters a different Gentile audience, one largely comprised of educated Stoic and Epicurean philosophers (Acts 17:16-34). Paul's ministry begins in the marketplace, where his polytheistic sparring partners completely misunderstand his message, accusing him of introducing foreign gods into the Greek Pantheon (Acts 17:18). Paul then delivers an evangelistic speech to the Areopagus ("Mars Hill") council, the body of leading citizens responsible for deciding religious questions in Athens.

Paul's sermon is exquisitely adapted to an educated pagan audience. His initial point of contact strikes a familiar chord to the Athenians, their altar to an unknown god (Acts 17:23). This serves as a springboard to the major thrust of the sermon, how the true God of the universe has made himself *known.* Paul's message both connects and collides with the worldview of his audience. Although the sermon is deeply rooted in Old Testament and Jewish teaching, he communicates that truth in ways that would make sense to biblically illiterate people. In addition, Luke's readers would recognize touch points with the teachings of Stoic philosophers, such as the notion that all people are in kinship with God (Acts 17:28). To support the point, Paul even borrows material from one of their own Stoic poets, first written in praise to Zeus ("We are his offspring," Acts 17:28)!

Yet Luke makes it abundantly clear that sermons to religiously plural Gentiles are not just about finding common ground. Paul, for example, subverts the Stoic belief in an impersonal, all-pervasive principle of divine reason by proclaiming a personal God who is "Lord of heaven and earth" (Acts 17:24). Above all, he delivers a devastating critique of Athenian idolatry (Acts 17:24-25, 29). Throughout the speech, Paul recruits the very language of the philosophers to confront and transform their worldview.

The speech crescendos to a climax in Acts 17:30-31: God has raised Jesus from the dead and appointed him to judge the world. For their part, the Athenians must "repent or face the music."[50] This proclamation of the good news echoes themes from previous sermons in Acts. But it also clashes with a Greek worldview. The gospel teaching on a bodily resurrection would have sounded disgusting, if not ridiculous, to many Greeks. The Christian message cannot be diluted simply to make it easier for the Athenians to swallow.

49. Rowe, *World Upside Down*, 140.

50. Richard J. Pervo, *Acts: A Commentary* (Minneapolis: Fortress, 2009), 430.

We have plotted a number of moments along the journey of Christian witness to Jesus's resurrection in Acts. Along the way, that mission crosses one cultural and ethnic barrier after another, forming faith communities out of peoples ranging from devout Jews to polytheistic Gentiles. But there is also a *geographical* movement to Luke's story. In Acts, Christian mission tracks from Jerusalem to *Rome*. Why Rome? Is it because Luke considers Rome to be "the end of the earth" (Acts 1:8)? Not exactly. As the hub of the Gentile world, Rome symbolizes the extension of the church's mission to the world at large. It is therefore a fitting place for Luke's story of Jesus and the early Christian mission to end.

In another sense, however, Luke tells an open-ended story. As Acts closes, we find Paul awaiting trial in Rome, continuing "to preach God's kingdom and teach about the Lord Jesus Christ" (Acts 28:31). Not much of an ending. Paul simply is doing what he's been up to all along. The ending of Acts, then, is more of an invitation than a closure. It beckons Luke's readers, in the first century and the twenty-first century, to embrace the mission of God that has been his subject all along. What God has done through Jesus and the apostolic church, God continues to do through communities of salvation today. *We*, in our diverse nations, cultures, and contexts, remain the *end of the earth*.

A Spirit-Empowered Mission

The Spirit in the Mission of Jesus

More than any other New Testament writer, Luke welds mission to the work of the Spirit. In Luke's narrative, the Spirit functions like a strong mountaineering rope, binding Jesus's mission to that of the church. In the early chapters of the Third Gospel, Luke spotlights the Spirit's vital role in the mission of Jesus. The Holy Spirit prophetically inspires key spokespeople, like Zechariah, Elizabeth, and Simeon, to bear witness to God's mission in Jesus (Luke 1:41-42, 67-79; 2:25-35). The Spirit, in the form of a dove, authenticates Jesus's divine sonship at his baptism (Luke 3:21-22). When Jesus announces his divine mission in Nazareth, he begins, "The Spirit of the Lord is upon me, because he has anointed me" (Luke 4:18 NRSV; cf. Isa 61:1).

This Spirit-presence and anointing is evident as the Spirit leads Jesus into the wilderness prior to his testing by Satan and empowers him when he returns to Galilee (Luke 4:1, 14; see Acts 10:38). Luke largely confines his *explicit* references to the Spirit's role in Jesus's mission to the beginning of his ministry. Joel B. Green is right, however, that this emphasis at the outset of the narrative of Jesus's mission carries through in all that follows.[51] Luke confirms this when he summarizes Jesus's entire ministry in Acts 10:38 as being "anointed with the Holy Spirit and endowed with power." Jesus's whole mission radiates the Spirit's guidance and power.

The Spirit also anoints Jesus's prayer life. Repeatedly, Luke sews together prayer and obedient service. Accordingly, in Luke 6, Jesus spends all night on a mountain in prayer before choosing twelve of his followers to be the apostles who will share his ministry. At once, Jesus comes down from the mountain and returns to serving crowds of desperate people (Luke 6:12-19; cf. 3:21; 5:16; 22:39-46).

The Spirit in the Mission of the Church

Just as Jesus's mission operates under the influence of the Spirit, those who *continue* his mission need the indwelling and empowering of the Holy Spirit. We begin to see this even in Luke's Gospel. Jesus promises, for example, that when his followers are hauled before "synagogues, rulers, and authorities," the Holy Spirit will give them the words to say (Luke 11:11-12). In Acts, that promise is fulfilled again and again (e.g., Peter, Acts 4:5-12; 5:27-32; Stephen, 6:8–7:53; Paul, 26:2-23).

Likewise, Jesus's parting words to his disciples in Luke's Gospel assure them that they will receive "power from on high" for their role as witnesses to Jesus's death and resurrection and the salvation he brings (Luke 24:46-49). Here all three persons in the Trinity are involved in the disciples' mission (see also Acts 1:7-8; 2:33). Jesus says, in effect, "*I* am sending you the blessing *my Father* promised—the empowering *Spirit*" (Luke 24:49).

What is anticipated in Luke's Gospel is realized in Acts. Almost four times as many references to the Holy Spirit fill the pages of Acts than occur in the Gospel.[52] In Acts, the Spirit initiates, directs, and empowers Christian mission. Let's look at each of these dimensions of the Spirit's work.

First, *the Spirit initiates the church's participation in the mission of God.* Right at the outset of Acts, Luke trumpets the pivotal role of the Spirit in his story of the church in mission. The disciples ask, "Lord, are you going to restore the kingdom to Israel now?" (Acts 1:6). The question is not surprising, in light of Jesus's teaching on the kingdom (Acts 1:3) and his promise of the Spirit (Acts 1:5), which had been prophesied as an end-time gift, ushering in

51. Green, *Theology of the Gospel of Luke*, 44–45.

52. Bock, *A Theology of Luke and Acts*, 219.

the age of salvation to come (e.g., Joel 2:28–3:1; Isa 32:15-17; 44:3; 59:21; Ezek 36:26-27; 37:1-14). In response, Jesus shifts the emphasis from *when* to *how* that restoration will happen (see Acts 1:8). "The outpouring of the Spirit," writes Michael Goheen, "signals that the blessings of the kingdom are about to be given, that the restoration has begun—and [the disciples'] role in this restoration is to be Jesus's witnesses in Jerusalem, Judea, Samaria, and on to the ends of the earth."[53]

In fulfillment of God's purpose, then, the Spirit gives birth to a community of mission, a restored Israel, which can embody Israel's servant role as a light to the nations of the earth (Isa 42:6; 49:6). The watershed event that enables this to happen is Pentecost. Just as the Spirit descended on Jesus in his baptism (Luke 3:22), so the Holy Spirit descends in a second, Spirit-baptism (Acts 1:5; cf. Luke 3:16). The risen and exalted Jesus receives and grants the Spirit as the transforming presence of God (Acts 2:33).[54] In fulfillment of Joel's promise, the Spirit of the last days is poured out, literally, on "all flesh"—the entire community of God's people (Acts 2:17). This means, on the one hand, that receiving the gift of the Spirit is essential for experiencing the salvation that God has provided through the death and resurrection of Jesus (Acts 2:38; 10:47; 11:14-15). Luke simply cannot imagine people being truly *Christian* apart from receiving the Spirit (see Acts 8:15-17; 19:2-3, 5-6). This is why Peter can defend God's saving work among the Gentiles as well the Jews by pointing to the evidence that God gave "them the Holy Spirit, just as he did to us" (Acts 15:8). It is the Spirit's work to forge a diverse, multicultural community of redeemed people.

On the other hand, the pouring out of the Spirit initiates a new era in the mission of God. Pentecost spawns mission. By the Spirit, the risen Christ continues his mission through the church, but now in an expanded, universal sense. The Spirit-community comes to mediate God's mission promise to Abraham long ago—to be a blessing to the nations. The Spirit in Acts is the Spirit of mission, a mission that in its very nature leans outward to the end of the earth (Acts 1:8).

Second, *the Spirit directs the church's participation in the mission of God.* At every point, the Spirit leads the apostolic church into ever-widening horizons of witness. "The Spirit," notes David Bosch, "becomes the catalyst, the guiding and driving force of mission."[55] The Holy Spirit leads Philip to an

53. Michael W. Goheen, *A Light to the Nations: The Missional Church and the Biblical Story* (Grand Rapids: Baker Academic, 2011), 126; see also Alan J. Thompson, *The Acts of the Risen Lord Jesus: Luke's Account of God's Unfolding Plan* (Downers Grove, IL: IVP Academic, 2011), 103–8.

54. Schnabel, *Acts*, 1092.

55. David J. Bosch, *Transforming Mission: Paradigm Shifts in the Theology of Mission* (Maryknoll, NY:

Ethiopian in the desert (Acts 8:29) and orchestrates an encounter between Peter and Cornelius that God uses to unlatch the door to the church's Gentile mission (Acts 10:19; 11:12). When the church wrestles over the issue of requiring Gentiles to be circumcised, the church testifies that its decision "seemed good to the Holy Spirit and to us" (Acts 15:28 NRSV).

The Holy Spirit guides a worshipping local church in Antioch to initiate the first itinerant mission, sending out Paul and Barnabas (Acts 13:2). And step-by-step the Spirit superintends Paul's missionary activity, both by blocking his entry into some locales (Acts 16:6, 7) and directing him to others (Acts 13:4; 16:9; 19:21; 20:22). The Spirit appoints local leaders to shepherd God's people (Acts 20:28) and speaks through scripture (Acts 1:16; 4:25; 28:25) and words of prophecy (Acts 11:27-28; 20:23, 25; 21:11). In short, without the guiding work of the Spirit, the narrative of Acts would be left with so many holes, it would fall apart.

Third, *the Spirit empowers the church's participation in the mission of God.* The Spirit of the risen Christ is also the power behind the mission of God's people in Acts. In fulfillment of Jesus's promise of divine power in Luke 24:49 and Acts 1:8, the Spirit energizes the church's witness from Jerusalem to the end of the earth (see Acts 4:8; 5:32; 6:10; 9:17; 13:9; 18:25).

One of the special ministries of the Holy Spirit in Acts is to infuse Christian witness with *boldness* in the face of adversity and opposition. In Acts 4, when the Jerusalem believers are threatened by hostile Jewish officials, they go to prayer. They ask for God's enabling to speak his word with "boldness" (*parrēsia*), that is, power and freedom (Acts 4:29-30). God's answer comes without delay. Their gathering place trembles, and they are "all filled with the Holy Spirit," so they can begin to speak God's word courageously (Acts 4:31). This passage is important, for at least two reasons. First, it shows that not only the apostles or missionaries, but also the wider believing community, are empowered by the Spirit for bold witness. Second, the vital linkage we saw between the Spirit, mission, and prayer in the life of Jesus now becomes the experience of the church.

Repeatedly in Acts, believers are "filled" with the Spirit on particular occasions in service of God's mission (e.g., Acts 4:8, 31; 6:5; 7:55; 13:9). While Paul and Barnabas, for example, engage in missionary work in Pisidian Antioch, Jewish opponents turn against them and kick them out of the city. Yet in spite of this persecution, their new converts are "filled with joy and with the Holy Spirit" (Acts 13:52 AT). Presumably this young community of

Orbis, 1991), 113.

believers stands "equipped to spread the word and meet further opposition (cf. Acts 14:22)."[56]

Furthermore, just as the anointing of the Spirit empowers Jesus to heal and drive out demons (Acts 10:38), so the coming of the Spirit on God's people enables signs and wonders to be performed in Jesus's name (Acts 2:17-19, 43; 4:30; 13:9-11). Luke also pictures the Holy Spirit as the Spirit of prophecy (Acts 2:17-21), who empowers God's servants to speak and act prophetically (Acts 2:17; 6:5, 8; 11:27-28; 13:46-47; 19:21; 21:11). Their prophetic ministry stands in continuity with Jesus, who has been raised up as a prophet like Moses (Acts 3:22; 7:37).[57]

Finally, a function of the Spirit that may not be as visible as inspired speech and miracles is the ministry of encouragement. In one of his summary statements, Luke makes it clear that it is "through the encouragement of the Holy Spirit that the church continued to increase in numbers" (Acts 9:31 AT). Given what we've seen in this brief survey, it's safe to say that virtually everything that happens in the mission of God that Luke narrates in Acts comes about through the presence, power, and guidance of the Holy Spirit, even when the Spirit is not specifically named.

Luke-Acts as an Instrument of the Divine Mission

To this point, we've focused primarily on how God's magnificent saving purpose is at work in Luke's story of Jesus and the early church. But this narrative also functions as an invitation. It calls concrete, missional communities—the audience of Luke-Acts—to faithfully participate in the divine mission in their own settings. The Spirit not only is active in the events Luke chronicles. The Spirit also works through the narrative to call readers, then and now, to join God's plan to bring the fullness of salvation to all people.

In the early chapters of Luke, for example, Spirit-inspired persons like Zechariah, Mary, and Simeon speak for God. As readers, we are not only invited to *understand* what Mary sings about God's purpose to lift up the lowly and bring down the lofty (Luke 1:52). We also are summoned to join the choir, so to speak, by aligning *ourselves* with God's redemptive purpose.

56. Brian Rapske, "Opposition to the Plan of God and Persecution," in Marshall and Peterson, *Witness to the Gospel*, 249.

57. See Luke Timothy Johnson, *Prophetic Jesus, Prophetic Church: The Challenge of Luke-Acts to Contemporary Christians* (Grand Rapids: Eerdmans, 2011), 61–64.

In Luke's Gospel, Jesus's own words and works dominate the landscape. Accordingly, when Jesus announces in his Nazareth manifesto (Luke 4) that he is anointed for a mission that touches the full range of human need, this is not simply a portrayal of his own ministry. Because the church continues what Jesus "began to do and teach" (Acts 1:1 NIV), Jesus's mission of good news of release to the poor and oppressed becomes our calling, as well.

Likewise, what Luke reveals about how Jesus served and the kind of people to which he was sent, in turn, shapes the agenda and practice of communities that read Luke's Gospel. Continuing Jesus's mission involves engaging in ministries that seek transformation at every level: offering forgiveness to sinners, caring for the sick and impoverished, embracing the excluded, and confronting both the power of the evil one and evil power structures that oppose God's reign. Embracing the mission of Jesus does not mean that we are compelled to try to imitate the specifics of Jesus's life and messianic ministry in a "cookie-cutter" fashion. But it does mean that those who would follow Jesus must follow him in his mission of compassion toward the least and the lost, the diseased and the defenseless, the ostracized and the oppressed. The open, embracing arms of Jesus continue to extend to the world through his church.

Perhaps in an even more direct way, the narrative of the book of Acts beckons us to join the saving project that God has unleashed in the world. Through the stories of the apostles' preaching and the church's Spirit-inspired witness to both Jews and Gentiles, Luke offers models for his readers as they live out God's mission in their own settings.

First, the *speeches* in Acts carry an exemplary role for Luke's audience. Luke features a series of representative sermons in Acts. Peter's message to Jews on the day of Pentecost (Acts 2) and Paul's synagogue sermon in Pisidian Antioch (Acts 13) provide examples of preaching to Jewish audiences for Luke's readers. Likewise, Paul's brief exposition to rustic polytheists in Lystra (Acts 14), and, more significantly, his address to a crowd of educated pagan Gentiles in Athens (Acts 17) serve as models of missionary preaching to Gentiles. Moreover, the evangelistic speeches in Acts demonstrate the ongoing need to contextualize the gospel for different audiences, without compromising the saving truth of God. They signal that the good news can speak to people of all cultures, worldviews, and life circumstances.

Second, Luke's portraits of *Christian communities* like those in Jerusalem (Acts 2:42-47; 4:32-37) and Antioch (11:19-30; 13:1-3) offer examples to congregations engaged in the mission of God. The Jerusalem community models uncommon unity, radical generosity, and joyful worship that result in a "missional magnetism" for the watching world.[58] Similarly, readers of Acts see in the Antioch congregation a spirit of acceptance of outsiders and an unselfish missionary vision that churches can learn from and emulate in every generation.

Third, Luke gives his readers positive and negative examples in the *characters* he portrays. For example, Luke places back to back the stories of the Spirit-filled and selfless Barnabas and the greedy and deceptive Ananias and Sapphira (Acts 4:36–5:11). The contrast could not be more striking. Stephen, the prophetic preacher and servant of the needy, exudes the fullness of the Spirit (Acts 6:3, 5, 10; 7:55) and follows his Lord by forgiving his executioners (Acts 7:59-60). Above all, Paul models an irrepressible desire to bring the good news of Jesus to all people, as well as a manner of life worth imitating (Acts 20:18-21, 34-35).

Fourth, the individual *stories* in Luke's narrative in Acts function as examples for the audience. Luke narrates an incremental journey of Christian witness, which addresses Jews, peripheral people like Samaritans and an Ethiopian eunuch, God-fearing Gentiles like Cornelius, and various groups of pagan Gentiles of the Greco-Roman world. These stories convey to Luke's readers that the gospel, by its very nature, crosses barriers. There is no "bridge too far" for the Christian mission, no one who is outside of the "target audience" for God's salvation. Furthermore, the story of mission in Acts reminds us that there is no one-size-fits-all way of telling or living out the good news. Christian mission, Acts shows us, takes sensitivity, flexibility, innovation.

Finally, Luke and Acts in tandem call followers of Jesus to a mission that is the work of God's Spirit from beginning to end. The Spirit anoints and empowers the entire ministry of Jesus. The Holy Spirit launches the church's mission, guides its progress, emboldens Christian witness, sustains God's messengers in suffering, energizes works of healing, inspires prophetic speech, overturns social and religious barriers, and forms a generous and joyful community. The Holy Spirit is so deeply embedded into the fabric of Luke-Acts that we, as Luke's readers, surely must expect the Spirit to energize and empower our own life of witness in the world.

In short, Luke's rich and elegant narrative invites his audience, in the first century and the twenty-first century, to enter a story and a mission that continues beyond the open-ended ending of the narrative in Acts 28:31. Luke's

58. Christopher J. H. Wright, *The Mission of God's People: A Biblical Theology of the Church's Mission* (Grand Rapids: Zondervan, 2010), 129.

story of God's plan to bring the fullness of salvation to all people through the redemptive mission of Jesus and the Spirit-endowed witness of the church is an unfinished story. It is a story "that is being lived out in London and Lagos and Lima and a myriad of other concrete settings that extend 'to the ends of the earth.'"[59]

---

59. Flemming, *Contextualization in the New Testament*, 55.

Chapter Three

Sent into the World: Mission in John

The Gospel of John is probably not the *first* place most Christians would go for an understanding of the church's mission. After all, it lacks the celebrated "Great Commission" of Matthew 28 to "go and make disciples of all nations" (28:19-20). Nor does it boast anything comparable to Jesus's personal mission statement in Luke 4, where he describes his anointing to "preach good news to the poor" and to "liberate the oppressed." Yet I tend to agree with Geoffrey Harris that John, of all the Gospel writers, "provides us with the most developed theological understanding of mission."[1] In this chapter, we'll explore why that is so.

A missional reading of John's Gospel aligns with its purpose. John's first audience was likely a new generation of Jewish and Gentile Christians, people who weren't eyewitnesses to Jesus's earthly ministry and mission.[2] John seeks in part to encourage and fortify the faith of these Christians, not least by helping them understand their role in the mission of God. This Gospel may also carry an indirect evangelistic aim. John's confessions of Jesus's identity and his narratives of people coming to faith through their encounters with Jesus would surely instruct John's readers in their own mission among

1. R. Geoffrey Harris, *Mission in the Gospels* (London: Epworth, 2004), 223.

2. See Marianne M. Thompson, "John, Gospel of," in *Dictionary of Jesus and the Gospels*, ed. Joel B. Green, Scot McKnight, and I. Howard Marshall (Downers Grove, IL: InterVarsity Press, 1992), 372–73.

unbelievers. Mission, then, is woven into the very fabric of the Fourth Gospel. Our missional reading looks first at John's witness to the mission of a loving, sending God. It then explores how John's Gospel seeks to inscribe Jesus's followers, in the first century and twenty-first century, into Jesus's own loving mission in the world.[3]

The Mission of the Triune God

In the Beginning

John could hardly be accused of holding a narrow perspective on God's mission. The Fourth Gospel begins with a sweeping vision of the eternal, missional God. Unlike Matthew, who opens his Gospel with a Jewish genealogy, or Mark, who introduces Jesus as a fully grown preacher, or Luke, who starts with an extended birth narrative, John immediately paints God's mission with broad brushstrokes on a cosmic canvas. Launching his Gospel with an elegant theological prologue (John 1:1-18), John grounds God's mission "in the beginning" of all things (John 1:1) and gives it a universal scope. God has a purpose for the whole of creation, and that missional purpose is fulfilled in the eternal Word (*logos*), the only Son. He is the Father's agent of creation and the source of life and light for all people (John 1:3-4, 9). The Word himself enters the created world, taking on "flesh" (John 1:14). The *logos* embodies God's grace and glory. He "exegetes" (*exegeomai*) the Father, making him known to the world (John 1:18).

At the same time, the Word, the eternal Son, fulfills Israel's specific missional role as a "light to the nations" (Isa 42:6; 49:6). Israel, according to her own prophets, often acted more like a smoldering candle than a floodlight of hope for the surrounding nations. But God's true servant, the Word, is the sun that shines on everyone, the *true* "light of the world" (John 1:9; 8:12; 9:5).

Sent from the Father

What the prologue ushers in, John unfolds throughout the rest of the Gospel. God is a missionary God, who in love sends his Son for the sake of the whole world. John captures the *missio Dei* in a nutshell in the celebrated summary of John 3:16: "God so loved the world that he gave his only Son,

---

3. For the following section, see the similar arguments in Dean Flemming, *Recovering the Full Mission of God: A Biblical Perspective on Being, Doing and Telling* (Downers Grove, IL: IVP Academic, 2013), 114–18.

so that everyone who believes in him won't perish but will have eternal life." The notion of "sending" is critical to John's understanding of mission. Verbs for "sending" occur some sixty times in the Fourth Gospel, and two-thirds of these speak of Jesus as the one being "sent" (see, e.g., John 3:17, 34; 4:34; 5:23-24, 30, 36-38).[4] Jesus's mission is utterly dependent on the Father and brings glory to the Sender. Jesus does the Father's will, completes the Father's work, speaks the Father's words, obeys the Father's will, and reveals the Father's heart. Like a spring rising from an underground pool, Jesus's mission flows out of the Father's sending love and gives it a visible expression. In John, the church's earthly mission is possible only because of the prior and more fundamental action of the Father sending the Son: "As you sent me into the world," Jesus prays, "I have sent them into the world" (John 17:18; cf. 20:21).

Embodying God's Mission

For John, who Jesus *is* takes precedence over what he *says* or *does*. Jesus is the embodied presence of the loving, seeking God. Everything hinges on his relationship with the Father. At one point, Jesus shouts to (or *at!*) a largely skeptical audience, "Whoever believes in me doesn't believe in me but in the one who sent me. Whoever sees me sees the one who sent me" (John 12:44-45). Jesus doesn't just *proclaim* a message; he *is* the message.[5] "*I am* the way, the truth and the life," Jesus declares. "No one comes to the Father except through me. If you have really known me, you will also know the Father" (John 14:6-7, italics added). Repeatedly, Jesus describes God's mission in strikingly personal terms. For example, Jesus's witness to his coming passion in John 12:32 bristles with personal pronouns: "When *I* am lifted up, *I* will draw everyone to *me*" (italics added). Mission in John, then, is profoundly *christological*. Jesus himself *is* the mission of God.

Furthermore, mission in John is *incarnational*. While this is certainly implied in the other Gospels (see Matt 1:23), John broadcasts it from the start. The same infinite, eternal Word that created all things and enlightened all people, stunningly, "became flesh and made his home among us" (John 1:14). In order to embody the mission of the Sender, Jesus had to enter human skin, bone, and blood. Richard B. Hays describes it well: "John gives us a Jesus who gets thirsty and asks a Samaritan woman for a drink (Jn 4:7; cf. Jn 19:38), a Jesus who weeps at Lazarus's grave (Jn 11:35), a Jesus who strips

---

4. See Craig S. Keener, "Sent Like Jesus: Johannine Missiology (John 20:21-22)," *Asian Journal of Pentecostal Studies* 12 (2009): 22–24.

5. See José Comblin, *Sent from the Father: Meditations on the Fourth Gospel*, trans. Carl Kabat (Maryknoll, NY: Orbis, 1979), 2–3.

55

off his clothes, takes a towel and washes the grimy feet of his followers (Jn 13:3-5)....He is a man who knows pain and the joys and sorrows of embodied existence."[6] Jesus in John is a Palestinian Jew, a member of an oppressed people, someone who participates in Jewish religious festivals and community celebrations, like weddings (John 2:1-11). In order to reveal a missionary God, Jesus becomes enmeshed in the coarse, and sometimes torn, fabric of human life. Our understanding of God's saving mission, therefore, must be anchored in Jesus's *incarnated life* as well as his atoning death.

Words and Works

Jesus's mission takes on a public face through what he does and says. Jesus repeatedly testifies that he speaks on behalf of the sending Father: "The one whom God sent speaks God's words because God gives the Spirit generously" (John 3:34; cf. 12:49-50; 14:10). John's Gospel contains a great deal of teaching, especially in the form of personal conversations and extended teaching sections. That teaching concentrates, not on the kingdom of God, as in the Synoptic Gospels, but on Jesus himself and the life he came to impart.[7]

John also spotlights Jesus's *witness* to the *truth*. To a Pontius Pilate who is bewildered at his identity, Jesus declares, "I was born and came into the world for this reason: to testify to the truth. Whoever accepts the truth listens to my voice" (John 18:37). When Jesus speaks God's truth, it carries the potential either to set people free (John 8:32) or to expose their ugly alliance with the devil, who is a "liar and the father of lies" (John 8:44; cf. 8:39-47; 15:22). Bearing witness to the truth, however, involves more than simply what is said. Behind the spoken word lies the *living* Word, Jesus himself (John 1:1, 14). And Jesus's testimony to God's truth is rooted in his own identity, as the one who *is* the truth (John 14:6). Ultimately, for John, truth is not a proposition, but a *person*—Jesus himself.[8]

Similarly, Jesus enacts God's mission through what he *does*. John frames this in terms of both *signs* and *works*. Jesus's "signs" refer to his miraculous deeds, all seven of which appear in the first half of the Gospel, during Jesus's public ministry. In John, Jesus's miraculous signs function not so much to demonstrate his compassion, as in the other Gospels, but rather to reveal God's glory and to lead people to put their faith in Jesus (John 2:11; 4:53).

---

6. Richard B. Hays, *The Moral Vision of the New Testament: Community, Cross, New Creation; A Contemporary Introduction to New Testament Ethics* (San Francisco: HarperSanFrancisco, 1996), 141.

7. See Craig R. Koester, *The Word of Life: A Theology of John's Gospel* (Grand Rapids: Eerdmans, 2008).

8. Darrell L. Guder, ed. *Missional Church: A Vision for the Sending of the Church in North America* (Grand Rapids: Eerdmans, 1998), 104.

What's more, John structures his Gospel in a way that tightly binds Jesus's signs to his teaching. In chapters 1–12, Jesus's signs are interlaced with his teaching discourses. In some cases, Jesus's words interpret his deeds, such as when his discourse on the "bread of life" (John 6:22-59) serves as a commentary on the miracle of feeding bread to the five thousand (6:1-15).

Jesus's *works* represent a broader range of activities in John, including both words and deeds (John 14:10-12; 15:22-24). Jesus leaves people in no doubt whatsoever that his works are not his own, but the Father's. "I assure you," Jesus answers his Jewish critics, "that the Son can't do anything by himself except what he sees the Father doing.... The Father has given me works to do so that I might complete them. These works I do testify about me that the Father sent me" (John 5:19, 36). Unlike the "signs," which only Jesus performs, his followers will continue to do his "works" after he leaves them (John 14:12). Jesus can even sum up his entire ministry as doing the Father's "work": "My food is to do the will of him who sent me and to finish his work" (John 4:34 NIV). In the immediate context, the Father's work involves reaping a harvest of mission among the Samaritan townspeople (see John 4:35-41). But in the broader horizon of John's Gospel, Jesus completes the Father's work by giving up his life on the cross. Only in John, Jesus ends his life with a cry of triumph: "It is finished" (John 19:30). By dying and rising from the dead, Jesus completes the mission for which he was sent, bringing glory to the Father (John 17:4).

Sending Love

If John were asked, "What motivates the mission of God that is embodied in Jesus?" his answer would surely be: *divine love*. "For God so loved the world" (John 3:16) he sent his Son to redeem it. John pictures divine love as both the *motive* and the *character* of Jesus's mission. Jesus gives the loving heart of the Father visible expression. In the first half of the Gospel, that love touches a varied cast of characters and a whole range of human needs. Jesus cares for the lowly and the great, insiders like religious leaders and royal officials, and, especially, outsiders like despised Samaritans, scorned sinners, low status women, hungry crowds, excluded Gentiles, and the physically disabled—the lame and the blind. His love reaches across barriers of social status, gender, ethnicity, belief, and moral reputation.[9]

Jesus's approach to people was one of invitation, never coercion. Two phrases sum up that attitude: "Come and see" and "Follow me." Early in

9. Richard A. Burridge, *Imitating Jesus: An Inclusive Approach to New Testament Ethics* (Grand Rapids: Eerdmans, 2007), 334.

Jesus's ministry, two disciples of John the Baptist, attracted by what John testified about this rabbi, and no doubt rather curious, begin to follow Jesus. When they ask Jesus where he is staying, he invites them to "come and see" for themselves (John 1:39). They stay with him the rest of the day and, as a result of that relational encounter, become convinced he is the Messiah (John 1:41). In turn, they bring others to Jesus (1:42).

It's noteworthy that the second phrase appears both at the beginning and end of the Gospel, like a pair of bookends. In chapter 1, Jesus seeks out Philip and invites him, "Follow me" (John 1:43). Then, in the Gospel's epilogue, Jesus twice tells Peter to follow him (21:19, 22). This comes hard on the heels of Jesus's restoration of Peter, the disciple who denied Jesus when it mattered most. In John, "Follow me" serves as an invitation to remain with Jesus in a long-term, intimate, loving relationship (see John 15:1-17).

John's portrait of God's missional love embodied in Jesus reaches a climax in the second half of the Gospel (chs. 13–21). With the cross looming before him, Jesus turns his focus to his own disciple community, whom he loves "to the end" (John 13:1 NIV). Jesus vividly displays that love in a kind of "acted parable" (John 13:4-17). Discarding his robe, he gets down on the floor like a lowly slave and washes his disciples' filthy feet, giving them an example to follow (John 13:14-16). Yet it is only in Jesus's sacrificial death on the cross that we see a wide-screen picture of what "loving to the end" entails.[10] John interprets the meaning of Jesus's death as an act of self-giving love. Jesus is the good shepherd who knows his flock intimately and voluntarily lays down his life for them (John 10:11-18). There is no greater love, Jesus insists, "than to give up one's life for one's friends" (John 15:13). Craig Keener reflects that as sinful people "pounded the nails in the hands of God's own Son, he was crying, 'I love you! I love you! I love you!'"[11] For John, mission is cruciform. The cross symbolizes that God accomplishes his purpose for the world through seeking, self-sacrificing love. Jesus's death on the cross is the embodiment of God's tenacious love.

Divine love, then, is the hallmark of the *missio Dei* in the Fourth Gospel. As I summarized elsewhere,

> Jesus's whole mission is a concrete expression of the loving character of God. For John, Jesus's words and works, his witness and his acts of service, his dwelling among us and his dying for us, are all seamlessly woven together as manifestations of divine love.[12]

10. The language of "to the end" (*eis telos*) in John 13:1 appears once again in verbal form in Jesus's cry from the cross in 19:30—"It is finished" (*tetelestai*). This forms a linguistic bracket, which binds Jesus's acted parable in the upper room to his act of dying for others on the cross.

11. Keener, "Sent Like Jesus," 26.

12. Flemming, *Recovering the Full Mission of God*, 118.

Contextualized Mission

John can give us a panoramic view of God's love for the whole world, but he can also zoom in on Jesus's ministry to specific individuals. John narrates a whole series of transforming personal encounters. In some cases, Jesus takes the initiative and seeks people out: Philip in Galilee, a woman in Samaria, a blind man in Jerusalem. On other occasions, people are drawn to Jesus and find *him*. These include Andrew the fisherman, who follows Jesus (John 1:40), Nicodemus the Pharisee, who comes at night (John 3:2), and some Greeks who want to "see" Jesus (John 12:21). What is truly striking is that in each case, Jesus tailors his approach to the person's life situation and need. For example, he confronts the religious leader Nicodemus with the need to be "born again" (John 3:1-8); he assures a man afflicted with blindness, "I am the light of the world" (John 9:5); and he announces to a woman drawing from a well that he can give her *living* water that bubbles up into eternal life (John 4:14). Ben Witherington III makes the convincing observation that this pattern of contextualizing the message for a varied procession of people serves as an example to John's readers, as they encounter different sorts of people in their own mission.[13] Likewise, Jesus's audience-sensitive approach to mission continues to speak to Christian communities as they participate in God's mission today.

Mission and the Spirit

In the Gospel of John, the Spirit has a mission, just as do the Father and the Son.[14] Not only is Jesus "sent," but so is the Spirit. The Son sends the Spirit in his name (John 14:26) in order to testify about Jesus (John 15:26). There are a number of dimensions to the Spirit's role in the *missio Dei* in John, and I will highlight several here.

1. *The life-giving Spirit.* John's Gospel pictures the Spirit as a gift from the Father and the Son, which imparts life to people. In particular, the gift of the Spirit is connected to the symbol of water. Early in the Gospel, John the Baptist contrasts his baptism in water with Jesus's superior baptism with the Holy Spirit (John 1:26, 33). In chapter 3, Jesus tells Nicodemus that the entry pass

13. Ben Witherington III, *John's Wisdom: A Commentary on the Fourth Gospel* (Louisville: Westminster John Knox, 1995), 31, 36. Jesus's evangelistic encounter with a woman in Samaria in ch. 4, in particular, carries important implications for the church in mission. See Flemming, *Recovering the Full Mission of God*, 119–20; Eckhard J. Schnabel, *Early Christian Mission*, vol. 1, *Jesus and the Twelve* (Downers Grove, IL: IVP Academic, 2004), 242–47.

14. See Mortimer Arias and Alan Johnson, *The Great Commission: Biblical Models for Evangelism* (Nashville: Abingdon, 1992), 84.

for the kingdom of God to be born "of water and the Spirit" (John 3:5). The language recalls Ezekiel 36:25-27, which links the sprinkling of clean water with the gift of the Spirit in the new age of salvation.[15] At a well-side, Jesus promises a Samaritan woman "living water" (John 4:14), which will result in true worship, in the sphere of the Spirit and truth (John 4:23-24).

Jesus makes the connection between "living water" and Spirit even more explicit at the Feast of the Tabernacles in Jerusalem. He shouts to the crowd of gathered pilgrims, "All who are thirsty should come to me! All who believe in me should drink! As the scriptures said concerning me, *Rivers of living water will flow out from within him*" (John 7:37-38). John quickly clarifies that Jesus was speaking about the Spirit, which believers would receive once he was glorified (John 7:39). God's mission in John involves imparting new life to those who believe in Jesus through the purifying water of the Spirit.

2. *The Spirit of revelation and witness.* We find the Fourth Gospel's fullest and most concentrated teaching on the Spirit in Jesus's "Farewell Discourse" to his disciples in John 14–16. Here Jesus usually refers to the Holy Spirit as the *Paraclete*, a notoriously difficult word to translate into English. He is the helper/advocate/strengthener, who will be forever present among them (14:16). The Father sends the Advocate in Jesus's name to teach believers and to remind them of Jesus's words (John 14:26). The *Paraclete* will guide them into all truth (16:13), particularly the truth of what God has done in Jesus (John 14:6), and so bring glory, not to himself, but to Jesus (John 16:12-15).

The Spirit's ministry of guidance and teaching, however, is not merely for the sake of the Christian community. The Spirit's role in the world is to bear witness to Jesus and to empower Jesus's followers for witness: "When the Companion [*Paraclete*] comes, whom I will send from the Father—the Spirit of Truth who proceeds from the Father—he will testify about me. You will testify too, because you have been with me from the beginning" (John 15:26-27). Note the trinitarian thrust of this statement. Jesus sends the Spirit from the Father to testify about Jesus himself. And we, his followers, will join in the Spirit's witness to the truth of God to those who do not yet belong to God (see John 15:18-25).

3. *The Spirit of conviction.* In John, truth has a "cutting edge," and part of the Spirit's witness involves exposing the world's sin (John 15:22, 24). The Spirit acts like a prosecutor, convicting the world "about sin, righteousness, and judgment" (16:8-11). Although the language in this passage is highly condensed, John likely pictures the Spirit's ministry in terms of proving the

15. Some Qumran texts also connect the cleansing ministry of the eschatological Spirit with "purifying waters" (e.g., 1QS 4:19-21).

unbelieving world wrong: (1) about its sin of rejecting Jesus and his saving mission; (2) about its false standards of righteousness; and (3) about its wrongheaded judgment, which fails to see that it is *Satan*, not Jesus, who stands condemned.[16] The Spirit as prosecutor, through the witness of Jesus's followers, capsizes the world's values and perceptions of the way things really are.

To sum things up, John's understanding of the mission of God is profoundly trinitarian. The Father, in love, sends the Son, and the Son sends the Spirit from the Father to bear witness to Jesus through his followers.

John as an Instrument of God's Mission

In John's Gospel, Jesus's disciples fulfill a paradigmatic role, representing the church to come.[17] More explicitly than the other Gospels, John shows interest in all those who will believe in Jesus through the disciples' message (John 17:20). Consequently, in John, Jesus's promise of doing "greater works" (14:12), his invitation to bear much fruit (15:8), or his sending followers into the world (17:18; 20:21), speak not only to the Twelve but also to the wider church. Christians in subsequent generations may not perform identical functions to Jesus's first companions, but John envisions them sharing in the same mission. When, therefore, we reflect on how John portrays the mission of the Twelve and other representative characters in its narrative, we also need to consider how this Gospel shapes and energizes the church in mission today.

Sharing in Jesus's Mission

Just as both the Gospels of Matthew and Luke conclude with a pivotal text for the church's mission in the world (Matt 28:16-20; Luke 24:44-49), so John's understanding of Christian mission reaches a climax in chapter 20:

> It was still the first day of the week. That evening, while the disciples were behind closed doors because they were afraid of the Jewish authorities, Jesus came and stood among them. He said, "Peace be with you." After he said this, he showed them his hands and his side. When the disciples saw the Lord, they were filled with joy. Jesus said to them again, "Peace be with you. As the Father sent me, so I am sending you." Then he breathed on them and

16. See, e.g., Colin G. Kruse, *John* (Grand Rapids: Eerdmans: 2003), 330–31.

17. Keener, "Sent Like Jesus," 41. For this section, see the similar arguments in Flemming, *Recovering the Full Mission of God*, 120–28.

said, "Receive the Holy Spirit. If you forgive anyone's sins, they are forgiven; if you don't forgive them, they aren't forgiven." (John 20:19-23)

In their narrative setting, these words address a cowering band of disciples inside a locked chamber in Jerusalem. But from John's perspective, Jesus speaks as the risen Lord of the church. Among the numerous implications of this passage for the church's participation in God's mission, three stand out.[18]

First, the mission of Jesus's disciples is anchored in the life and character of the triune God. Jesus, the one sent by the Father, now becomes the sender. And as the crucified and risen one, still bearing the wounds of the cross, he imparts the Holy Spirit to them (John 20:22). In this passage, the gift of the Spirit remains the crucial element of continuity between Jesus's commission and the church's mission of forgiving and retaining sins.

Not to be missed is that Jesus bestows the Spirit by *breathing* on his disciples. This act recalls God's initial breath of life into humanity in creation (Gen 2:7; cf. Ezek 37:1-10). "Now," explains N. T. Wright, "in the new creation, the restoring life of God is breathed out through Jesus, making new people of the disciples, and, through them, offering this new life to the world."[19] The church, then, endowed with the Spirit, participates in the life-giving mission of the triune God.

Second, the mission of God's people is defined above all by their *relation-ship* to Jesus, rather than by their words or deeds. The mission of Jesus and that of his followers are tightly stitched together: "As the Father sent me, so I am sending you" (John 20:21). John's Gospel contains no account of Jesus sending out his disciples to preach and heal on their own, such as we find in the Synoptic Gospels (see Matt 10:1-42; Mark 6:1-6; Luke 9:1-6). For John, the church's "sent-ness" is a continuation of Jesus's sent-ness.[20] Disciples who share Jesus's life, abiding in him, also share his mission of bearing fruit (John 15:1-8). As Andreas Köstenberger wisely observes, for John, the church not only *represents* Jesus in the world but also *re-presents* him; Christ is present in the church's mission by the Spirit.[21] To make this practical, John calls the church "to see itself more consciously in relation to the mission of Jesus."[22] If

18. For an excellent reflection on the implications of John 20:19-23 for Christian mission, see Ross Hastings, *Missional God, Missional Church: Hope for Re-evangelizing the West* (Downers Grove, IL: IVP Academic, 2012).

19. N. T. Wright, *John for Everyone, Part 2: Chapters 11–21* (London: SPCK, 2002), 150.

20. Ibid.

21. Andreas J. Köstenberger, *The Missions of Jesus and His Disciples according to the Fourth Gospel* (Grand Rapids: Eerdmans, 1998), 191.

22. Andreas J. Köstenberger and Peter T. O'Brien, *Salvation to the Ends of the Earth: A Biblical Theology of Mission* (Leicester: Apollos, 2001), 224.

the church is rightly related to Jesus, it will *be* missional. Mission, in all of its diverse and concrete forms, flows out of relationship.

Third, Jesus twice "passes the peace" to his frightened followers (John 20:19, 21; cf. 14:27; 16:33). This peace—God's wide-ranging *shalom*—signifies more than simply a conventional greeting or a calm state of mind. In the context, it speaks forgiveness of their failures, a restored relationship, and freedom from fear of the hostility of others. Ultimately, however, it signals the wholeness and the harmony associated with God's coming kingdom. But Jesus's followers not only *experience God's shalom*—they also give it away. Jesus's second bestowal of peace introduces his commission to participate in his own sending mission (John 20:21). What's more, Jesus promises that, by the Spirit, they will extend the *shalom* of forgiveness to others (John 20:23). In other words, Jesus calls them to live as both a reconciled and a reconciling community, to share the peace and restoration they have received.[23]

Sent into the World

Jesus's post-Easter commission in John 20 is mirrored by his pre-crucifixion prayer for his disciples in John 17: "As you sent me into the world, so I have sent them into the world" (John 17:18). Here Jesus clarifies where they are sent—into *the world*. In the Fourth Gospel, the "world" (*kosmos*) is a double-edged sword. On the one hand, it often represents an arena of spiritual blindness and of open hostility toward God and his people (see John 7:7; 8:23; 12:31; 15:18-19). On the other hand, the world—especially the people in it—remains the object of God's missional love (John 3:16-17; 10:36; 12:47). As Geoffrey Harris memorably puts it, "'The world' is a mission field for the disciples, but it is also a minefield for the Christian community."[24]

Consequently, Jesus's followers carry out their mission in the midst of this arresting tension: they don't *belong* to the world, but they are sent *into* the world (John 17:16, 18). They engage the world as a people who are unmistakably separate (John 17:17, 19), but they never isolate or insulate themselves from it. In John's missional vision, the church is *both* a holy, contrast community *and* God's loving presence in an unfriendly world.

Does John's "world" include non-Jews? In chapter 4, a crowd of Samaritans recognize Jesus as "savior of the world" (John 4:42). This amounts to a confession of Jesus's universal salvation, embracing not only Jews and Samaritans, who are culturally on the fringes of Judaism, but, by implication, Gentiles, as

23. Hastings, *Missional God*, 26.
24. Harris, *Mission in the Gospels*, 175.

well. Indeed, some Roman emperors also used the title "savior of the world" to claim their sovereignty over all peoples.[25] Elsewhere in John, Jesus speaks of "other sheep that don't belong to this sheep pen" (John 10:16); Greeks come to "see Jesus" (John 12:20-21; cf. 7:35); and John takes pains to point out that the inscription on Jesus's cross is written in Hebrew, Latin, and Greek (John 19:20). Craig Keener's conclusion therefore seems justified: "John's mention of the 'world'... is as much a summons to reach all peoples as Matthew's or Luke's call to the 'nations.' Isaiah's light to the nations (Isa 42:6; 49:6; cf. 60:2-3) is in John the 'light of the world' (Jn 8:12; 9:5; 11:9; 12:46)."[26]

Speaking Jesus's Words

How does John envision the disciples' specific mission in the world? What are they supposed to *do*? At the very least, they are to *speak Jesus's words, do his works,* and *love the way he loves.* First, just as Jesus came to bear witness to the truth about his divine mission (John 18:37), so his followers will testify to the truth about Jesus (John 15:27; cf. 17:20). Apart from their relationship with the triune God, this verbal witness is devoid of power. God's people will testify only because they have been *with Jesus* and because their witness is joined to the testimony of the "Spirit of Truth," whom Jesus sends from the Father (John 15:26-27).

Some will come to believe in Jesus through the disciples' word (John 17:20). But because they live in an unfriendly world, God's witnesses can expect to meet exclusion, persecution, and rejection (John 16:1-3). Such a prophetic witness unleashes momentous consequences. Jesus declares, "If you forgive anyone's sins, they are forgiven; if you don't forgive them, they aren't forgiven" (John 20:23). This represents less a promise of special authority than a statement of fact. When the church calls people to repentance, those who receive the message will be forgiven; those who reject it remain in their sins. At a time when the *proclamation* of the gospel, whether through personal evangelism or public preaching, is sometimes ushered to a back row seat by Christians in the West, we need to hear John's emphasis on the power of the *word* in Christian mission.

One way that John equips his audience for witness is by offering them concrete examples. In the first half of his Gospel, we encounter a parade of people who bear witness to Jesus. Headlining the list is John the Baptist, whose chief role in the Gospel is to give testimony to Jesus (see John 1:7-8,

---

25. Andrew T. Lincoln, *The Gospel according to Saint John* (Peabody, MA: Hendrickson, 2005), 181.
26. Keener, "Sent Like Jesus," 30.

19, 32, 34). When he announces to two of his disciples that Jesus is the Lamb of God, they immediately follow Jesus (John 1:35-37). Later, Philip testifies to Nathanael, "We have found the one Moses wrote about in the Law and the Prophets," and invites him into a personal encounter with Jesus (John 1:45-46). In John 4, as the light gradually dawns on a Samaritan woman that Jesus may indeed be the Messiah, she abandons her water jar and invites her whole town to "Come and see" him (John 4:28-29). John reports that "many Samaritans in that city believed in Jesus because of the woman's word" (4:39). This prepares the way for them to hear Jesus's "word" and to recognize that he is indeed "savior of the world" (4:42). For John, such examples of personal witness surely served a paradigmatic role for John's audience, helping to equip them for their own mission in the world.

In addition, Keener rightly points out that John himself offers a model of verbal witness by how he proclaims Jesus's identity in the Gospel.[27] John narrates, for example, a whole string of christological confessions, from John the Baptist's, "Look! The Lamb of God who takes away the sin of the world!" (John 1:29) to Thomas's cry of recognition, "My Lord and my God!" (John 20:28). Beyond that, John draws attention to Jesus's own testimony about himself: "I am the light of the world" (John 8:12; 9:5), "I am the resurrection and the life" (11:25), and so forth. In various ways, then, the Fourth Gospel calls Christians to a mission of proclaiming Jesus to others.

Doing Jesus's Works

Another way the disciple community shares in Jesus's mission is by engaging in practices that continue his ministry in the world. John spotlights three metaphors that help to shape the church's missional practice.[28] First, Jesus sends his disciples to *gather the harvest*, to "harvest what you didn't work hard for" (John 4:38). Since this commission immediately leads into John's report of many Samaritans believing in Jesus (John 4:39; cf. 4:41), it especially focuses on the harvest of people entering a life of genuine faith in "the savior of the world" (4:42).

Second, Jesus appoints his disciples to "go and *produce fruit*" (John 15:16, italics added; cf. 15:5, 8). Does this "fruit" refer to a loving Christian character (see John 15:9-10, 17), similar to the "fruit of the Spirit" (Gal 5:22)? Or are they to bear the fruit of mission, including leading people to believe in Jesus (see John 12:24)? Surely the answer to both questions is yes! On the

---

27. Ibid., 41–42.

28. See the similar arguments in Flemming, *Recovering the Full Mission of God*, 124–25.

one hand, Jesus maintains that love for one another remains a powerful form of Christian witness (John 13:34-35; cf. 17:21, 23). On the other hand, Jesus's commission to "go" and produce fruit implies that, at least in part, this involves bearing the fruit of mission. What this text highlights, however, is not the specific nature of the fruit, but rather, the *source* and the *aim* of fruit-bearing. This practice flows out of the church's relationship with Jesus, their abiding in him and his love (John 15:4-5, 7, 9). And its goal is to bring glory to the God the Father (John 15:8).

A third metaphor that defines the church's missional practice is Jesus's commission to "shepherd the flock." Three times in the epilogue of the Gospel, Peter declares to Jesus, "You know I love you," and three times Jesus responds by telling him to feed or care for his sheep (John 21:15-17). It's possible to take this shepherding ministry as something *only* relating to the nurture of Christians. In John 10, however, Jesus says that the mission of the Good Shepherd involves gathering "other sheep" into the fold (John 10:16). This implies that the church's shepherding ministry includes seeking out scattered sheep in the world in order to bring them into Jesus's flock. What's more, Peter fulfills a representative role in John 21, signaling a future ministry for the church as a whole to gather the dispersed flock of Jesus.[29]

John records another task of Jesus's followers: to *do his works*. To be precise, Jesus promises that those who believe in him will not only "do the works that I do," but "they will do even *greater* works" (John 14:12, italics added). There's been no shortage of suggestions about what these "greater works" entail. Are they more *spectacular* works? Surely not. Are they greater in *number*? Or works covering a wider *geographical* scope? Perhaps. More likely, however, the key is located in the last part of John 14:12: "because I am going to the Father." The disciples' works are "greater" because they arise out of Jesus's *finished* work of salvation (John 19:30), accomplished by the cross and the empty tomb. These are the works of the risen and exalted Lord *through his people*, now empowered by the gift of the Spirit (John 20:22). This promise shapes the mission, not only of Jesus's original disciples, but also the church to come. Presumably, these "greater works" are not limited to deeds of power, in answer to prayer. They also include works of love and service (John 13:15, 35), as well as the miracles of regeneration that happen again and again through the church's Spirit-energized witness among the nations (John 15:26-27).[30]

29. Köstenberger, *Missions of Jesus and His Disciples*, 160.
30. See Hastings, *Missional God*, 279–30.

Loving as Jesus Loves

John gives special accent to a third aspect of the church's missional practice: the Christian community's *unity* and *love for one another*. Some of the most striking language appears in Jesus's prayer of consecration for his disciples in John 17. Beginning in verse 20, Jesus expands the horizon of his prayer to embrace, not only his first disciples, but future generations of Christians, as well:

> I pray they will be one, Father, just as you are in me and I am in you. I pray that they also will be in us, *so that the world will believe that you sent me....* I've given them the glory that you gave me so that they can be one just as we are one. I'm in them and you are in me so that they will be made perfectly one. *Then the world will know that you sent me and that you have loved them just as you loved me.* (John 17:21, 23, italics added)

In this remarkable passage, Jesus includes the church in the very union that exists between the Father and the Son. It is out of their union with Christ, who is in the Father, that the community's oneness flows. And *why* does Jesus pray that the church might be one? In Jesus's words, "so that the world will believe that you sent me" (John 17:21; cf. 17:23). Here the church's union with the triune God and with one another leans outward. The goal of unity is mission.[31] In the midst of a fragmented, alienated, and divided world (see John 7:43; 9:16), the unity of Christ's church offers a compelling witness to the healing, reconciling love of God, a love that is visible in the way God's people treat one another.

In John, missional unity walks hand in hand with missional love. In the discourse that precedes Jesus's intercessory prayer in John 17, Jesus urges his disciples to love one another in the same way that he has loved them (John 13:34). The *new* aspect of this "new commandment" (John 13:34) is that the disciples' mutual love is to be patterned after Jesus's own love for them and flows out of it. Within the narrative, Jesus's companions have just witnessed an earthy and unforgettable demonstration of that love in Jesus's act of washing his disciples' grimy feet (John 13:3-17). But that act foreshadows something even greater, Jesus's ultimate expression of self-giving love on the cross. Likewise, Jesus challenges his followers to live out their love for one another by laying down their lives for others (John 15:12-13).

The community's mutual love, however, is not an end in itself. Jesus continues, "This is how everyone will know that you are my disciples, when you

---

31. Ibid., 285.

love each other" (John 13:35). The same self-sacrificing love that Jesus will soon demonstrate through his nailed-pierced hands and feet "becomes the trademark and credential of the missionary community."[32] Then and now, such cruciform love causes a self-absorbed world to sit up and take notice. As Richard A. Burridge reflects, love for others "has remained the acid test, whether it is said admiringly about Christian caring in practice, or sarcastically in frustration at the church's inner wranglings."[33]

The community's life of unity and love, suggests Ross Hastings, offers "the New Testament's most neglected evangelistic strategy."[34] The church is missional when, and only when, it truly *is* the church, a church indwelt by the Father, Son, and Spirit, a church whose oneness and uncommon love visibly demonstrates the embracing love of God to a watching world. The church's mutual love, above else, showcases the reality and the character of God's mission in Jesus.

Being Sanctified for Mission

We return to Jesus's magnificent prayer for his followers in John 17. On the cusp of the cross, Jesus prays, "Sanctify them in the truth; your word is truth. As you have sent me into the world, so I have sent them into the world. And for their sakes I sanctify myself, so that they also may be sanctified in truth" (John 17:17-19). If the disciples are to continue Jesus's mission (John 17:18), they must be sanctified in continuity with Jesus (John 17:17, 19). Being sanctified (*hagiazō*), in the first place, means being "set apart" or "consecrated" for God's purposes and God's mission. Jesus consecrates himself to his loving, saving mission, above all by his sacrificial death "for their sakes" (John 17:19). And that saving action makes possible—indeed, has as its *goal*—the disciples' consecration to the same saving mission for which Jesus has been sent into the world (John 17:18). As D. Moody Smith observes, like Jesus, they are "set apart from the world and for the sake of the world."[35] In John's Gospel, holiness is inseparable from mission.

In addition, the notion of ethical holiness is not foreign to Jesus's prayer that his followers might be "sanctified" (see CEB, "so that they also would be made holy," John 17:19). If Jesus's disciples are to be set apart from the world and its sin (John 17:14-16; cf. John 15:22-25), if they are to be wholly dedi-

---

32. Arias and Johnson, *Great Commission*, 93.
33. Burridge, *Imitating Jesus*, 328.
34. Hastings, *Missional God*, 284–85.
35. D. Moody Smith Jr., *John* (Nashville: Abingdon, 1999), 316.

cated to God and his mission in the world, then this surely involves a moral cleansing from sin and lives lived in obedience to what pleases a holy God. What's more, if Jesus's own sanctification includes laying down his life in self-giving love for others, then for us to partake in his loving mission implies the need for inner transformation and a sharing in his own love and holiness.

This sanctified mission all takes place "in the truth" (John 17:17, 19). In the Fourth Gospel, "truth" is profoundly personal. It is manifested, above all, in God's revelation in Jesus, who not only bears witness to the truth (see John 18:37) but also *is* both the Word (John 1:1-2, 14) and the truth (John 14:6; cf. John 17:17, "your word is truth"). The sanctification of God's people, then, is anchored in Jesus himself, who embodies the truth. It flows out of his self-giving death on the cross, and it thrusts them into the world to continue Jesus's own mission. That's missional holiness.

Incarnational Mission?

If John expects the church to continue Jesus's own mission in the various ways I have just noted, then how far does that identification go? In particular, does John's theology of Jesus's incarnation, the Word made flesh (John 1:14), offer us a paradigm for Christian mission? Put differently, should we talk about *incarnational* mission? Recently, some interpreters have pushed back against the notion of "incarnational" ministry. Todd Billings, for example, insists that to use the language of the term *incarnation* in relation to the mission of God's people risks confusing Jesus's singular ministry with our own. The incarnation of the eternal Word into human flesh, he points out, is a unique and unrepeatable event. Consequently, it cannot serve as a model to be applied to the ongoing ministry of the church.[36]

Fair enough. Billings is right that there are inappropriate ways of applying "incarnational" language to Christian mission.[37] It is not up to individual Christians, for example, to "make Christ incarnate" among a particular group of people, as if their own presence becomes redemptive, apart from the work of the Spirit. There are some things about Jesus's sending into the world that we cannot imitate; we can only bear witness to them.

Does this mean, however, that Jesus's incarnation has *no* application to the church's participation in the mission of God? That would seem to be a case of throwing out the theological baby with the bathwater. Perhaps we

---

36. J. Todd Billings, *Union with Christ: Reframing Theology and Ministry for the Church* (Grand Rapids: Baker Academic, 2011), 124. See also, David J. Hesselgrave, *Paradigms in Conflict: Ten Key Questions in Christian Missions Today* (Grand Rapids: Kregel, 2005), 141–65.

37. See Billings's comprehensive discussion of this issue in *Union with Christ*, 123–60.

should view Jesus's incarnation more as a *theological lens* that helps shape our understanding of mission than as a *model* to strictly imitate. At the very least, mission in light of Jesus's "making his home among us" (John 1:14) is characterized by both *identification* and *contextualization*.

1. *Identification.* As the "Word become flesh," who "made his home among us" (John 1:14), Jesus radically identified with the human situation. "The incarnation," write Peskett and Ramachandra, "speaks of a God who *is* entangled with our world."[38] In particular, Jesus stood in solidarity with the poor and the powerless, the sick and the suffering. Ultimately, he suffered "not only *for* but *with* humanity in the lowest and most horrible form of death."[39] Likewise, the church must enter into the bloodstream of humanity, in all its dimensions. Like Jesus, the Christian community must live "for and with" others, whether poor or rich, gay or straight, Muslim or Sikh. Jesus's incarnation reminds us that "as Jesus got tangled up in our human vulnerability, hopes and sufferings, the church must be present in all the messiness of human life."[40]

2. *Contextualization.* In his incarnation, Jesus embraced the human situation in all of its scandalous particularity. He was no Melchizedek, a shadowy figure without a cultural past (Heb 7:3). Rather, Jesus was fully immersed in his Palestinian Jewish culture. He spoke his native Aramaic with a Galilean accent. His teaching oozed with earthy illustrations from rural Palestinian life.[41] Yet he regularly scandalized cultural and religious norms, for example, by sharing drinking vessels and conversing with a marginalized Samaritan woman (John 4). Mission in light of the incarnation, then, will seek to radically identify with every human culture, even as it challenges those cultures from within.

Conclusion

John offers us a magnificently rich and deep understanding of God's mission. More explicitly than the other Gospels, John portrays Christian mission as a natural outflow of the very character of a loving, seeking God. Like the motion of breathing out and breathing in, God sends his Son in love into the world and, in turn, draws people back to himself. At the same time, Jesus, the sent one, becomes the divine sender. He sends us, the community he has

---

38. Howard Peskett and Vinoth Ramachandra, *The Message of Mission: The Glory of Christ in All Time and Space* (Downers Grove, IL: InterVarsity Press, 2003), 86.

39. Orlando E. Costas, *Christ outside the Gate: Mission beyond Christendom* (Maryknoll, NY: Orbis, 1982), 13.

40. Flemming, *Recovering the Full Mission of God*, 115.

41. See Dean Flemming, *Contextualization in the New Testament: Patterns for Theology and Mission* (Downers Grove, IL: IVP Academic, 2005), 20–21.

formed, to participate in and to continue his own self-giving mission. And he breathes the Spirit on the church to make embodiment of his mission possible (John 20:21-22).

A missional reading of John's Gospel speaks compellingly to the church in mission today. It reminds us that mission, in the first place, is about *identity* rather than *activity*. It is anchored in who God *is* and our participation in the life of God, not in what we do *for* God. We are consistently tempted to shrink the mission of God—to view mission(s) as simply one among many assigned tasks carried out by the church. Or to think that by joining an annual mission trip or by giving an offering to support people who are serving across an ocean, we will fulfill our mission responsibility. Such activities may be well and good. But if God is a loving, seeking, sending God, then the church must recognize that mission "is not a certain set of activities but a way of life that has God at the center."[42]

It's striking that John's version of Jesus's postresurrection commission to his followers is short on specific activities, such as preaching, teaching, baptizing, or making disciples. John drives us deep, placing the weight on our intimate relationship with Jesus: "As the Father sent me, I am sending you" (John 20:21). We embody *his* mission in the world, through the enabling of the Spirit. Our mission strategies, structures, and methods will vary, according to our circumstances. Indeed, they *must* vary. But whatever form they take, they will only bear fruit if we remain embedded in the vine.

John also reminds us that our missional life is a *shared* life. For John, the world's recognition of God's sending love in Jesus is riveted to how Christians relate to one another (see John 13:34-35; 17:20-23). Particularly in the kind of individualistic, increasingly postmodern cultures, that prevail in the West, Christian communities that reflect authentic unity and love have the potential, by the Spirit's working, to magnetically attract people outside the church. This is particularly true when we demonstrate love for those who are not like us, people we are not *expected* to love. John's Gospel shows us that witness cannot consist of verbal proclamation alone. Our love and our lives *speak*.

---

42. Hastings, *Missional God*, 262.

Chapter Four

Living Out the Story: Mission in Philippians

T ell me a story!" If you are like me, you spoke those words more times than you can count when you were a child. But there is something in human beings that never stops saying, "Tell me a story!" Nor should it. Stories are foundational to who we are and how we see the world around us. They both shape and interpret our world and our lives. Within his letter to the Philippians, the apostle Paul, in effect, tells a story. It is not just *any* story, however. For Paul, it is *the* defining story. It is a "V-shaped" narrative, in which Christ travels from the heights of heavenly glory to the utter depths of death on a cross. But he is then exalted by God the Father to the highest possible status (Phil 2:6-11). As we will discover in the course of this chapter, that "story" lies at the very heart of how Philippians unfolds God's mission and the church's participation in it.

But why focus on Philippians? Certainly, if my task in this book were simply to discuss the New Testament theology of mission, then we would need to consider the whole body of Paul's writings. But since my goal is to offer missional readings of representative New Testament writings, I will treat Philippians as a kind of "case study" for reading Paul's letters through missional eyes.[1] Perhaps no other letter of Paul, with the possible exception of

1.   For one attempt to do a missional reading of Paul's letters as a whole, see Dean Flemming, *Recovering the Full Mission of God: Biblical Perspectives on Being, Doing and Telling* (Downers Grove, IL: IVP Academic, 2013), 159–207. See also the excellent, in-depth treatment in Michael J. Gorman, *Becoming*

Romans, gives us such a clear and multifaceted picture of God's mission and the local church's participation in it. Certainly, for its size, it is unsurpassed in this regard. In this chapter, we'll consider Philippians first as a *product* of mission, second, as a *witness to* God's mission, and third, as an *instrument* of the mission of God.[2]

Philippians as a Product of God's Mission

Apart from the *missio Dei*, there would have been no reason for Paul to send a letter to the church in Philippi. As with all of Paul's writings, Philippians is an extension of his apostolic and gospel ministry. That ministry began when Paul gave birth to a community of Christ followers in this highly Romanized city. And although Paul is no longer physically present—indeed, he is in prison—he continues to fulfill his God-given mission among the Philippians by means of written correspondence.

This assumes that Paul's ministry of the gospel isn't exhausted with initial evangelism and planting communities of faith. Paul's mission seeks to form growing and mature Christian communities (Phil 3:12-16), which are conformed to the cross-shaped life of Christ (Phil 2:1-11), even until "the day of Christ" (Phil 1:6, 10). Christian formation, then, is essential to Paul's missionary calling.[3] In modern terms, he desires converts to *belong* and *behave*, as well as to *believe*.

The particular *shape* that Paul's community-forming ministry takes in Philippians is linked to circumstances "on the ground." This is a church that Paul holds close to his heart (Phil 1:3-8; 4:1). He writes in part to thank them for their generosity and care, which came to him through their representative Epaphroditus (4:10-20). But what Paul says to his friends in Philippi is also related to the specific challenges of the church. Paul's exhortations to the Philippians give us a window into their likely circumstances. Here is a faith community that faces internal tensions (Phil 4:2-3), potential danger from Jewish Christian agitators (Paul calls them "dogs," Phil 3:2-3), and suffering as a result of opposition from those outside. Like Paul, these Christians endure suffering "on behalf of Christ" (Phil 1:29-30). Most likely, their af-

---

the Gospel: Paul, Participation, and Mission (Grand Rapids: Eerdmans, 2015).

2. This chapter significantly depends on material adapted from Dean Flemming, "Exploring a Missional Reading of Scripture: Philippians as a Case Study," *Evangelical Quarterly* 83 (2011): 9–17.

3. See Michael Barram, "The Bible, Mission, and Social Location: Toward a Missional Hermeneutic," *Interpretation* 61 (2007): 53–57; David G. Peterson, "Maturity: The Goal of Mission," in *The Gospel to the Nations: Perspectives on Paul's Mission*, ed. Peter Bolt, Mark Thompson, and Peter T. O'Brien (Downers Grove, IL: InterVarsity Press, 2000), 185–204.

fliction came at the hands of the Roman populace of Philippi. This city was a Roman colony, a miniature Rome, where loyalty to Caesar and his empire was intense. Christians, who dared to worship another "Lord" than Caesar, would likely be viewed as dangerously un-Roman and a threat to the colony:

> Christians could have experienced harassment from their neighbors and various forms of economic suffering. We might imagine that Christian tradespeople would lose their customers. Pagan owners might punish Christian slaves. Patrons could withdraw financial support from Christian clients. Magistrates might drag believers to court. In short, Christians in Philippi might experience the kind of ostracism, discrimination, or even violence that has accompanied loyalty to Christ in many times and places.[4]

Paul, then, seeks the formation of a young Christian community, in light of challenges from both inside and outside the church. As Paul puts it, he desires their "progress and joy in the faith" (Phil 1:25 NIV; cf. Rom 1:11-13). But the advance of their faith is also inextricably linked to the advance of the gospel (Phil 1:12).[5] Only if these Christians live in a manner "worthy of the gospel" (Phil 1:27), steadfast and united, can they expect to be a part of the progress of the gospel in the world.[6] The letter to the Philippians, therefore, extends Paul's missionary work. It aims to lead God's people into full maturity in Christ and to encourage their ongoing "partnership in the gospel" (Phil 1:5)—in short, to form a faithful "colony of Christ" within the Roman colony of Philippi.

Philippians as a Witness to God's Mission

How does this letter *bear witness* to the sweeping story of God's purpose to redeem a missional people and to reconcile all things? As I noted at the beginning of the chapter, Philippians 2:6-11 forms the missional nerve center of the letter. In this celebrated text, Paul tells the "Master story" of God's loving and self-giving mission in Jesus Christ.[7] This V-shaped story first chronicles a journey of descent. The narrative describes one who shared divine status and glory, yet "did not consider being equal with God something to exploit"

---

4. Dean Flemming, *Philippians: A Commentary in the Wesleyan Tradition* (Kansas City, MO: Beacon Hill, 2009), 28.

5. The two phrases "for the progress of the gospel" (Phil 1:12 AT) and "for your progress...in the faith" (1:25 NIV) form striking literary "bookends," which frame Paul's narrative in ch. 1 of how God is advancing the gospel in the midst of adverse circumstances.

6. See Robert C. Swift, "The Theme and Structure of Philippians," *Bibliotecha Sacra* 141 (1984): 250.

7. Michael J. Gorman, *Cruciformity: Paul's Narrative Spirituality of the Cross* (Grand Rapids: Eerdmans, 2001), 88, 164.

(Phil 2:6). Instead, he "emptied himself," taking on human form (Phil 2:7). What is more, he "humbled himself" to the extreme—dying a slave's death by crucifixion, in obedience to God the Father (Phil 2:8). Jesus's "death on a cross" (Phil 2:8) is the nadir of his downward journey. Suddenly, the story shifts direction, veering upward. It shouts that, in response to Christ's costly obedience, God exalted him supremely. The one who made himself nothing is now granted divine status as Lord of all (Phil 2:9-11). The story line reaches its glorious conclusion when all of creation unites in acknowledging "Jesus Christ as Lord," to God the Father's glory. In Philippians, the way *up* is *down*.

We can add several further reflections on how Phil 2:6-11 bears witness to the mission of God. First, this is one of the clearest expressions of the *missio Dei* in Paul's letters. It narrates God's gracious activity on behalf of human beings and the whole of creation. Michael Gorman is surely right that it functions as a narrative summary of the gospel that Paul wants the Philippians to proclaim and live out (see Phil 1:27).[8]

Second, this poetic text makes it clear that Christ is at the center of God's mission. It is the incarnate, humble, crucified, exalted Messiah who puts into effect God's redeeming mission in the world.[9] Philippians 2:6-11 likely reflects a theological interpretation of Isaiah 52:13–53:12 and 45:22-23.[10] Jesus fulfills the mission of Isaiah's suffering messianic servant in order that he might be worshiped by the nations. And because God's mission centers on Jesus, so does Paul's preaching. In fact, he can sum up his proclamation of the gospel with the bare-bones phrase "preaching Christ" (Phil 1:15, 17, 18).

Third, God's mission is *cruciform*. The one who was in the form of *God* is the very one who emptied himself and in obedience embraced the cross. And it is precisely *because* Christ humbled himself that he was exalted as sovereign Lord. This means that Jesus's self-emptying and humiliation are not a temporary step *away* from his true character as God. Rather, they show us what God is like, just as much as Christ's heavenly exaltation does. Moreover, if God's *identity* is fundamentally cruciform, then so is God's *mission*.

This is crucial knowledge for the Philippians. In the status-hungry Roman world, crucifixion was the most degrading, dishonorable death imagin-

8. Gorman, *Becoming the Gospel*, 115. See also Alistair I. Wilson, "An Ideal Missionary Prayer Letter: Reflections on Paul's Missionary Theology," in *New Testament Theology in Light of the Church's Mission: Essays in Honor of I. Howard Marshall*, ed. Jon C. Laansma, Grant Osborne, and Ray Van Neste (Eugene, OR: Cascade, 2011), 249–50.

9. Michael J. Gorman, *Inhabiting the Cruciform God: Kenosis, Justification, and Theosis in Paul's Narrative Soteriology* (Grand Rapids: Eerdmans, 2009), 38.

10. See Richard Bauckham, *God Crucified: Monotheism and Christology in the New Testament* (Grand Rapids: Eerdmans, 1999), 56–61.

able—the so-called "slave's punishment."[11] Rome sought to bring about its promised salvation in the world through self-glory and violence. God fulfills his saving purpose through self-giving and a *cross*. The two "stories" collide, like a couple of trains barreling toward each other on the same track.

In Philippians 3:20-21, Paul revisits the ending to the story told in Philippians 2. The exalted Christ will return from heaven as Savior and Lord (Phil 3:20). He will transform human life in its wholeness, including the body. And by the power given to him by the Father, Christ will "subject *all things* to himself" (Phil 3:21, italics added). At that time, God in Christ will fully restore his loving sovereignty over the whole of creation. This is the breathtaking goal of the *missio Dei*. God's mission is good news, not only for people but also for all of creation.

Paul makes it clear that the Philippians themselves are caught up in this story of God's redeeming, restoring purpose in Christ. God, who has begun a "good work" of salvation in and among them, will faithfully bring it to completion on the day of Christ Jesus (Phil 1:6; cf. 1:10; 3:14). God is presently working in them, empowering them to work for his good pleasure (Phil 2:13). And they live in hope of the heavenly Savior's return. At that time, the bodies of their humiliation—now like the "humbled" and vulnerable body of their Lord while on earth (2:8)—will be conformed to his own body of glory (Phil 3:21). From start to finish, their salvation originates "from God" (1:28). The only fitting response is to give God all the glory (Phil 1:11; 2:11; 4:20).

Paul does not skimp when he describes the richness of God's saving purpose for his people. In Philippians, some of his most compelling language comes in the form of autobiography. Paul's singular passion is "the superior value of knowing Christ" (Phil 3:8, 10). Indeed, for Paul, living *is* Christ (Phil 1:21). This intimate, profoundly personal knowledge of Christ involves participating in his suffering and death (Phil 3:10). It also means sharing in Christ's resurrection life, both now and in the future (Phil 3:10, 11). But this is not just Paul's story. Paul's own experience of Christ has a paradigmatic role in Philippians (see below). Paul believes it is God's purpose that his audience shares that same kind of intimate, transforming relationship to God in Christ. This is part of what it means to be "in Christ," both as persons and as a community (Phil 1:1, 14; 3:9; 4:21).

Paul can also talk about God's saving work as a "righteousness," which comes graciously "from God" and is brought about either "through *faith in*

11. Joseph H. Hellerman, *Reconstructing Honor in Roman Philippi:* Carmen Christi *as* Cursus Pudorum, Society of New Testament Studies Monograph Series 132 (Cambridge: Cambridge University Press, 2005), 146–47.

Christ" (most translations) or "through the *faithfulness of* Christ" (Phil 3:9 CEB, italics added). In the context, this righteousness is tightly tethered to the experience of knowing Christ (see Phil 3:8, 10). It therefore entails more than simply the righteous *status* that God gives sinners. It involves the restoring of a right *relationship* with God through the work of Christ, which enables people to *live rightly*. The latter includes being in *right, loving relationships* with others (see Phil 1:11, "the fruit of righteousness"). God's activity of "putting things right" also encompasses a future dimension. The God who is faithful to his covenant will vindicate his people in the end, when the dead are raised (3:11), and God sets right the whole cosmos (Phil 3:20-21).

What's more, the Philippians are active players in God's saving and transforming activity in the world. At the outset, Paul thanks God for their "partnership in the gospel" from the time of their conversion (Phil 1:5 NIV).[12] This does not simply mean that they have embraced the grand gospel narrative, but, in particular, that they have partnered *with* Paul in the ministry of the good news. In Philippians, "the gospel" is dynamic language.[13] It is the "word of life," that is, the word that brings life and salvation (Phil 2:16), or, as Romans puts it, the "power of God for salvation" (Rom 1:16). Paul's own priority is the "advance of the gospel" (Phil 1:12 AT), and the Philippians have shared in that dynamic progress. What form did this gospel partnership take? Taking into account the letter as a whole, it likely includes the following:

• Practical support of Paul's mission, both through financial gifts (Phil 4:15-16) and by sending coworkers like Epaphroditus to minister to him (Phil 2:25-30)

• Intercessory prayer on Paul's behalf (Phil 1:19)

• Suffering along with Paul for the gospel's sake (Phil 1:30; 4:14)

• Living in a way that is worthy of the gospel (Phil 1:27)

• Evangelistic witness to the gospel in Philippi (Phil 1:27, 28)[14]

12. James Ware notes that the term "gospel" (*to euangelion*) appears more often in Philippians than any other letter of Paul; see 1:5, 7, 12, 16, 27 (twice); 2:22; 4:3, 15. James P. Ware, *Paul and the Mission of the Church: Philippians in Ancient Jewish Context* (Grand Rapids: Baker Academic, 2011), 165–66.

13. Paul speaks, for example, of the gospel's "defense" (1:7, 16) and "confirmation" (1:7), its "advance" (1:12), its "work" (2:22; 4:3), and of the "beginning" of his gospel mission in Philippi (4:15).

14. See Peter T. O'Brien, *The Epistle to the Philippians: A Commentary on the Greek Text* (Grand Rapids: Eerdmans, 1991), 63.

Moreover, they have become Paul's "partners in God's grace" (Phil 1:7), not only by aiding him financially but also by participating in the "defense and support of the gospel" (Phil 1:7).[15] This shared grace involves withstanding hostility from the Romans in their own setting, even as Paul has in prison (Phil 1:29-30). The congregation, then, already has a track record of participating in God's gospel mission in Philippi. But Paul desires this gospel partnership to continue and strengthen. This brings us to a third aspect of a missional reading of Philippians. How does this letter shape and equip its readers for their missional calling in the world?

Philippians as an Instrument of God's Mission

A Past to Recall

Paul draws upon a fistful of strategies in Philippians in order to form a mature, missional community. He begins by reminding his converts of their past faithfulness in mission. The mention of their role as "partners in the ministry of the gospel" (Phil 1:5) in the opening thanksgiving section of the letter (rhetorically, the *exordium*) not only previews a key theme that will unfold as the letter progresses. It also reinforces the Philippians' ongoing attachment to the gospel and its mission. Ultimately, the questions of how this letter bears witness to God's mission in Philippi and how it shapes the congregation for that mission are inseparable, like light and the sun.

Examples to Follow

Another key strategy for the forming of missional identity in Philippi is Paul's use of examples. This begins early on. Paul's personal narrative in Philippians 1:12-18a gives his readers a pattern to emulate. He tells his friends that his present suffering, far from hampering the progress of the gospel, has only served to enhance it. As sharers in a common struggle with Paul, they are able to face their own suffering for the sake of Christ with confidence (Phil 1:29-30). If they are faithful, the power of the gospel will likewise be released in Philippi. Paul's own imprisonment testifies that God's mission cannot be derailed, even by apparent catastrophes. On the contrary, his incarceration under Caesar's Roman nose has enabled the gospel to penetrate into the very

---

15. Markus N. A. Bockmuehl, *The Epistle to the Philippians* (Peabody, MA: Hendrickson, 1998), 60, 64; Flemming, *Philippians*, 55–56.

bloodstream of imperial power: "The whole Pretorian Guard and everyone else knows that I'm in prison for Christ" (Phil 1:13; cf. 4:22). This would surely be an encouragement to a church situated in the midst of a Roman colony.

Likewise, part of the reason that Paul continues to "preach Christ," even in the face of personal attacks (Phil 1:15-18), is so that the Philippians will be faithful to make Christ known in their own sphere of influence.[16] What is more, Paul spotlights the fearless testimony of his fellow believers in Rome, who, because of his example, "have had more confidence through the Lord to speak the word more boldly and bravely" (Phil 1:14). This serves as a model for his Philippian friends. They, like their counterparts in Rome, should partner with Paul in daring to speak the word boldly, in spite of opposition.[17] Of course, the supreme example for shaping a missional identity is Christ himself (Phil 2:5-11). But we'll return to that shortly.

Exhortations to Embody

Above all, Philippians forms the church for its missional calling in the section of pastoral exhortation that runs from 1:27 through 2:18. Verse 27 sounds the keynote for the unit, and, for that matter, the whole letter: "Live out your citizenship in a manner worthy of the gospel of Christ" (AT).[18] This is a "mission statement," if there ever was one. But its missional impact is often overlooked. Unfortunately, most English translations give Paul's verb a rather generic rendering, such as "live your life" (NRSV) or "live together" (NEB). This could easily lead us to think that Paul is only concerned with how Christians conduct their private lives or their interactions with one another. But Paul draws on *political* language here. The verb "live out your citizenship" (*politeusthe* in Greek) plays on Philippi's status as a Roman colony. Paul reminds the church that, although they conduct their public, common life—their citizenship—in a setting where Caesar seems to hold all the cards, they must do so according to a higher loyalty and a different lifestyle. Their true citizenship is in heaven (Phil 3:20). They worship the Lord of heaven and earth (Phil 2:10-11). Consequently, they must visibly live out the values of

16. I. Howard Marshall, *New Testament Theology: Many Witnesses, One Gospel* (Downers Grove, IL: IVP Academic, 2004), 360.

17. Ware, *Paul and the Mission of the Church*, 184–85. Differently, John Dickson maintains that the "brothers" that Paul refers to in Phil 1:14 are Paul's "missionary colleagues," not "ordinary believers." Dickson, *The Best Kept Secret of Christian Mission: Promoting the Gospel with More Than Our Lips* (Grand Rapids: Zondervan, 2010), 146. But there is nothing in the context that requires such a narrow identification.

18. Rhetorically, 1:27-30 functions as the thesis statement or "proposition" for the letter, with 1:27a as the headline imperative.

the kingdom of Christ, not the empire of Caesar. Whether within the church or in the public square, their lives must embody the good news of *Christ*.

Paul unfolds what it means to live a gospel-worthy life (Phil 1:27) in the rest of the section. He calls them to be united and steadfast in the midst of harassment and suffering (Phil 1:27-30). They must stand firm, enabled by "the one Spirit" (Phil 1:27).[19] Facing pressure from their opponents, they must struggle together, literally, "for the faith of the gospel" (Phil 1:27). This likely involves not only promoting and defending the truth of the gospel to outsiders (cf. Phil 4:3) but especially refusing to compromise the gospel's integrity through unworthy living.[20] They bear witness to the gospel with both their lips and their lives. Furthermore, the Philippians' unified faithfulness becomes a twofold "sign" to their persecutors (Phil 1:28). It shows on the one hand that their adversaries are on the highway to destruction (cf. Phil 3:19); on the other, it demonstrates that God will vindicate his people in the end. Their communal life "speaks," even to those who seek them harm.

But Paul pulls no punches. A faithful witness to the gospel is costly. It will mean embracing the severe grace of suffering on behalf of Christ, even as it has for Paul (Phil 1:29-30). Is Paul concerned that the Philippians might *not* stay firm under fire and live worthily of the gospel? Given Paul's language in 1:27-30, this is a real possibility.[21]

Throughout Paul's exhortations, there is a vital link between the Philippians' "inside" and "outside" conduct. Unity within the Christian community is inseparable from public witness and steadfastness. A "therefore" at the beginning of chapter 2 (Phil 2:1) binds Paul's appeal to Christian love, oneness, and humility in 2:1-4 to his exhortations to public faithfulness in 1:27-30. Michael Gorman is right that "the exhortations to unity in the community are not intended merely to create internal harmony; they serve to ensure the community's public witness to the gospel 'in one Spirit' (Phil 1:27)."[22]

Living worthily of the gospel entails working out their own salvation through God's enabling power (Phil 2:12-13). How that "works out" in practice is unpacked in 2:14-16. On the negative side, the congregation must learn from Israel's misadventures in the desert and avoid a pattern of complaining and arguing (Phil 2:14). Such internal frictions could blunt their witness before a watching world. Positively, they must live as God's holy

---

19. It is better to take this phrase as a reference to the Holy Spirit than to understand it metaphorically ("in one spirit"). See Gordon D. Fee, *Paul's Letter to the Philippians* (Grand Rapids: Eerdmans, 1995), 163–66.

20. I. Howard Marshall, *Philippians* (London: Epworth, 1991), 37.

21. See Gorman, *Becoming the Gospel*, 113–15; Ware, *Paul and the Mission of the Church*, 222–23.

22. Gorman, *Becoming the Gospel*, 123.

people, above reproach, in the midst of a twisted and corrupt environment (see Deut 32:5). If they do, they will "shine like stars in the world" (Phil 2:15).[23] Even as Israel was set apart to become a "light to the nations" (Isa 42:6; 49:6), so the church's unity and embodied holiness "will enable them to have a light-bearing witness among their pagan contemporaries."[24] Like Israel, their distinctive, God-shaped lives will challenge the surrounding world by their very difference. At the same time, the church's holy character will shine as a light in the darkness, attracting others to their Lord, like moths to a flame.

This brings us to the most controversial phrase in the passage, one that is especially important for understanding how Paul sees the missional role of God's people. Does Paul want the Philippians to hold steady in their faith, as they "hold on to" the word of life (so most English translations)? Or does he envision them "holding out" the word (see NIV84), in an active evangelistic sense (the minority view)? Both translations are possible, and both make good sense in the context.

This disagreement over the meaning of the verb "hold out/fast" (*epechō*) in Philippians 2:16 provides a window into a larger debate. Several recent studies insist that Paul expected the believers in Philippi—as well as the rest of his congregations—to actively evangelize and proclaim the gospel.[25] In contrast, Brian K. Peterson argues that the Philippians' mission was *not* "to tell [their neighbors] about Jesus" in order to win converts. Instead, they were simply to "be" the church and let their shared life do the talking. In other words, congregations were to embody the gospel as loving communities, not proclaim it.[26]

But does this need to be an "either/or" question? Regarding the translation of verse 16, I find the arguments by James Ware and others that Paul wants the Philippians to spread the good news by "holding forth" the word of life to be quite compelling.[27] Among other reasons, the phrase "the word of life" refers to the gospel, which imparts life to others. It is a message that Paul expects God's people to "hold out" to their non-Christian neighbors.

23. The phrase "stars in the world" points to Dan 12:3, which prophesies that those who lead many to righteousness will shine like heavenly lights.

24. Flemming, *Philippians*, 134.

25. See Ware, *Paul and the Mission of the Church*; Robert L. Plummer, *Paul's Understanding of the Church's Mission: Did the Apostle Paul Expect the Early Christian Communities to Evangelize?* Paternoster Biblical Monographs (Milton Keynes: Paternoster, 2006), esp. 72–77, 134–35; Mark J. Keown, *Congregational Evangelism in Philippians: The Centrality of an Appeal for Gospel Proclamation to the Fabric of Philippians*, Paternoster Biblical Monographs (Milton Keynes: Paternoster, 2008).

26. Brian K. Peterson, "Being the Church in Philippi," *Horizons in Biblical Theology* 30 (2008): 169. Unfortunately, Peterson seems to think that "evangelism" is primarily about numerical growth and success (pp. 169–71, 177–78).

27. See Ware, *Paul and the Mission of the Church*, 256–84.

But even if Paul is urging the church to hold firmly *to* the gospel, this doesn't rule out an active mission. Being faithful to the gospel surely includes sharing the word that imparts life when the opportunity arises.[28] What is more, Gorman rightly asks whether we can imagine the Philippian congregation regularly worshipping Jesus as Lord, living a countercultural lifestyle in Philippi, without *ever* explaining their strange behavior or introducing their pagan friends to the story of Jesus.[29] It is not hard to imagine Christians describing to "family members, associates, fellow slaves or masters, coworkers in the trade guilds, and so on why they no longer sacrifice to the deities that protect the Empire, including the Emperor. Some may have even explained their new beliefs, behaviors, and community in terms of an alternative gospel, lifestyle, and family to that offered by Rome."[30] Can we account for such a stiff opposition to these Christians if there were *no* active and verbal aspect to their witness? It's doubtful. What's more, we have already seen that Paul's argument from example in chapter 1 suggests that he wants his friends in Philippi to join him and other Christians in courageously speaking the word in the face of adversity (Phil 1:12-18). Finally, Paul says near the beginning of the letter that the Philippians share with him in "the defense of the gospel" (Phil 1:7), which surely includes answering objections to the Christian message.

At the same time, "holding forth" the life-bearing word is not *simply* about verbal witness. Paul expects his audience to hold out the good news to their pagan neighbors, not only by the words they speak but also by the lives they live (Phil 2:14-15). Later in Philippians, Paul writes of the contagious influence of a gentle spirit, one that refuses to retaliate in the face of opposition. The Philippians must let their "gentleness show in [their] treatment of all people" (Phil 4:5). In this way, the church bears witness to the good news about a Savior whose unwillingness to assert his rights led him all the way to a cross.[31] The Philippians' partnership in the gospel involves both showing and telling the good news.

A Story to Enter

Right in the midst of Paul's mission-oriented exhortations of Philippians 1:27-30 and 2:12-18, we find the foundational story of Jesus (Phil 2:5-11). This hymn-like narrative, above all else in the letter, forms the readers'

---

28. Keown, *Congregational Evangelism*, 146.

29. Gorman, *Becoming the Gospel*, 127.

30. Ibid., 290. Gorman's comments originally describe Christians in Rome, but he notes the similarity of their witness to that of believers in Philippi.

31. Flemming, *Philippians*, 220.

identity as a people through whom God can work. It not only tells the story of the divine mission (see above); it also shows God's people the attitude and conduct they must embrace in order to participate in the *missio Dei*. Before Paul talks about how Jesus emptied himself and humbled himself and obediently suffered death on a cross (Phil 2:6-8), he says this to the church: "Adopt the attitude that was in Christ Jesus" (Phil 2:5). Only by assuming the mindset of Christ will the congregation become a visible interpretation of the gospel in Philippi. Only when they embody Jesus's self-giving love for others, both inside and outside the community, can they hope to live in a manner worthy of the gospel in the public square (Phil 1:27). If the good news is the story of cross-shaped love, then that's the story that must be lived out, both within the community and before the watching world. Like Christ, like Christians.

I agree, then, with Michael Gorman that we can't limit what it means to follow the example of Christ in Philippians 2:6-11 to interpersonal relationships within the church.[32] The same self-giving love that led Jesus to stay faithful, even to the point of death, will compel the Philippians to faithfully bear witness to the gospel of Christ, in both word and life. This is a story that must be proclaimed *and* practiced by the church.

What's more, this passage implies that just as God exalted Jesus in response to his obedience unto death on a cross, so also God's people, if they remain steadfast in the face of suffering at the hands of the Romans, will be vindicated by God in the end (see Phil 1:6; 3:20-21).[33] And the assurance that one day every created being will confess Jesus as Lord draws the church into God's mission. They must proclaim and embody Christ's lordship even now, in joyful anticipation of what is to come. They do so in a setting where declaring Jesus's lordship hurls them on a collision course with Rome, whose emperors were acclaimed "lord of the world."[34] The story of a crucified Savior, who rules not by universal domination but by self-emptying love, confronts Rome's entire vision of the world. If the crucified Jesus is Lord of all, that reality, by its very nature, challenges all other competing stories, all other claims to ultimate allegiance. *Living* the story of Jesus in Caesar's colony is a risky business.

What does participation in God's mission by imitating Christ look like in practice? To make this clearer, "Paul parades before their eyes a series of examples for imitation, people in their own context who embody the pattern

32. Gorman, *Becoming the Gospel*, 123–25.

33. Ibid., 125.

34. On the challenge to imperial sovereignty in Phil 2:9-11, see Peter Oakes, *Philippians: From People to Letter*, Society for New Testament Studies Monograph Series 110 (Cambridge: Cambridge University Press, 2001), 149–50, 171–72.

of Christ."[35] These include Paul's coworker Timothy, who puts the interests of Christ and others before his own (Phil 2:21-22); the Philippians' messenger Epaphroditus, who, risking his very life, comes within a hair's breadth of death in service to Christ (Phil 2:25-30); and, above all, the apostle himself (Phil 3:4-14, 17; 4:9). Even as Jesus relinquished equality with God and became a slave for others (Phil 2:6-7), so Paul, Christ's "slave" (Phil 1:1), trashes all he once valued for the sake of knowing Christ (Phil 3:7-11). He now participates in Christ's suffering and Christ's mission.[36] Paul explicitly urges his audience to practice whatever they "learned, received, heard, or saw" in him (Phil 4:9). This likely includes both how Paul *lived* the gospel and how he *witnessed to* the gospel before them. All of these examples point back to the defining story of Jesus's cruciform love. By joyfully reenacting the drama of Christ in their own setting, God's people can *be* the good news in Caesar's colony—in both word and deed.

Values to Engage

There is one more text to consider, which carries implications for how the church participates in the mission of God.[37] Near the end of the letter, Paul lists a set of virtues that were widely valued in Greco-Roman culture (Phil 4:8). He uses them to instruct the Philippians as to how they should think and live. They should focus their attention on things, for example, that are "excellent" or "admirable" or "worthy of praise." Paul doesn't reject such publicly recognized virtues, even though they are connected to the popular moral teaching of the Roman world. Instead, he says, in effect, "Recognize what is good and beautiful, wherever it is found. Use it as a point of contact with your unbelieving neighbors, *as long as it is compatible with the self-giving pattern of Christ*" (see Phil 4:9). Such critical engagement with the culture will enable Paul's audience to fulfill their calling to shine as beacons in the midst of a dark and crooked world (Phil 2:14-16).

Paul's positive use of language shared by Christians and their pagan friends implies an overlap between the values found in human cultures and those of God's kingdom. Let me illustrate this with a contemporary example. While living in the Philippines, I was struck by the Filipinos' practice of naming their shared cultural values. One such virtue was called *pakikipagkapwa-tao* (literally, "being a fellow to others"). It embraces attitudes like sharing with others, treating them with respect, and giving aid to those in need. It's

35. J. Ross Wagner, "*Missio Dei*: Envisioning an Apostolic Reading of Scripture," *Missiology* 37 (2009): 25.

36. Ibid., 26.

37. For the following section, see Flemming, *Philippians*, 223, 226, 230–31.

not hard to see the common ground between these attributes and the Christian notion of "partnership" (*koinōnia*). God's people can affirm such values and use them as touch points for the gospel of Christ. Similarly, Paul doesn't hesitate to tap into the best in Roman culture and thought in the service of the gospel.

At the same time, Paul does not want believers to understand what is "lovely" or "admirable" just like the Romans do. If we read on in verse 9, we see that Paul interprets this list by urging God's people to learn from his example, even as he reflects the pattern of Christ (Phil 2:6-11). Ultimately, all of the virtues listed in Philippians 4:8 are embodied in the character of Jesus. The language and values that Christians share with the wider culture are always transformed in some way by the gospel of Christ crucified. In other words, Paul intends for these "cultural" virtues to be filled with Christian content.

To summarize, Paul's formation of a cross-shaped community enables the Philippians to *be* the visible manifestation of God's reconciling purpose for the world. Part of what that means is to actively bear witness to the word of life (Phil 2:16). But, as citizens of heaven (Phil 3:20), they are also called to publicly live out the life of heaven on earth—a life of love, unity, and holiness. They are the embodiment of the *missio Dei* on Roman streets.

Reading Philippians as Missional Communities

No other letter of Paul shines as bright a spotlight on the role of the local church in God's mission as does Philippians.[38] If that is true, then a missional reading of this letter would be incomplete without touching on how the letter *continues* to equip Christian communities to participate in the *missio Dei*. Here are some brief reflections, which you can contextualize for your own setting:

Embodying God's Mission as United, Holy, and Loving Communities

In Philippians, the church's mission is bound to its Christlike character. First, a church that lives out its shared life with a common mindset (Phil 1:27; 2:2; 4:2), without "complaining and arguing" (Phil 2:14), is a church whose witness to those outside will ring true (Phil 2:15; cf. John 17:20-23). Conversely, divisions within the community become a stumbling block to our reconciling mission. "The world watches, Christians bicker, the flame of witness smolders."[39]

---

38. See Marshall, *New Testament Theology*, 359.
39. Flemming, *Philippians*, 140.

Second, a church in mission is a church that embodies holiness (Phil 1:10-11; 2:14-15). On the one hand, our lives of integrity, both personally and as a community, will stand out in a sinful and crooked world by their very difference. On the other hand, people who reflect the holy character of Christ will positively give light to their world (2:15). Christian families, for example, can model faithfulness and self-giving in societies where conflict, abuse, and disposable relationships are too often the norm. Christian leaders who demonstrate integrity in finances, speech, and sexuality will offer a winsome alternative to many cultural patterns of leadership.

Third, the cruciform love of Jesus Christ, so powerfully narrated in Philippians 2:6-11, shapes both our gathered life in community and our scattered life in witness. Communities that reflect self-giving love will "interpret" the gospel faithfully in their spheres of influence. Genuine love is contagious, attractive, magnetic. And that same others-oriented love of Christ will compel us, by the power of the Spirit, to engage in God's healing and reconciling mission in the world (2 Cor 5:14-20).

Living and Telling the Gospel Story

The pendulum of Christian mission tends to career between a narrow focus on verbal proclamation and church planting on the one hand, and on Christian presence and loving deeds on the other. Paul resists all such dichotomies. For the apostle, a church that is "on mission" is a church with a seamless witness of word and life. Brian Peterson is right to deny that Paul presents doing good and loving others simply as a means for the church to accomplish its real mission of conversion.[40] But he is wrong to imply that we must choose between the two. The alternative to faulty forms of evangelism is not silence. A public and communal life that is "worthy of the gospel of Christ" (Phil 1:27) means "being" the new creation of God. But it also involves confidently announcing Jesus as Lord in the midst of seemingly hopeless situations, even as we joyfully anticipate his coming rule over the whole universe.

Critically Engaging Our Cultures

The church is not called to completely reject the culture or cultures in which it is found. Paul's use of popular cultural virtues to promote Christian thinking and living (Phil 4:8) assumes that the whole world belongs to God. God's grace is active in the world he has created, including human cultures.

40. Peterson, "Being the Church," 171.

We should therefore not be afraid to celebrate what is true and beautiful in our cultures, or to enlist "secular" ideals or art forms in the service of the gospel.

At the same time, we dare not embrace the values of the wider culture uncritically. If we are already "citizens of heaven" (Phil 3:20), then our daily life in Philippi, Philadelphia, or the Philippines will embody the character and ideals of the kingdom of God, rather than those of the present world. Whenever the church becomes too cozy with the values of the culture around it, it loses its credibility to prophetically challenge that culture. "As citizens of heaven, we will have one foot firmly planted *inside* our culture, so that we can identify with the people around us and make sense to them. At the same time, we will have one foot *outside* of the culture, as we model a cross-shaped alternative to the spirit of the world."[41]

Conclusion

Philippians calls the church to get caught up in the magnificent pageant of what God is doing in the world. That mission comes to expression above all in a V-shaped drama about the self-giving, dying, exalted Christ. This is the gospel message that God's people, then and now, are to proclaim. But it is also the story the church must live out, if it is to publicly and faithfully embody the good news in its world. A missional reading of Philippians cannot stop with *understanding* God's mission in the text. Indeed, we haven't truly *understood* this text, until we let the Spirit form us into people who reenact the self-giving story of Christ. Not until we begin to live out our heavenly citizenship in ways that display the gospel of Christ—in word and deed.

---

41. Flemming, *Philippians*, 209; cf. Miroslav Volf, *Exclusion and Embrace: A Theological Exploration of Identity, Otherness, and Reconciliation* (Nashville: Abingdon, 1996), 49.

Chapter Five

Mission for Misfits: A Missional Reading of 1 Peter

Mission is not just about what we *do*. First and foremost, it's about who we *are*. And nowhere in the New Testament is that clearer than in 1 Peter. This letter pictures its Christian audience as "immigrants and strangers in the world" (1 Pet 2:11). They are Christians who, because of their new life in Christ, are no longer at home in their own cultures. Christians who live under siege from their unbelieving neighbors. Christians who know something about *suffering*. But 1 Peter is more than simply a pastoral message designed to encourage believers facing hard times. The letter trots out what it means for Christian communities to live out their identity and witness in a society that treats them like strangers, even intruders. Peter wrestles with how the church embodies God's mission in an unfriendly world. If that's true, then this fascinating letter is not only *open* to a missional reading. It *clamors* for it.

How, then, does 1 Peter witness to God's mission? And how does it serve as an instrument of the *missio Dei* for "exiles in mission"? These are the key concerns of this chapter.[1]

---

1. This chapter includes material adapted from Dean Flemming, "'Won Over without a Word': Holiness and the Church's Missional Identity in 1 Peter," *Wesleyan Theological Journal* 49 (2014): 50–66; and Dean Flemming, *Recovering the Full Mission of God: A Biblical Perspective on Being, Doing and Telling* (Downers Grove, IL: IVP Academic, 2013), ch. 9.

1 Peter as a Witness to God's Mission

Overlapping Stories

One vital strategy for helping hard-pressed Christians to live out their calling is to remind them of their part in a larger story. No less than in Philippians, 1 Peter offers the church a defining narrative, a magnificent vision of what God is up to in the world. But whereas Paul spells out that narrative quite explicitly in a passage like Philippians 2:6-11, in 1 Peter the "story" is more behind the scenes. It provides a kind of narrative framework for Peter's message.[2] Actually, we discover several stories in 1 Peter, which are fully intertwined.

The primary narrative is the story of God's saving purpose for humanity and the world—the *missio Dei*. God is the lead actor in this drama, but God acts through Jesus Christ.[3] Peter articulates that gospel narrative, particularly in the early stages of the letter, and it serves as bedrock for everything else he says to the church. The story of God's mission in Christ sweeps from creation to the consummation of all things. It begins with what the redeeming God has done in the past. God, the gracious creator (1 Pet 4:19), chose Christ before the foundation of the world for God's saving purposes (1 Pet 1:20). In fulfillment of scripture (1 Pet 1:10-12), God revealed Jesus Christ in human history "in these last times" (1 Pet 1:20 NIV). This revelation becomes the midpoint and focus of the story. Peter especially accents Jesus's suffering, death, and resurrection from the dead, the events that give meaning to the entire narrative.[4] In the present, the risen and exalted Jesus sits at the right hand of God, and all created beings and powers are subject to him (1 Pet 3:22). And the story of God's mission will reach a glorious climax in the future. God will reveal Jesus Christ in glory (1 Pet 1:7, 13; 5:4) and will impartially judge all people in the end (1 Pet 1:17; 2:23; 4:5-6).

But Peter is not interested in this grand narrative for its own sake. It is the story of God's *salvation*, after all (1 Pet 1:5, 10). Peter inscribes his audience into this divine drama of redemption. Over and over, Peter shows how

---

2. In recent years, a number of scholars have recognized the importance of 1 Peter's "narrative" for understanding the letter's theological message. See, e.g., Joel B. Green, "Narrating the Gospel in 1 and 2 Peter," *Interpretation* 60 (2006): 262–67; Joel B. Green, *1 Peter* (Grand Rapids: Eerdmans, 2007), 197–202; M. Eugene Boring, "Narrative Dynamics in 1 Peter: The Function of Narrative World," in *Reading First Peter with New Eyes: Methodological Assessments of the Letter of First Peter*, ed. Robert L. Webb and Betsy Bauman-Martin (London: T&T Clark, 2007), 7–40; Abson Prédestin Joseph, *A Narratological Reading of 1 Peter*, Library of New Testament Studies 440 (London: T&T Clark, 2012).

3. Lewis R. Donelson, *1 & 2 Peter and Jude* (Louisville: Westminster John Knox, 2010), 20.

4. Eugene Boring reckons that no less than twenty-two times in 1 Peter, we encounter the "what" and the "why" of Jesus's death ("Narrative Dynamics," 29).

the two stories, the story of God in Christ and the story of Christians, are intertwined. Here is just a sampling (italics added):

- God the Father chose *you*... through the Holy Spirit's work... and because of *the faithful obedience and sacrifice of Jesus Christ* (1 Pet 1:2).

- *You* have been born anew into a living hope through *the resurrection of Jesus Christ* (1 Pet 1:3).

- Hope completely on the grace that will be brought to *you* when *Jesus Christ is revealed* (1 Pet 1:13).

- *Christ was... revealed* at the end of time...*for you* (1 Pet 1:20).

- *Christ suffered on your behalf.* He left you an example so that *you* might follow in his footsteps (1 Pet 2:21).

- *Christ suffered* on account of sins... to bring *you* into the presence of *God* (1 Pet 3:18).

- When the *chief shepherd appears, you* will receive an unfading crown of glory (1 Pet 5:4).

It's plain that Peter wants his audience to realize they are caught up in the grand story of God's saving mission in Christ. God's mission bears fruit in their salvation.

But there is another story that 1 Peter tells—the story of Israel. Addressing a primarily Gentile audience, Peter connects them to what God has already been doing in the life of his people Israel. This connection, however, is not so much a *continuation* of Israel's story as it is an *embodiment* of that story. Peter reads the experience of these Christians directly *into* Israel's narrative. God's people then and God's people now are one. Using Old Testament images, he says, in effect, "*You Gentile Christians* are God's 'chosen exiles'" (1 Pet 1:1 AT; see 1:17; 2:11). *You* are a "chosen race, a royal priesthood, and a holy nation" (1 Pet 2:9; cf. Exod 19:5-6). Peering through the lens of Israel's story, Peter shapes the church's identity as the people of God. Peter, in effect, is doing creative theological reflection, contextualizing the Old Testament scriptures for new circumstances.[5]

---

5. Lee Beach, *The Church in Exile: Living in Hope after Christendom* (Downers Grove, IL: IVP Academic, 2014), 122–24.

By placing his audience within the stories of Israel and of Christ, Peter enables these Gentile Christians to see their context of suffering on behalf of Christ from a whole new vantage point. As Joel B. Green puts it, their "present circumstances make sense only on the expansive canvas of the whole of God's purpose and activity, from the very foundations of the world to the eschaton."[6] In particular, Peter shines a spotlight on the themes of redemption, suffering, and hope.

Redemption in Christ

First Peter's witness to the *missio Dei* fixes its sights, in particular, on God's redeeming work in the death and resurrection of Christ. Peter lays out a bountiful table of images to express the significance of what Christ has done. For example, Peter recontextualizes language from God's deliverance of his people in the exodus to convey the meaning of Christ's death for his audience. God has "liberated" them, not from slavery to the taskmasters of Egypt, but from bondage to the empty and debauched lifestyle they inherited from their ancestors (1 Pet 1:18-19; 4:3-4). The means of their liberation is "the precious blood of Christ (1 Pet 1:19; cf. 1:2). Here the imagery shifts from the exodus event to Israel's sacrificial system. Christ's death is an atoning sacrifice, like that of an unblemished and spotless sacrificial lamb (1 Pet 1:19). Peter wants his audience to know that their redemption is truly "precious"; God has provided it at enormous cost.

In addition, 1 Peter pictures God's saving activity as a triumph over the powers of evil. In a passage that has proved to be an interpretive hornet's nest, Peter announces that Christ, having been "put to death as a human [literally, 'in [the] flesh'], but made alive by the Spirit[7] . . . went to preach to the spirits in prison" (1 Pet 3:18-19). Traditionally, this text has been used to support the notion that, between his death and resurrection, Jesus descended to Hades and preached to the spirits of dead humans imprisoned there. I agree, however, with most recent interpreters that Peter has something else in mind. The "spirits" that hear the message in verse 19 are probably not human spirits, but instead evil cosmic powers (see 1 Pet 3:22).[8] "Their imprisonment,"

---

6. Green, *1 Peter*, 201.

7. I prefer the NEB translation "by the Spirit" to the NRSV's "in the spirit"; that is, the spiritual aspect of Jesus's human person. Here Peter seems to stress that Christ's death has been vindicated in his resurrection by the life-giving power of the Holy Spirit.

8. Most interpreters think Peter may be drawing on Jewish traditions from *1 Enoch* about fallen angels and evil spirits connected with the time of Noah and the flood (see Gen 6:1-4; 1 Pet 3:20). For a fuller discussion of the exegetical issues behind 1 Pet 3:18-22, see Donald P. Senior, "1 Peter," in *1 Peter, Jude, and 2 Peter*, ed. Donald P. Senior and Daniel J. Harrington (Collegeville, MN: Liturgical Press, 2008), 99–111.

argues Karen Jobes, "represents in spatial terms God's restraining power over them."[9] Jesus's proclamation to the spirits, then, is not an offer of forgiveness, but rather, "a triumphant announcement of victory over the forces of death and evil hurled at the hostile powers."[10] It anticipates the assurance in 1 Peter 3:22 that the risen and enthroned Jesus rules over all angels, authorities, and powers at the right hand of God.

What does this say to Peter's audience about God's mission? First, through the death, resurrection, and exaltation of Christ, God has liberated his people from the power of evil and death. And second, because Christ has decisively defeated all threatening powers, they can enjoy the daily confidence of victory in the end. The hostility they currently face may threaten to overwhelm them. But it is a hollow threat—a mouse roaring like a lion. Jesus's resurrection and exaltation proclaims to all hostile powers, whether human or cosmic, that they are *already* subject to Jesus Christ. They cannot derail God's redeeming purpose for his people.

The Suffering of Christ

Above all, Peter connects God's work of salvation with the *suffering* of Christ. This is good contextual theology. Addressing Christians for whom un-deserved suffering is a familiar companion, he reads their experience through the lens of God's ongoing purpose. For Peter, the mission of God is accomplished precisely through suffering, with its ultimate expression in the cross. On the one hand, Christ's suffering brought about their salvation: "Christ himself suffered on account of sins, once for all, the righteous one on behalf of the unrighteous. He did this to bring you into the presence of God" (1 Pet 3:18; cf. 2:21-24; 4:1; 5:1). Taking up language that recalls the role of God's suffering servant in Isaiah 53, Peter assures them that it is "by his wounds" they were healed (1 Pet 2:24). In fact, the ancient prophets long ago foresaw Christ's sufferings, which would result in their salvation (1 Pet 1:10-11).

On the other hand, Jesus's suffering becomes a *model* for how the church participates in God's mission. Even as Jesus suffered unjustly on behalf of others, so, at times, must God's people. Peter couldn't make it any clearer: "You were called to this kind of endurance, because Christ suffered on your behalf. He left you an example so that you might follow in his footsteps" (1 Pet 2:21; cf. 4:13). In particular, Christians refuse to retaliate when others wrong them. Instead, they offer grace and blessing to their enemies (1 Pet 3:9). Christian

---

9. Karen H. Jobes, *1 Peter* (Grand Rapids: Baker Academic, 2005), 244.

10. Senior, "1 Peter," 109.

slaves, for example, are free *not* to treat a harsh master in kind (2:18), because this is the Jesus way: "When he suffered, he did not threaten revenge" (2:23). By means of their enemy love, the Christian community "proclaims" the gospel of a Messiah who in love suffered without cause in order to bring his enemies to God (1 Pet 3:18).

Ultimately, the church's suffering and how it responds to that suffering becomes a compelling form of witness. Peter links suffering to the conversion of unbelievers. Godly behavior in the midst of suffering may lead slanderers to glorify God in the end (1 Pet 2:12). Believing women who display a holy lifestyle in the face of hostility may win their unbelieving spouses to Christ (1 Pet 3:1-2). Indeed, Peter could hardly conceive of engaging in God's mission *without* suffering. This in no way implies that Peter thinks Christians should seek out suffering or that suffering is good in itself. Peter understands, however, that God can transform suffering into something he can use to further his missional purpose and to conform his people to the pattern of Christ.

Peter is unequivocal that God's reconciling mission could only be accomplished through the costly suffering of Jesus Christ, who "bore our sins in his body on the cross" (1 Pet 2:24 NRSV). And those who wish to participate in God's mission must also be willing to bear the cost of suffering with and for the sake of Christ (see 1 Pet 4:13). This is still the reality for a vast array of faithful Christians across the global church. As Christopher Wright reflects, the church's suffering in mission is no less than a participation in the suffering mission of the suffering God.[11]

Hope and Judgment

First Peter not only emphasizes that God's mission involves past and present suffering. It also draws attention to the "hope-full" conclusion of that mission. Because Jesus's sufferings are followed by glory (1 Pet 1:11), those who walk in his steps will surely receive vindication and glory in the end. This exuberant hope frames the letter like brass bookends. Peter's opening "blessing" in 1:3-5 spotlights the eschatological character of God's salvation: God, in his mercy, has given them a living *hope* (1 Pet 1:3; cf. 1:13, 21), an unfading *inheritance* (1 Pet 1:4); and a future *salvation*, ready to be revealed on the last day (1 Pet 1:5; cf. 1:9). And the letter's conclusion soars with the

---

11. Christopher J. H. Wright, *The Mission of God's People: A Biblical Theology of the Church's Mission* (Grand Rapids: Zondervan, 2010), 240–41.

assurance that beyond their present suffering lies an eternal glory in Christ. The "God of all grace" will surely restore them in the end (5:10).

It shouldn't surprise us, then, that 1 Peter features what Joel Green calls "backshadowing," in which God's final purpose for his people casts its long shadow on their *present* lives.[12] God's future glory *already* rests on them (1 Pet 4:14; 5:10). Their coming salvation *presently* is being kept safe for them, even as they themselves are protected by God (1 Pet 1:4-5). At the same time, they are called to live out their everyday lives in ways that are consistent with God's glorious future. That includes both a holy lifestyle and faithful participation in the mission of God (1 Pet 1:13-16; 2:11-12).

At the same time, 1 Peter pictures God not only as a gracious savior, but also as a righteous judge (1 Pet 1:17; 2:12, 23; 3:12; 4:5-6, 17-18). This is the other side of his saving mission. God's redemptive purpose for his people will not be frustrated by evildoers. Those who oppress God's people will stand before the judge of the living and the dead in the end (1 Pet 4:4-5; cf. 2:7-8; 4:17-18). But God's reconciling love refuses to give up even on blasphemers and oppressors. Touched by the life witness of God's people, even some of those who slandered them may worship God on the day he comes to judge (1 Pet 2:12).

The Gospel Proclaimed

First Peter declares that God's great salvation has taken root in his audience through the preaching of the word. Long ago, the ancient prophets gave advance notice of God's gracious work in Christ. But, Peter affirms, "these things have now been proclaimed to you by those who *brought you the good news*" (1 Pet 1:10-12, italics added). What's more, Christians have been born anew through "God's life-giving and enduring word" (1 Pet 1:23). This abiding word, attested by the prophet Isaiah, is the very word "that *was proclaimed to you as good news*" (1 Pet 1:24-25, italics added). Both 1:12 and 1:25 feature the same key term for proclaiming the gospel (*euangelizomai*), which regularly describes Jesus's preaching in the Gospels, the early Christian proclamation in Acts, and the letters of Paul. It is through the proclamation of the good news that Peter's audience obtains the goal of their faith, the salvation of their souls (1 Pet 1:9). Peter leaves no doubt that God's saving mission has borne fruit among them. But how does this letter seek to shape these Christians to participate in the mission of God?

12. Green, "Narrating the Gospel," 274–75.

95

Chapter Five

1 Peter as an Instrument of God's Mission

An Identity to Embody

Immigrants and exiles. Peter anchors the mission of God's people in who they *are.* In part, Peter answers the identity question by picturing the church as "aliens" and "exiles" (1 Pet 2:11 NRSV; cf. 1:1, 17).[13] We have already noted that Peter characteristically reads his primarily Gentile audience into Israel's story. Like Abraham, whom God called to leave his homeland and live among strangers, they, too, are "immigrants" and "temporary residents" (Gen 23:4; cf. 1 Pet 1:1; 2:11). They are one with God's people Israel, who became "immigrants in the land of Egypt" (Lev 19:34). And like the Jewish exiles in Babylon, they are strangers in a strange land (1 Pet 1:17). Moreover, Peter addresses them as exiles of the *diaspora* ("dispersion," 1 Pet 1:1). In Peter's world, this language described the experience of Jews who were scattered and dislocated from their home country throughout the Roman Empire. Stacked together, these images portray Peter's Christian audience as a displaced people. Foreigners. Outsiders. Misfits.

We need to be clear, however, about what this identity as "foreigners" and "exiles" means for Peter's audience. This is *not* primarily a reference to their political or social status, either before or after they were born anew in Christ.[14] Instead, Peter pictures them as people who used to fit in to their social world, but who do so no longer. God has given them a new identity as his "chosen strangers in the world" (1 Pet 1:1). Formerly they spent their time "doing what unbelievers desire" (1 Pet 4:3). But God has called them to a new, distinctive way of living, which has set them at odds with their unbelieving family members and friends. They are like the proverbial "square peg" in the round hole of their own culture. Their true homeland is their new life "in Christ" (1 Pet 3:16; 5:10, 14).

What does this new identity imply about how God's people engage their world? This is not a call to withdraw from their social world into a cocoon of pious irrelevance. They still live "among the unbelievers" (1 Pet 2:12), and that is the arena of their mission. As Miroslav Volf wisely observes,

13. Despite frequent attempts to make a distinction in the meaning of the terms *aliens* and *exiles,* there seems to be little difference in how they function in 1 Peter. See Moses Chin, "A Heavenly Home for the Homeless: Aliens and Strangers in 1 Peter," *Tyndale Bulletin* 42 (1991): 110.

14. Against, e.g., John H. Elliott, *A Home for the Homeless: A Sociological Exegesis of 1 Peter, Its Situation and Strategy* (Philadelphia: Fortress, 1981); John H. Elliott, *1 Peter: A New Translation with Introduction and Commentary* (New York: Doubleday, 2000), esp. 312–13, 476–83.

Christians do not come into their social world from outside seeking either to accommodate to their new home (like second generation immigrants would), shape it in the image of the one they have left behind (like colonizers would), or establish a little haven in the strange new world reminiscent of the old (as resident aliens would). They are not outsiders who either seek to become insiders or maintain strenuously the status of outsiders. Christians are the *insiders* who have diverted from their culture by being born again.[15]

As John's Gospel would frame it, these Christians are "in the world" but not "of" it (see John 17:11-19).

And in their "world," the dominant player was Rome. Asia Minor, the social and political setting of Peter's audience (see 1 Pet 1:1), was a thoroughly Romanized region.[16] Rome was master of the universe, and its subjects were expected to play by Rome's rules regarding how life should be lived in the empire. Those rules demanded certain allegiances and practices: honoring Rome's gods and lords, including the emperor himself; buying into Rome's codes of what constituted honor and status; submitting to Rome's systems of power, which maintained the "peace" through coercion and violence. But these people were "Christians" (1 Pet 4:16)—a label that invoked suspicion and hostility in the Roman world.[17] They bore the name of Christ, not of Caesar. They refused to adopt Rome's ways of thinking and behaving. And that choice pushed them to the margins of their society. It was as if a target were painted on their backs, marking them out for exclusion and contempt. In the empire of Caesar, misfits suffer (1 Pet 4:12-19).

But that's only part of the story. Christians may be foreigners in their own culture, but they are still actively engaged in that culture. As Volf puts it, they "live an alternative way of life" within the various institutions of their social, political, religious, and cultural world.[18] For Peter, these Christian communities embody a missional presence in their societies, "among the unbelievers" (1 Pet 2:12). They are both connected and disconnected with their world.[19] They sing the melodies of their culture with new lyrics. It is precisely this

15. Miroslav Volf, "Soft Difference: Theological Reflections on the Relation between Church and Culture in 1 Peter," *Ex Auditu* 10 (1994): 18–19.

16. See Green, *1 Peter*, 192. See also 5:13, in which Peter refers to Rome by the Old Testament name *Babylon*—the Old Testament symbol of an empire that arrogantly defies God and the place of Israel's exile.

17. See C. Kavin Rowe, *World Upside Down: Reading Acts in the Graeco-Roman Age* (Oxford: Oxford University Press, 2009), 129–35.

18. Volf, "Soft Difference," 20.

19. Ross Hastings, *Missional God, Missional Church: Hope for Re-evangelizing the West* (Downers Grove, IL: IVP Academic, 2012), 290.

life of paradox that enables *outsiders* to live a missional existence *within* their world.

A holy people. A second aspect of the missional identity that Peter envisions for his audience is their character as a *holy priesthood.* First Peter 1:14-16 is an identity-shaping text for God's people:

> Don't be conformed to your former desires, those that shaped you when you were ignorant. But, as obedient children, you must be holy in every aspect of your lives, just as the one who called you is holy. It is written, *You will be holy, because I am holy.*

Here Peter identifies Israel's mandate to be holy as God is holy (Lev 19:2) as God's calling for the church. In the Old Testament, Israel, rescued from slavery by God's grace, was to display the holy character of God to the nations by its distinctive way of life. Similarly, the Christian community, liberated by the lamb's precious blood (1 Pet 1:19), is called to embody the holiness of God "among the Gentiles" (1 Pet 2:12 NRSV). In the first place, to be holy means to be different and distinctive. If God's people are going to make a *difference* in their unbelieving neighbors, they must be *different* from their neighbors. But holiness in 1 Peter also means being conformed to the character of a holy God. It means displaying the self-giving love of Christ. Christians are to "follow in the footsteps" of the one who suffered unselfishly for others (1 Pet 2:21).

This God-shaped holiness is more than just a "spiritual" activity. It penetrates every "nook and cranny" of their lives (1 Pet 1:15).[20] This is not the type of holiness that hangs a sign on the office door that says, "Please do not disturb. I'm being *holy!*" Instead, Peter envisions a church whose distinctive, self-giving, God-reflecting life, lived out "among the unbelievers," becomes an attractive witness to the surrounding world (see 1 Pet 2:12; 3:1, 13-17).

We find an even more explicit link between holiness and mission in 1 Peter 2:9-10:

> But you are a chosen race, a royal priesthood, a holy nation, a people who are God's own possession. You have become this people so that you may speak of the wonderful acts of the one who called you out of darkness into his amazing light. Once you weren't a people, but now you are God's people. Once you hadn't received mercy, but now you have received mercy.

Once again, Peter draws on Israel's experience to define the identity and calling of the church. The images of a "royal priesthood" and a "holy nation"

---

20. Green, *1 Peter,* 44.

are anchored in the foundational covenant passage of Exodus 19:4-6. Like Israel, the church's fundamental calling as a people chosen and redeemed by God is not to *do* certain things, but to *be* a certain kind of people.

What does it mean that the church is a "holy" or "royal *priesthood*" (1 Pet 2:5, 9)? Here Peter is not promoting the modern notion of the priesthood of each individual believer within the church. Rather, his concern is the priestly role of the whole people of God. For Israel, the function of a priest was, above all, to stand in the middle.[21] Israel, as priest, was to mediate God's presence and knowledge to the nations. At the same time, Israel was to bring the nations to God, interceding for them and bringing them to a means of atonement.

In the same way, the church is called to be a bridge, mediating the knowledge and blessing of God's salvation to the world. Christians are to declare God's mighty acts through word and deed (1 Pet 2:9), and they are to magnetically draw unbelievers to God through the witness of their holy lives. Like Israel, the church's calling as a "holy nation" is not for its own sake. Rather, God's people are to be "Exhibit A" for the abundant, transformed life that God wants *all* people to live. The "spiritual sacrifice" the church offers, notes Douglas Harink, "is its holy, cruciform life as a godly people in the midst of the nations, and for their sake."[22]

Consequently, the church's call to be holy in 1 Peter does not live in tension with the church's mission to the world. On the contrary, the two are inseparable. For Peter, Christian holiness is not a retreat *from* the world into a safe house of individual spirituality. Nor is it a crusade *against* the world, treating it as a foe to be defeated.[23] Instead, Peter envisions a church that is "radically different, yet fully engaged, for the sake of others."[24]

A Lifestyle to Practice

The mission of "doing good." For Peter, *who we are* leans out into the world in terms of *how we live.* In the section of exhortations that begin in 1 Peter 2:11, he unpacks how the church's missional identity works out in practice. "Live honorably among the unbelievers," Peter urges. "Today, they defame you, as if you were doing evil. But in the day when God visits to judge they

21. See Wright, *Mission of God's People*, 120–22.

22. Douglas K. Harink, *1 & 2 Peter* (Grand Rapids: Brazos, 2009), 69.

23. See Joel B. Green, "Living as Exiles: The Church in the Diaspora in 1 Peter," in *Holiness and Ecclesiology in the New Testament*, ed. Kent E. Brower and Andy Johnson (Grand Rapids: Eerdmans, 2007), 324.

24. Flemming, *Recovering the Full Mission of God*, 214.

will glorify him, because they have observed your honorable deeds" (1 Pet 2:12). This appeal clearly builds on what comes before it in chapter 2. Peter says, in effect, "As people who have been lavished with God's abundant mercy (1 Pet 2:10), as a priesthood, chosen to mediate God's holy presence to the world (1 Pet 2:5, 9), as 'strangers' who no longer ride the current of your culture (1 Pet 2:11), put that new identity into action. Live such godly and obedient lives that even some of your fiercest critics may join the celebration of God's glory on the last day" (cf. 1 Pet 2:12).[25]

Peter spotlights two key terms that describe the church's missional practice: Christian "conduct" (1 Pet 1:15; 2:11; 3:1-2, 16) and the notion of "doing good" (see 1 Pet 2:12, 14-15, 20; 3:10-17; 4:19). The latter, in particular, becomes a major theme in the letter. For modern readers, "doing good" may sound like a rather innocuous way to talk about the church's witness. But for Peter, it represents much more than "Be nice to others!" What, then, does it mean for God's people to "do good"?

In the Roman world, "doing good" was often defined as performing acts of public benefaction—wealthy citizens giving to advance the good of the city. It's been argued that Peter is urging well-to-do Christians to engage in precisely this kind of public service as a form of Christian witness (see especially 1 Pet 2:14-15).[26] But Peter's notion of "doing good" is far too general to be limited to the actions of rich Christians. Slaves and wives are also expected to "do good" (1 Pet 2:20; 3:6). Nevertheless, if "doing good" involves more than just public benefaction, it clearly has a public face. For Peter, good conduct is an outward oriented kind of witness. First Peter 2:12, for example, refers to good behavior "among the Gentiles," as well as outsiders "observing" Christians' honorable deeds. Peter goes on to explain that "doing good" before public authorities has the potential to "silence the ignorant talk of foolish people" (1 Pet 2:15).

Paradoxically, "doing good" both repels and attracts outsiders. On the one hand, a Christ-honoring lifestyle provokes opposition and slander. God's people "suffer *for doing good*" (1 Pet 3:16-17, italics added). They are misrepresented as *evil*-doers (1 Pet 2:12). Their godly behavior pricks and offends. It is as incompatible with their old way of living as oil is with water. As a result,

25. See Wright, *Mission of God's People*, 127.

26. See Bruce W. Winter, *Seek the Welfare of the City: Christians as Benefactors and Citizens* (Grand Rapids: Eerdmans, 1994), 25–40; cf. 11–23. Winter takes 1 Pet 2:14-15 as a reference to wealthy Christians positively engaging their social world by "doing good" in the form of civic benefaction. In turn, they would receive "praise" from ruling authorities (2:14) in the form of public accolades on inscriptions. See Torrey Seland's critique of Winter's reading: "Resident Aliens in Mission: Missional Practices in the Emerging Church of 1 Peter," *Bulletin for Biblical Research* 19 (2009): 577–78.

their pagan compatriots are baffled when they discover these Christians no longer join in with the partying crowd (1 Pet 4:3-4).

On the other hand, Peter is convinced that the church's good conduct attracts unbelievers to the faith. The point he seems to make in 1 Peter 2:12 is, "Even some of those who currently malign you are watching your lives. And because of the honorable deeds they see, they may come to glorify God on the day of judgment."[27] Here "glorifying God" is conversion language (see 1 Pet 4:16).[28] These words remind us of Jesus's appeal in the Sermon on the Mount to "let your light shine before others, that they may see your good deeds and glorify your Father in heaven" (Matt 5:16 NIV). Peter, then, recognizes the evangelistic impact of a Christian community that engages in a lifestyle of "doing good" (see 1 Pet 3:1-2). As Lee Beach points out, Peter nowhere offers a vision of sweeping social change. Rather, he "envisions an alternative community that offers witness to the world through its collective life."[29]

Witness "without a word." What does a lifestyle witness look like within ordinary family, social, and political relationships in the Roman world? Peter answers that question in the section of instructions relating to the ancient household in 2:13–3:7. Such "household codes" were a familiar form of teaching throughout the Greco-Roman world, and sometimes they were extended to include obligations to the state.[30] Peter's use of this form differs somewhat from those in Colossians and Ephesians, in that it more explicitly addresses how Christians relate to those *outside* the family of God. The whole section builds on Peter's headline appeal in 2:11-12 to live honorably "among the unbelievers" so that outsiders might be transformed through observing Christians' good deeds.

But *how* do believers engage others in their society? Peter answers that question with the signature verb "be subject" (*hypotassō*; "submit," CEB). God's people should subordinate themselves to "every human institution," including political authorities, like emperors and governors (1 Pet 2:13-17). Slaves should be subject to their masters (1 Pet 2:18). Wives should submit to their husbands (1 Pet 3:1). Admittedly, the notion of "submitting" to others prickles many modern readers, particularly in more individualistic societies.

---

27. Literally, "on the day of visitation" (1 Pet 2:12).

28. Differently, e.g., Eckhard J. Schnabel, *Early Christian Mission*, vol. 2, *Paul and the Early Church* (Downers Grove, IL: IVP Academic, 2004), 1522n124, who maintains that 1 Pet 2:12 does not refer to Gentile conversion but rather to "their forced acknowledgment of God on the day of judgment." However, the language of "glorifying God" normally speaks of the voluntary worship of God's people (see 1 Pet 4:16).

29. Beach, *Church in Exile*, 131.

30. Green, *1 Peter*, 70.

What, however, did the appeal to "be subject" mean for Peter's audience? Is it about getting in line with the expectations of the Roman social order? Some interpreters think so. Peter's advice, it is claimed, seeks to fend off the accusations of outsiders by showing that Christians are orderly people; they practice what's considered to be good and acceptable behavior in Roman society.[31] But this is not the best reading of the passage. Not at all.

We cannot forget that the repeated calls to "be subject" in 1 Peter 2:13–3:7 are addressed to "immigrants and strangers" (1 Pet 2:11)—people who, by definition, no longer fit in to the expectations of their culture. It is no accident that the cord that binds together Peter's instructions to Christian slaves (1 Pet 2:18-20) and Christian wives (1 Pet 3:1-7) is his appeal to the example of Christ (1 Pet 2:21-25). Peter defines what it means to "do good" in the midst of harassment with the pattern of Jesus. For Peter's audience, good conduct involves "freely" subordinating themselves, enduring undeserved suffering without retaliating, and loving their enemies. In short, "being subject" is an expression of what it means to follow in Jesus's steps (1 Pet 2:21). What this amounts to is a profound contextualization of the gospel of Christ for Peter's powerless and suffering audience.

This christological basis for missional living helps us grasp Peter's advice to specific groups in his social world, like slaves and women. When he tells them to "be subject," he says, in effect, "Don't withdraw from your roles within society. Engage your world. But do so with a Christ-shaped difference." The connection between mission and *sub*mission is especially clear in the instructions to Christian spouses in 3:1-2:

> Wives, likewise, submit to your own husbands. Do this so that even if some of them refuse to believe the word, they may be won without a word by their wives' way of life. After all, they will have observed the reverent and holy manner of your lives.

Here Peter imagines a household in which the wife is a believer and the husband is not. In the Roman world, this domestic arrangement is like a powder keg just waiting to be ignited. Plutarch expresses widely held cultural expectations in his "Advice to Bride and Groom": "A wife ought not to make friends of her own, but to enjoy her husband's friends in common with him. Their gods are the first and most important friends. Therefore it is becoming for a wife to worship and to know only the gods that her husband believes in, and to shut the door tight upon all strange rituals and outland-

---

31. See especially, David L. Balch, *Let Wives Be Submissive: The Domestic Code in 1 Peter* (Atlanta: Scholars Press, 1981).

ish superstitions."[32] Given the expectation that wives practice their husbands' religion, it's clear that "being subject" doesn't mean abandoning one's higher loyalty to Christ. Moreover, Peter describes some of these husbands as "disobedient to the word" (1 Pet 3:1 NASB). This implies not mere indifference, but an active rejection of the gospel. Presumably, they are hostile to the faith.[33]

Nevertheless, Peter is convinced that some of these husbands may be won to Christ, because of "the eloquent witness of a good way of life."[34] In other words, their wives' daily behavior can bear fruit in evangelism. As John Elliott notes, given that these spouses may well be their husbands' first and only contact with the Christian community, such conduct is especially crucial.[35] In the Greco-Roman context, then, voluntary submission becomes a gently subversive act "that has the potential for a wife to lead a husband in a religious choice rather than the other way around."[36]

Peter stresses that this lifestyle witness will happen "without a word" (1 Pet 3:1). This is not intended to prevent wives from speaking the gospel under any circumstances (see 1 Pet 3:15). Nor does it assume that husbands will be won over by actions alone. The fact that they have disobeyed the *word* implies they have already heard the gospel message. Peter's point is that, in the face of opposition, *behavior*, not *words*, will do more to effect conversion.

In the same breath, Peter describes this missional lifestyle, not in terms of Roman values, but in terms of Christlike virtues: *reverence* for God and *purity* of life (1 Pet 3:2). "The wife's aim," writes Douglas Harink, "is not to manipulate the husband into believing the word—he may finally refuse—rather, she takes up the gracious action of subordination because this is the way of Jesus Christ. . . . It is the gospel proclaimed."[37]

Such a lifestyle witness is not limited to wives alone. Joel B. Green perceptively observes, "What is said to believing wives in relation to their disbelieving husbands is applicable to all believers in relation to a disbelieving world."[38] On the one hand, believers are to "be subject to every human institution" (1 Pet 2:13 AT). They are to continue to engage their world within society's roles and structures, using them as platforms to demonstrate the gospel with their lives. On the other hand, their behavior displays the

---

32. *Moralia* 140D; translation adapted from Plutarch, *Moralia*, vol. 2, trans. Frank Cole Babbitt, Loeb Classical Library (Cambridge: Harvard University Press, 1928), 311.

33. Green, *1 Peter*, 94.

34. Senior, "1 Peter," 85.

35. Elliott, *1 Peter*, 558.

36. Beach, *Church in Exile*, 126.

37. Harink, *1 & 2 Peter*, 87.

38. Green, *1 Peter*, 90.

magnetic beauty of the gospel, not because their lifestyle conforms to society's expectations, but because it is *different*. Their conduct is missional precisely because it bears the brand of Christ's self-giving love.

A Message to Proclaim

First Peter's focus, we have seen, is on missional identity, which spawns a missional lifestyle. That doesn't mean, however, that Peter snubs the importance of proclaiming the good news. Two passages, in particular, bear this out. The first is 1 Peter 2:9:

> But you are a chosen race, a royal priesthood, a holy nation, a people who are God's own possession. You have become this people *so that you may speak of the wonderful acts* of the one who called you out of darkness into his amazing light. (italics added)

As we noted earlier, Peter's first concern in this passage is with who God's people *are*. But their identity as God's chosen, holy people also gives them a purpose in the world. This community of priests exists *so that* it might declare the liberating deeds of God. But what does it mean to "proclaim" (*exangellō*) God's mighty acts in this context? Does it refer to the kind of speaking that happens when God's people praise him in public worship?[39] Or is it about declaring the good news to unbelieving family members and friends?[40]

I would be hard pressed to make an "either/or" choice. Rather, Peter's words suggest *both* a "vertical" sense—praising God for his wonderful deeds—*and* a "horizontal" dimension of witnessing to unbelievers. In the former case, the Old Testament background for the passage points to the act of public worship. The Psalmist, for example, speaks of "declaring" (*exangellō*) God's praises publicly "in the gates of daughter Zion" (Ps 9:14; cf. Isa 43:21). Surely the kind of "proclaiming" Peter envisions in 1 Peter 2:9 includes the activity of worshipping God. Yet even the community's worship carries a missional thrust. Christopher Wright notes that in both the Old Testament and 1 Peter, "such declarative praise is not a private affair between God and the worshippers, but it spills out into the public arena as one of the means by which God draws the nations to himself."[41] Through worship, God's people publicly announce God's power to save to all who are listening in.

---

39. So, e.g., Balch, *Let Wives Be Submissive*, 133; J. Ramsey Michaels, *1 Peter* (Waco, TX: Word, 1988), 110.

40. Seland, "Resident Aliens in Mission," 585; see also Schnabel, *Early Christian Mission*, 2:1524.

41. Wright, *Mission of God's People*, 250.

At the same time, we cannot limit the church's proclamation to the context of public worship. As a priesthood, God's people are to mediate the knowledge of God to the world, and this surely includes declaring his salvation blessings in various contexts (see 1 Pet 3:13-16). As Donald Senior insists, "The Christian mission is to proclaim publicly to the world the 'great deeds' of God, that is, the acts of salvation that have given life to the Christians and are offered to all who would accept the gospel."[42] Moreover, Peter moves directly from the theme of proclaiming God's salvation to the call to live godly lives among unbelievers that they may see the good news embodied (1 Pet 2:11-12). In this context, missionary proclamation flows out of the church's identity as a holy priesthood (2:9a), and it partners with a lifestyle that draws outsiders into the sphere of God's grace (2:11-12). Proclamation and demonstration of the gospel walk hand in hand.

We discover a second key "speaking" text in chapter 3:

> Instead, regard Christ as holy in your hearts. Whenever anyone asks you to speak of your hope, be ready to defend it. Yet do this with respectful humility, maintaining a good conscience. Act in this way so that those who malign your good lifestyle in Christ may be ashamed when they slander you. (1 Pet 3:15-16)

Peter here reads a page from the everyday life of Christians, one that requires a verbal testimony. God's people must be ever prepared to give a "defense" (*apologia*) of their faith to those who ask a "reason" (*logos*; literally, "word") for it. Although there are times when a wordless witness is appropriate (see 1 Pet 3:1-2), on other occasions believers must be ready to speak a "word" of witness. This apology is not a formal defense, as might take place before authorities or a judge (see, e.g., Luke 12:11-12). Rather, "Peter sees his readers as being 'on trial' every day as they live for Christ in a pagan society."[43] When unbelievers question the reason for their hope, Christians must be ready with an explanation.

What might prompt such questions from outsiders? The context talks about Christians who "suffer because of righteousness" (1 Pet 3:14) and who are maligned for their "good lifestyle in Christ" (1 Pet 3:16). At least in part, then, believers are likely being questioned about their distinctive behavior, which swims against the current of the culture.[44] Christians, for example, might be challenged for refusing to participate in various forms of idolatry.

---

42. Senior, "1 Peter," 62.

43. Michaels, *1 Peter*, 188.

44. Paul J. Achtemeier, *1 Peter: A Commentary on First Peter* (Minneapolis: Fortress, 1996), 233.

Or former friends might demand to know why these believers don't party anymore (1 Pet 4:3-4). Followers of Christ need to be prepared to give an answer in the face of unsympathetic, or even hostile, questions.

That explanation, Peter affirms, needs to focus on the *hope* within God's people (1 Pet 3:15; cf. 1:3, 21). This is not so much a matter of piling up airtight arguments as it is narrating the good news—the story of Jesus's suffering and death, his resurrection and return (see 1 Pet 1:3-12).[45] Such a Christ-centered hope spawns a way of life that is so radically distinctive that it demands an explanation. The marriage between what Christians say and what they do is unmistakable in verse 16. Peter tells the church, in effect, "Always be prepared to explain the reason you put your hope in Christ, but do so with gentleness and reverence."

The term *gentleness* in 3:16 describes an attitude of humility and courtesy, even in the face of unjust treatment. Such a gentle stance toward others is fortified by their "reverence" (literally, "fear") for God. The way in which God's people respond to unbelievers is often as important as what they actually say. Their manner of answering others must be consistent with the self-giving story of Christ. It is an expression of what it means to "sanctify Christ as Lord" (1 Pet 3:15 NRSV)—the Christ who endured abuse without retaliation, the Lord who suffered, entrusting himself to the righteous judge (1 Pet 2:23). For Peter, a gentle defense is part of "good conduct in Christ" (1 Pet 3:16 NRSV). The point is clear: answers worth hearing flow from lives that are worth questioning.[46]

Conclusion

Reading 1 Peter through the lens of God's mission gives us, above all, a vision of the church's *missional identity*. That identity is anchored in the sweeping story of God's salvation, enacted by the suffering, death, and glory of Christ. But having been liberated by God from sin and the power of evil, God's people are called to *be* a missional community. Peter paints a distinctive portrait of Christians who are caught up in the mission of God. They are

- *exiles* and *strangers*, people who engage in God's mission from the margins of their social world;

45. Green, *1 Peter*, 117; Harink, *1 & 2 Peter*, 94–95.

46. John Dickson, *The Best Kept Secret of Christian Mission: Promoting the Gospel with More Than Our Lips* (Grand Rapids: Zondervan, 2010), 188.

- a *holy* people, who display the character of a holy God before the gaze of a watching world. In particular, they live out their missional identity by "doing good"—modeling a distinctive, Christlike way of life;

- an *engaged* people, radically different, but fully involved in the public life, institutions, and relationships of their cultures;

- a *suffering* people, a community that follows in the footsteps of a savior who also was maligned, mistreated, and misunderstood;

- a *magnetic* people, whose visible embodiment of the good news has a profound impact on others, drawing even some of their opponents to worship the true God (1 Pet 2:11; 3:1);

- a *witnessing* people, who don't shy away from declaring the good news (1 Pet 2:9) or from gently explaining their hope in Christ to those who question it.

First Peter speaks a compelling and timely word to Christian communities in the twenty-first century, not only in the majority world, but also in the West. For Christians in the post-Christendom settings of North America, Western Europe, or Australia/New Zealand, Peter's exilic imagery holds increasing relevance. In such contexts, the church once played a significant role in shaping the values of the culture. Now, however, the church is being pushed to the margins of rapidly changing, pluralistic societies. Many of the people with whom we rub shoulders either don't know the Christian story or they are already biased against it. Some of them are openly opposed to historic Christian values. At the same time, our role as foreigners and exiles provides the opportunity to meet the challenges of our new circumstances in fresh and creative ways. [47]

Doing mission as holy exiles is filled with tensions. We are called to embody the good news of Christ *within* the public life or our culture, knowing full well that we are *not at home* in that culture. We live out the mission of God as *engaged strangers*. We demonstrate the self-giving love of Christ—with words or without—in every "nook and cranny" of our world. At times, we may suffer. Yet we engage our world with the assurance that the Spirit can give our vulnerable witness an attractive quality, so that others will join the communion of exiles who worship God (1 Pet 2:12).

---

47. For a valuable reflection on mission in an exilic, post-Christendom context, see Beach, *Church in Exile*, ch. 11.

Chapter Six

The Triumph of the *Missio Dei*: Mission in Revelation

I f the question that prompts this book is "Why mission?" then maybe the obvious question to open this chapter is "Why *Revelation*?"[1] Does a *missional* reading of Revelation make any sense? After all, most popular interpretations of John's Apocalypse tend to focus on predicting imminent future events. Revelation is regularly viewed as a kind of playbook for the end times. As a result, God's mission and the church's place in it seldom appear on the "radar screen."[2]

Even those who seek to take seriously the message of Revelation for the church often downplay its importance for mission. For example, some Bible scholars hold that Revelation's sharp polarization between the church and the hostile world shows that John offers little hope for outsiders before they are judged by God (Rev 22:11).[3] Missiologists, for their part, have sometimes

1. This chapter is adapted from Dean Flemming, "Revelation and the *Missio Dei*: Toward a Missional Reading of the Apocalypse," *Journal of Theological Interpretation* 6 (2012): 161–78.

2. Popular dispensationalism, for example, generally confines missionary activity in Revelation to a group of 144,000 Jewish converts to Christianity (Rev 7:1-8; 14:15), who will evangelize a multitude of people from other nations (Rev 7:9-17). This often coincides with the belief that the church is "raptured" to heaven at the beginning of ch. 4 ("Come up here," Rev 4:1).

3. See, e.g., Jan Lambrecht, *Collected Studies on Pauline Literature and on the Book of Revelation*, Analecta Biblica 147 (Rome: Pontifical Biblical Institute, 2001), 381.

settled for culling the Apocalypse for "missionary texts" (e.g., Rev 5:9; 7:9; 14:6), which might help provide a "biblical basis for missions." But seldom do they look to Revelation as a whole for a theology of mission.

I want to propose a different approach. What if, instead of trying to ferret out "missionary texts" within the visions of the Apocalypse, we approached the *entire book* as a "mission text"? In other words, might a missional reading of Revelation offer a key to unlocking the theological message of this weird and wonderful exclamation point to the Christian canon? This chapter will try to show that we interpret Revelation more faithfully when we read it in light of the comprehensive mission of God. As in previous chapters, I'll first look at the Apocalypse as a *witness* to the *missio Dei*, and then as an *agent* of that mission.

Revelation as a Witness to God's Mission

The whole Bible tells the sweeping story of God's purpose to redeem and form a missional people and to restore all things. The book of Revelation narrates the climax and triumph of that story. Actually, as Michael J. Gorman observes, Revelation "consists of several overlapping, simultaneous, and inextricably interrelated stories."[4] These include the stories of creation and new creation, the story of redemption, the story of judgment, and the story of God's people.[5] In order to tease out the contours of God's mission in Revelation, I will treat these stories separately. Keep in mind, however, that they are closely intertwined.

Creation and New Creation

Revelation places God's saving mission in Christ within a cosmic framework. The God who redeems Israel and the church is the creator of all things. The magnificent heavenly throne room scene in chapters 4 and 5 shout that message. Here we find the theological heart of Revelation. John's vision declares that God's sovereignty is anchored in his creative and life-giving power:

> You are worthy, our Lord and God,
>> to receive glory and honor and power,
>>> because you created all things.
>>>> It is by your will that they existed and were created.
>>>>> (Rev 4:11)

---

4. Michael J. Gorman, *Reading Revelation Responsibly: Uncivil Worship and Witness; Following the Lamb into the New Creation* (Eugene, OR: Cascade, 2011), 38.

5. See ibid.

Because God is creator, God's saving work is not simply about rescuing people *out of* this wicked world so they can escape to the safe harbor of heaven. Rather, "the Creator seeks the liberation of the world itself from the forces that hold it captive."[6]

For John, God's judgment of the powers that "destroy the earth" (Rev 11:18) is a necessary prelude to his ultimate purpose. And that purpose is *new creation*. Revelation 21 and 22 envision the ultimate triumph of God's mission, foretold long before by the prophet Isaiah (Isa 65:17-19; 66:22-23). Indeed, Genesis and Revelation form canonical bookends to scripture's story of a loving creator's purpose for the whole of creation.[7] That story begins with creation and climaxes with *re*-creation. It starts with God forming the heavens and the earth; it ends with God preparing a *new* heaven and a *new* earth. It commences in a garden, with two people communing with God. It finishes in a city, an urban garden, complete with a "green-belt" (Rev 22:1-2), in which people from every tribe and nation dwell in the immediate presence of God. Originally, the tree of life was "out of bounds" to humans. But in the new Eden, the world's nations find healing in its leaves (Rev 22:2). And whereas the first garden became a source of death and a curse upon the earth, the paradise of the new holy city is a vision of life and of the curse reversed: "There will no longer be any curse" (Rev 22:3).[8]

God's mission in Revelation, then, is *creation focused*. The New Jerusalem *comes down* from heaven to earth, even as earth and heaven merge into one (3:12; 21:2). Unlike some pictures of the end time today, John is intensely concerned about *this* world and its ultimate destiny.[9] The *missio Dei* only reaches its fulfillment when God reasserts his rule over the whole creation and God's glory fills every corner and crevice of the earth (see Rev 5:13; 11:15; 22:1-5).

Redemption

The Apocalypse portrays God's mission not only in terms of new creation but also of redemption. Revelation's story of redemption creatively reworks the story of God and Israel, especially God's mighty, delivering act in the

6. Craig R. Koester, *Revelation and the End of All Things* (Grand Rapids: Eerdmans, 2001), 113.

7. See Robert W. Wall, *Revelation* (Peabody, MA: Hendrickson, 1991), 30; Gorman, *Reading Revelation Responsibly*, 161.

8. Gorman, *Reading Revelation Responsibly*, 161.

9. Donald Senior and Carroll Stuhlmueller, *The Biblical Foundations for Mission* (Maryknoll, NY: Orbis, 1983), 304–5.

Exodus (Rev 8:6-12; 15:3; 16:1-21). But the master narrative that gives meaning to all of history is the story of Jesus, the Lamb who was slain. [10]

For John, the epicenter of Jesus's mission is his death, resurrection, and exaltation. And the heavenly throne room scene in chapter 5 brings God's redemption in Christ into sharpest focus. John the seer weeps because no one is found worthy to open the scroll that symbolizes God's saving purpose for the world (Rev 5:4). One of the elders, however, assures John that one indeed stands worthy, "the Lion of the tribe of Judah, the Root of David," who "has emerged victorious" (Rev 5:5). These two messianic titles evoke nationalistic Jewish hopes of a powerful figure who will crush the enemies of God's people. But in a stunning reversal of expectations, we see instead a *lamb*—a slaughtered Lamb (Rev 5:6).

This is the magnificent mystery of the Apocalypse. God on the throne has chosen to redeem through the spilled blood of the Lamb (Rev 1:5; 5:9; 12:11). "The sovereign God of the universe is driven by self-giving love and is able to be wounded in reaching out to humanity."[11] Through his death, Christ the sacrificial Lamb (see Exod 12; Isa 53:7, 10) has ransomed a multinational people of God (Rev 5:9-10). Furthermore, the crucified redeemer is also the risen, exalted Lord. He is the "firstborn of the dead" (Rev 1:5; cf. 2:8), who has conquered sin, death, and evil (Rev 1:18; 5:5).

Yet the story of the slaughtered Lamb is an unfinished story. Satan and the self-deifying power of empire continue to rebel against God. Christ's triumph awaits its goal. In John's future vision, when the pernicious powers of this world, represented by the beast and the ten kings, wage war against the Lamb, he will conquer them (17:14). In the final battle scene in Revelation 19, Christ appears as a divine Warrior. He wears "a robe dipped in blood," and his name is "the Word of God" (19:13 NIV). Once again, Revelation turns our expectations upside down. As Joseph Mangina explains,

> The blood in which the rider's robe is dipped is not the blood of his enemies. It is *his own* blood.... We see no sword flashing in the hand of this warrior. The only weapon he wields is the word of truth, issuing from his mouth (19:15).[12]

The conquering Warrior is still the slaughtered Lamb.

---

10. On the role of narrative in Revelation, see M. Eugene Boring, "Narrative Christology in the Apocalypse," *Catholic Biblical Quarterly* 54 (1992): 702-23.

11. John Christopher Thomas and Frank Macchia, *Revelation* (Grand Rapids: Eerdmans, forthcoming).

12. Joseph L. Mangina, *Revelation* (Grand Rapids: Brazos, 2010), 221-22.

112

The slaughtered Lamb becomes the governing metaphor of John's visions.[13] This image leaves no doubt whatsoever as to *how* God carries out his missional purpose for the world. The Lamb conquers all evil, not by coercion, not by violence, but through suffering love (Rev 1:5; 12:11). This message poses a direct challenge to the ways of the empire. Rome rules by the power of violence and military conquest. But Jesus overcomes God's enemies through weakness and sacrificial death, in solidarity with the weak and the oppressed.

In Revelation's visions, the same slaughtered Lamb who in love has redeemed his people will come for them in the future (Rev 22:7, 12, 20) and take them as his bride (Rev 19:7, 9; 21:9). Along with God the Father, he will welcome them and tenderly care for them in the New Jerusalem. And they will worship him forever (Rev 21:23; 22:1, 3). The story of God's redemption in Christ has a glorious climax.

Judgment

God's redeeming love in Revelation has a flip side. Chapters 6–20 are salted with terrifying visions of judgment. Some interpreters reproach Revelation for being violent and sub-Christian. John Dominic Crossan, for example, argues that Revelation turns "the nonviolent resistance of the slaughtered Jesus into the violent warfare of the slaughtering Jesus."[14]

But are Revelation's scenes of judgment and God's saving purposes necessarily in conflict? On the contrary, Revelation treats judgment as an integral dimension of the loving mission of God and the Lamb. God's unrelenting faithfulness to creation and to humanity makes necessary a divine war against evil and empire. Nothing will abort God's purpose to redeem the world. God's judgment is therefore a necessary *means*, not an end.[15] Beyond the destruction of evil lies the new holy city, where people from every nation will dwell together in God's holy presence.

God's missional purpose in Revelation is dominated by redemptive love, symbolized by the slaughtered Lamb. Nevertheless, "divine love is a holy love that does not compromise with evil but overcomes it through merciful and righteous judgments."[16] Those who seek to destroy the earth will be destroyed

13. J. Nelson Kraybill, *Apocalypse and Allegiance: Worship, Politics, and Devotion in the Book of Revelation* (Grand Rapids: Brazos, 2010), 122.

14. John Dominic Crossan, *God and Empire: Jesus against Rome, Then and Now* (San Francisco: HarperSanFrancisco, 2007), 224. For a balanced discussion of the theme of violence in Revelation, see Warren Carter, *What Does Revelation Reveal? Unlocking the Mystery* (Nashville: Abingdon, 2011), 124–27.

15. Gorman, *Reading Revelation Responsibly*, 153–54.

16. Thomas and Macchia, *Revelation*.

(Rev 11:18). It is as if John tells his audience, "If you persist in worshipping the beast and the idolatrous systems it symbolizes, ultimately you will perish, along with those systems" (Rev 14:7-11; 19:17-21).[17] Yet for John, even judgment seeks repentance, and beyond that, mercy. Revelation's warnings and visions of judgment are not only intended to assure Christians of God's final triumph over evil. They also serve as a loud "wake up call" to the church—a call to *repent* (see Rev 2:5, 16, 21-22; 3:3, 19; cf. 9:20-21; 16:9-11).

The Scope of God's Mission

Revelation envisions the fulfillment of God's covenant promise to Abraham that through his descendants all nations on earth would be blessed (Gen 12:3; 18:18; 22:18). The horizon of God's mission stretches far beyond Israel and the followers of the Lamb to whom John writes. The focus of Christ's liberating work in chapter 5 is to call into being a servant people "from every tribe, language, people, and nation" (Rev 5:9-10; cf. 7:9). Those who conquer the beast celebrate God as "king of the nations." As a result, "all nations will come and fall down in worship" before him (Rev 15:2-4). In the New Jerusalem, the nations will walk by the light of God and the Lamb (Rev 21:24). There the leaves of the tree of life bud not just for healing, as in Ezekiel's prophecy (Ezek 47:12), but also "for the healing *of the nations*" (Rev 22:2, italics added). Indeed, when a voice from the throne thunders the traditional covenant promise of God's presence (Rev 21:3), we hear a surprising twist. God dwells, not just with his "people" (Lev 26:12; Jer 24:7) but also with his "peoples," in the plural. The Lamb's bride will be gathered from all the peoples of the world.

But there's a tension here. On the one hand, a strand running through the visions of chapters 6–20 appears to give the nations little hope of turning to God.[18] The nations rage against God (Rev 11:18), they are deceived by Satan (Rev 20:3, 7, 10; cf. 18:23), and they worship the dragon and the beast (Rev 13:4, 7-8). In the face of God's judgments they stubbornly refuse to repent (Rev 9:20-21; 16:9, 11). One of the last exhortations of the Apocalypse sounds as though there is less opportunity for the wicked to change their status than for a leopard to change its spots: "Let those who do wrong

17. Richard Bauckham, *The Theology of the Book of Revelation* (Cambridge: Cambridge University Press, 1993), 102.

18. See the balanced treatment of the role of the nations in Grant R. Osborne, "The Mission to the Nations in the Book of Revelation," in *New Testament Theology in Light of the Church's Mission: Essays in Honor of I. Howard Marshall*, ed. Jon Laansma, Grant Osborne, and Ray Van Neste (Eugene, OR: Cascade, 2011), 347–67.

keep doing what is wrong. Let the filthy still be filthy" (Rev 22:11). This has led some interpreters to conclude that Revelation offers no true repentance and conversion to the disobedient nations, only the fury of God's wrath (e.g., Rev 19:15; 20:7-9).[19]

On the other hand, Revelation offers considerable evidence that the church's testimony to outsiders will bear genuine fruit. In John's vision of the two witnesses (Rev 11:3-13), their faithful testimony unto death, along with God's judgment through an earthquake, lead the terrified survivors to give glory to God (Rev 11:13). In similar language, a gospel-bearing angel calls out to the nations: "Fear God and give him glory" (Rev 14:6-7). And in the song of Moses and the Lamb, the worship of all nations is couched in terms of fearing and glorifying the name of the one true God (Rev 15:3-4). Fearing God, honoring his name, worshipping him—all of these actions point to genuine repentance and conversion, not simply a forced confession.[20] Furthermore, in chapter 14, the redeemed followers of the Lamb are the first-fruits of a much greater harvest of salvation to follow (Rev 14:4, 14-16). As elsewhere in the New Testament (Matt 9:37-38; Mark 4:29; John 4:35-38), reaping a harvest is a positive symbol, referring to God's mercy in gathering believers into the kingdom.[21]

Yet the extent of God's mercy reaches its summit in John's vision of the New Jerusalem in Revelation 21 and 22. Without warning, unlikely characters begin to appear on "Broad Street" of the future city—the nations and the "kings of the earth" (Rev 21:24-26). John's readers would be well aware that the rebellious nations already had been judged by God (Rev 11:18; 16:19; 19:15) and destroyed by heavenly fire (Rev 20:7-15). But now John envisions the nations walking by the light of God's glory in the holy city (Rev 21:23-24; cf. Isa 60:3). More astonishing still is that the kings of the earth bring their glory into the eternal city (Rev 21:24). To this point, the earthly kings have consistently been portrayed as enemies of God, destined for doom (Rev 6:15; 17:2, 18; 18:3, 9; 19:9). But here their "glory" represents not material riches (see Isa 60:5) but their worship of the one true God.[22]

---

19. See, e.g., Greg Carey, *Elusive Apocalypses: Reading Authority in the Revelation to John*, Studies in American Biblical Hermeneutics 15 (Macon, GA: Mercer University Press, 1999), 160–62.

20. David deSilva, *Seeing Things John's Way: The Rhetoric of the Book of Revelation* (Louisville: Westminster John Knox, 2009), 77; see also Bauckham, *Theology*, 86–88, 98–104. Differently, Eckhard J. Schnabel, "John and the Future of the Nations," *Bulletin for Biblical Research* 12 (2002): 254–57, 262–65, who reads the language of "fearing" and "giving glory" to God in passages such as 11:13 and 15:4 as a forced acknowledgment of God's sovereignty resulting from judgment.

21. See Richard Bauckham, *The Climax of Prophecy: Studies on the Book of Revelation* (Edinburgh: T&T Clark, 1993), 290–96.

22. Greg K. Beale, *The Book of Revelation* (Grand Rapids: Eerdmans, 1999), 1095.

No doubt, such a vision "would stretch the imaginative abilities of the hearers to their limits."[23] Revelation's final picture of the nations is not the terrifying judgment of chapter 20 but "the healing of the nations" (Rev 22:2). This involves the removal of humanity's curse (Rev 22:3) and the healing of all wounds resulting from rebellion against God.[24] The Apocalypse concludes with a vision of breathtaking hope. God's missional purpose to redeem the nations will be realized in the end. To be sure, John is no universalist. His repeated warnings that not all are morally fit to enter the holy city make that clear (Rev 21:8, 27; 22:15). He does not try to resolve the tension between the visions of the healed nations on the one hand and of those who are barred from the city on the other. Nevertheless, the assurance that the nations will walk in the divine light of the New Jerusalem would be of enormous encouragement to John's readers. Despite present hostility, their faithful witness ultimately will result in an unthinkable harvest, as God's mission reaches its glorious triumph.[25]

God's Mission and the Church

John believes the church on earth is caught up in the story of God's mission in Christ. By virtue of his sacrificial death and victory, Christ has made the church "a kingdom and priests" engaged in faithful service to God (Rev 5:10; cf. 1:5-6; 20:6). These images recall the defining covenant passage of Exodus 19:5-6, which spells out the missional identity of God's people. As a *kingdom* people, the church both shares in God's reign and bears public witness to that rule as an alternative to the "kingdom of this world" (Rev 11:15). As a community of *priests*, it is called to mediate between God and the world. Just as Israel was marked out to be a holy and priestly nation, mediating divine light to the Gentiles, the new priestly people conveys God's presence to the nations by a witness of word and life (Exod 19:5-6; Rev 5:9-10; cf. 11:3-13).[26]

23. John Christopher Thomas, "New Jerusalem and the Conversion of the Nations: An Exercise in Pneumatic Discernment—Revelation 21.1–22.5" (paper presented at the Annual Meeting of the Society of Biblical Literature, Atlanta, GA, November 22, 2010), 8.

24. Ibid., 12.

25. Ibid., 13–14.

26. Dean Flemming, "'On Earth as It Is in Heaven': Holiness and the People of God in Revelation," in *Holiness and Ecclesiology in the New Testament*, ed. Kent E. Brower and Andy Johnson (Grand Rapids: Eerdmans, 2007), 347. Stephen D. Moore notes that the priesthood of Christians in Revelation stands in bold contrast to the role of priests in the official emperor cult of Rome ("The Revelation to John," in *A Postcolonial Commentary on the New Testament Writings*, ed. Fernando F. Segovia and R. S. Sugirtharajah [London: T&T Clark, 2009], 441–42).

Closely related is Revelation's picture of the churches of Asia as seven "lampstands" (Rev 1:12, 13, 20; cf. 11:4). In the Old Testament, Zechariah envisioned Israel as a seven-branched golden menorah (Zech 4:2). John, however, sees not a single lampstand, but seven, suggesting that each local church represents God's people as a whole.[27] As lampstands, these churches are to *be* the light of God to the world around them.

John portrays the church's missional vocation most explicitly in the vision of the two witnesses (Rev 11:3-13), a passage we will take up shortly. In this story, God's people share in the Lamb's victory by bearing "lamblike" witness, even to the point of death. In this way, they play an active role in God's purpose to draw people from all nations to come before him in worship (Rev 11:13; 15:3-4). This brings us to a second dimension of a missional reading of Revelation. *How* do John's visions shape and equip his audience to engage in the *missio Dei?*

Revelation as an Instrument of God's Mission

What Is Revelation Trying to Do?

For John's readers, the call to participate in God's mission is lived out on the dusty streets and in the crowded tenements of the Roman Empire. Contrary to a great deal of traditional interpretation, the chief problem facing the churches to which John writes is not systematic persecution from Rome, although sporadic local hostility was a real and present possibility (Rev 2:10, 13; 3:10). An even greater threat for most of these churches was the temptation to accommodate to the dominant Roman ideology and culture (e.g., Rev 2:14-16, 20-23; 3:1-3, 15-19), perhaps as a way of avoiding persecution.[28] Christians in Western Asia Minor faced everyday pressures to participate in Roman public life, which was laced with the "civil religion" of the emperor cult and the worship of traditional gods.[29] What John sees—and many of his hearers don't—is that by accommodating, they are sucked into an entire system of imperial political, religious, and economic power. They become guilty

---

27. Stephen S. Smalley, *The Revelation to John: A Commentary on the Greek Text of the Apocalypse* (Downers Grove, IL: IVP Academic, 2005), 53.

28. Craig R. Koester, "Revelation's Challenge to Ordinary Empire," *Interpretation* 63 (2009): 6–9; Beale, *Book of Revelation*, 28–33.

29. See Wes Howard-Brook and Anthony Gwyther, *Unveiling Empire: Reading Revelation Then and Now* (Maryknoll, NY: Orbis, 1999), 101–18.

of colluding with another kingdom/empire, which lays claim to a loyalty that only the true God deserves.

John's aim in writing, then, has both a negative and a positive dimension. On the one hand, he seeks to distance these Christian communities from the empire's ways of thinking and behaving.[30] On the other hand, he calls them to an unrivaled worship of the one sovereign God and to bear prophetic witness to God and his mission in the world. Michael Gorman wisely notes that Revelation "is above all a community-forming document, intended to shape communities of believers in Jesus as the Lamb of God into more faithful and missional communities of...worship and witness."[31] Such community formation is a crucial dimension of mission. God's mission simply cannot be fulfilled in Asia unless congregations both resist the temptation to compromise and faithfully follow the Lamb as genuine disciples. How, then, does Revelation seek to shape missional communities?

Reimagining the World

Drawing on the symbolic resources of apocalyptic literature, John offers his audience an alternative vision of the world from the deceptive imperial worldview that demands their allegiance. In effect, John says to his readers, "This is the way things *really* are," from the vantage point of God's future and God's throne. As Richard Bauckham puts it,

> John (and thereby his readers with him) is taken up into heaven in order to see the world from the heavenly perspective....He is also transported in vision into the final future of the world, so that he can see the present from the perspective of what its final outcome must be, in God's ultimate purpose for human history.[32]

Consider, for example, John's vision of a multinational multitude in heaven, worshipping the true God day and night in Revelation 7:9-17. This is not only a picture of the church's hope for the future. It also transforms their perception of who they are as God's people in the present and what God is about in the world. It is a vision of the peoples of the earth, in all their ethnic and linguistic diversity, reconciled to one another and to their sovereign Lord and Savior. That vision shapes their identity and mission. John's audience faces an urgent question: Which version of reality will shape how you imagine

30. deSilva, *Seeing Things John's Way*, 71, 90.
31. Gorman, *Reading Revelation Responsibly*, 176.
32. Bauckham, *Theology*, 7.

the world and live out your faith? Will it be the vision of God's new creation or the values of the earthly empire?[33]

Babylon—Left Behind

Part of John's strategy for forming missional communities is to spotlight the difference between the godly community and the ungodly empire. Perhaps no other New Testament book defines the boundaries between the church and the world so sharply. Not surprisingly, then, John's portrayal of Rome/empire is consistently negative. He critiques the entire imperial system of power, with its intertwining religious, political, and economic dimensions.[34] With scathing symbolism, he exposes the empire for what it truly is.

For example, the familiar symbol of *Babylon* (chs. 17–18) represents the proud and fallen human city that opposes God's rule. We see biblical harbingers in cities like Babel, Sodom, and Babylon itself. But its present manifestation is Rome, whose evil outstrips them all. Babylon takes the guise of a woman, but not the goddess Roma, the noble mother figure who was worshipped in the temples of Asia. In John's mocking parody, Rome is a tawdry whore, "the mother of prostitutes and the vile things of the earth" (Rev 17:5). In Revelation, the symbol of Babylon is particularly related to the empire's system of commerce. The harlot Babylon personifies a city and an empire that turns relationships into mere commodities.[35] People are bewitched by Rome's riches and by the prosperity they gain from trading with her. From John's prophetic perspective, however, Babylon is a city that amasses her wealth by oppressing the weak and exploiting the peoples of the empire. She slakes her unquenchable thirst for luxury by using others, even by trafficking in human lives (Rev 18:3, 7, 13).[36] Revelation's cutting critique of the empire shouts that God opposes the oppressive and dehumanizing use of wealth and power, wherever it is found.

But it's not enough for Christian communities simply to open their eyes and see the ungodly powers for what they are. The churches of Asia Minor must actively "come out" of Babylon (Rev 18:4). This is not so much a physical exodus as a flight from complicity with Babylon's idolatry, greed, and injustice. It is a call to forsake Babylon-living.

33. Flemming, "'On Earth as It Is in Heaven,'" 344–45.

34. See Bauckham, *Theology*, 35–39.

35. Koester, "Revelation's Challenge," 17.

36. On Revelation's economic critique, see Bauckham, *Climax of Prophecy*, 338–83. See also J. Nelson Kraybill, *Imperial Cult and Commerce in John's Apocalypse*, Journal for the Study of the New Testament Supplement Series 132 (Sheffield: Sheffield Academic Press, 1996).

For John's audience, that would involve separating from such normal cultural activities as eating food sacrificed to idols (Rev 2:14-15, 20-21), with its attachment to imperial worship. It would also mean dislodging themselves from unjust economic practices. And, as John's message to Laodicea spotlights, it calls God's people to forsake the kind of arrogance and selfish consumption that boasts, "'I'm rich, and I've grown wealthy, and I don't need a thing'" (Rev 3:17). Emigrating from Babylon requires leaving behind all values and practices that prop up imperial idolatry and oppose the claims of God and the Lamb. In short, John calls the church to be a contrast community, living in ways that reflect the holiness of God. Such holiness is inseparable from mission. On the one hand, only people who have not climbed in bed with the beast can authentically bear witness to God's truth. As Gorman elegantly frames it, "The church cannot be the church *in* Babylon until it is the church *out of* Babylon."[37] On the other hand, those resisting captivity to fallen Babylon create an opportunity for outsiders to take a second look at the empire around them and perhaps also renounce belief in the lordship of the empire.[38]

Bearing Faithful Witness

If Revelation urges God's people to "come out" of Babylon, what does this mean for how they relate to the world around them? Is this simply "an extremist call, requiring a radically sectarian mode of discipleship"?[39] Is John lobbying for an isolating, navel-gazing, world-renouncing brand of holiness? He is not. In Revelation, the church's participation in the mission of God has a double dimension: both separation and engagement. These Christians are not only to *come out* of Babylon but also to *call out* to an unbelieving world through their prophetic witness.[40]

Being a faithful witness is the church's fundamental calling in the book of Revelation. Bearing witness, in the first place, means giving verbal testimony to the word and truth of God, as well as obeying God's commands (Rev 12:17). But their witness is grounded in "Jesus Christ—the faithful witness" (Rev 1:5; cf. 3:14; 19:11), and Jesus's steadfast testimony took him to the cross. To follow the slain Lamb, likewise, means to bear witness and suffer.

37. Gorman, *Reading Revelation Responsibly*, 185.

38. deSilva, *Seeing Things John's Way*, 78.

39. Greg Carey, "Teaching and Preaching the Book of Revelation in the Church," *Review and Expositor* 98 (2001): 90. Cf. Moore: "In Revelation's hyperdualistic cosmos . . . Christian culture and Roman culture must be absolutely separate and separable" ("Revelation to John," 444).

40. deSilva, *Seeing Things John's Way*, 71.

God's people cling to "the witness of Jesus" (*hē martyria Iēsou*, Rev 12:17; 19:10; cf. 1:2, 9). This rich phrase refers not only to their testimony *to* Jesus. It also involves bearing Jesus's *own* testimony to the truth in word and spilled out life.[41] And it is the prophetic Spirit who calls and empowers the church to fulfill its mission of witnessing to Christ in the world (Rev 19:10).[42]

John gives his audience other examples of costly witness to emulate: Antipas of Pergamum, who was killed among them (Rev 2:13); the faithful witnesses and martyrs now in heaven (Rev 6:9-11; 7:13-14; 12:11; 17:6); and John himself, exiled on the rugged rock of Patmos (Rev 1:9). Witness *to* God is always witness *against* idolatry. And John is persuaded that when the church prophetically testifies to Gods' truth, when it resists the beast's challenge to God's rule over the world, the result may be the shedding of the blood of the saints (Rev 6:9). But through their suffering witness, God's people participate in the Lamb's triumph: "They gained victory over him [Satan] on account of the blood of the Lamb and by the word of their witness. Love for their lives didn't make them afraid to die" (Rev 12:11). As with their Lord, victory comes by way of the cross, or it doesn't come at all.

Above all, John's vision of the two witnesses (Rev 11:1-13) spotlights the church's prophetic testimony. The two witnesses represent the church as a whole in its function of witness bearing.[43] This remarkable passage unfolds like a four-part drama, in which the church embodies the story of Jesus in the form of witness.[44] The two prophets/witnesses initially demonstrate miraculous power and great authority in their testimony (Rev 11:4-6). The consuming fire that pours from their mouths represents the word of God (Rev 11:4; cf. Heb 12:29). It reminds us of the victorious sword of the word that issues from the mouth of Christ (Rev 1:16; 2:16; 19:15, 21). Here the witnesses recall not only the prophetic careers of Elijah and Moses (Rev 11:6) but also the earthly ministry of Jesus, "in which he enjoyed unparalleled success against his foes... and in which he was widely celebrated for the liberating, authoritative power of his preaching."[45] John encourages the marginalized churches in Asia; like Jesus, they are sent to bear witness with the authority and transforming power of God.

41. See Allison A. Trites, *The New Testament Concept of Witness*, Society for New Testament Studies Monograph Series 31 (Cambridge: Cambridge University Press, 1977), 156–64.

42. Smalley, *Revelation to John*, 487.

43. The two witnesses are called "lampstands" (11:4), a symbol that represents the seven churches (1:12, 20).

44. See Mangina, *Revelation*, 137–39, who distinguishes three acts to the drama: life, death, and resurrection.

45. Ibid., 138.

The second act in the drama brings a dramatic turn in events: God's witnesses are killed by the beast and publicly humiliated by the inhabitants of the earth (Rev 11:7-10). As Christ's mission of bearing faithful witness to God's kingdom led to his death at the hands of his enemies, the church in mission can expect no different from the beastly powers. God's faithful witnesses follow the Lamb *wherever* he goes (Rev 14:4)—and that path may take them to the cross. *How* the church carries out its witness is as important as the content of its testimony. Although the church's witness is powerful, it is non-coercive and cruciform, the testimony of suffering love.

Act three spells resurrection. As God raised Jesus from the dead, the creator God breathes new life into the slain witnesses (Rev 11:11). And in the final act, the faithful witnesses ascend to heaven at God's own calling (Rev 11:12), even as God exalted the crucified, victorious Lamb. John's vision offers a bittersweet assurance to a church under fire. If they persevere in their faithful witness even to the point of death, they will in the end be vindicated by God. But not only will *they* be saved. Their costly testimony, along with God's judgment through an earthquake, will draw people from every tribe and nation into the worship of the one true God (Rev 11:9, 13).[46] It is not the church's verbal proclamation alone that leads others to repent. By their sacrificial witness, they visibly embody the narrative of the crucified Lord. It is a witness of word and poured out life.

In the Apocalypse, the church's mission takes place in the public square. Three times in 11:3-13 we find the spectators gazing on the witnesses (Rev 11:9, 11, 12). Elsewhere the people of God have "[the Lamb's] name and his Father's name written on their foreheads" (Rev 14:1; cf. 22:4). They wear God's "seal" (Rev 7:3-8; 9:4) as an outward, visible sign of divine ownership. Public mission, however, has another face in Revelation. It's the face of *worship*.

The Witness of Worship

The witness of God's people in Revelation is intertwined with worship.[47] Worship is not only a liturgical practice. It's also a political act. Worshippers declare allegiances. Throughout Revelation, worship of the one true God in heaven is set over against the worship of the beast on earth (Rev 13:3, 4, 12, 15; 14:9, 11; 16:2; 19:20), embodied for John's audience in the imperial cult.[48] John's world was thoroughly saturated with worship of the em-

---

46. Brian K. Blount, *Revelation: A Commentary* (Louisville: Westminster John Knox, 2009), 217–18.

47. See Olutola K. Peters, *The Mandate of the Church in the Apocalypse of John*, Studies in Biblical Literature 77 (New York: Peter Lang, 2005), 142–44.

48. Revelation's heavenly throne room scene bears so many resemblances to the practices of the Ro-

peror and praise for the power of Rome. Coins announced Caesar's deity, poets extolled Rome's invincibility, and choral societies shouted the emperor's praise.[49] In Revelation, when the community sings its songs of worship, it announces to the world that God is on the throne and Caesar is not.

Worship is also missional. First, worship is the *goal* of God's mission.[50] The gracious purpose of God is that people of every tribe, language, and nation would come to love and adore the triune God for all of eternity. The many worship scenes in Revelation visualize this aim in stunning fashion. When a multinational choir of the redeemed stands before the throne of God to "worship him day and night" (Rev 7:15; cf. 22:3), or when the whole created order unites to offer glory to God and the Lamb (5:13), we see the ultimate goal of the *missio Dei* in which the church is caught up.

Second, worship is a *means* of fulfilling God's mission. Revelation extends the call to worship, not only to the church, but also to the world. John pictures this vividly in chapter 14. In the midst of visions of people worshipping the beast (Rev 13:1-18; 14:9-11), the redeemed of humanity lift a thunderous new song of praise to God (Rev 14:1-5). Immediately, an angel bids the earth dwellers of every tribe and nation to join in giving glory to God (Rev 14:7). They are invited to change loyalties and join the chorus of worshippers that encircles God's throne (Rev 4:11; 5:11-14; 7:9-12). Far from a purely private matter, worship in Revelation projects outward as a public means of testimony. Michael Gorman puts it well: "As a call to join the ongoing heavenly worship of God, Revelation is simultaneously a presentation of the divine drama that is celebrated in worship, and therefore also a summons to enter the story and mission of God."[51] The community's worship seeks to bring glory to God *and* to bring others into the orbit of worshipping God.

Reading from the Back Page

John's vision of the new heaven and the new earth (Rev 21 and 22) reveals the climax of the entire biblical story and the goal of God's mission. But how does this picture of the New Jerusalem energize God's people to participate in God's mission? If the New Jerusalem is simply a picture of the

man imperial court that John's readers could not miss the connection. See Howard-Brook and Gwyther, *Unveiling Empire*, 202–7.

49. J. Nelson Kraybill, "The New Jerusalem as Paradigm for Mission," *Mission Focus Annual Review* 2 (1994): 129.

50. See Christopher J. H. Wright, *The Mission of God's People: A Biblical Theology of the Church's Mission* (Grand Rapids: Zondervan, 2010), 244–47.

51. Gorman, *Reading Revelation Responsibly*, 37.

future destiny of Christians, without much connection to the current life and mission of the church, then it has little to say to us. But that is not the case. Although the holy city belongs to the future, it offers a vision of reality that profoundly shapes the church's present identity and mission.

In one sense, we need to read the Apocalypse, and, for that matter, the entire biblical story of God's mission, *from the back*. We saw earlier that this reading strategy made sense of the Gospel of Matthew. But it pertains to the book of Revelation, as well, particularly chapters 21 and 22. By embracing the future of God's mission, which these chapters portray, God's people receive the grace to live as a foretaste of God's coming reign here and now. John's audience must "enter" the heavenly Jerusalem in order to gain a perspective from which to resist the illusions of the earthly empire. John's vision of the new heaven and earth equips the church, in effect, to live out Jesus's prayer, "Your kingdom come, your will be done, *on earth, as it is in heaven*" (Matt 6:10 NIV, italics added).

John's description of the new holy city stands in stinging contrast to that of the wicked city of Babylon. Note some of the ways in which the character of the New Jerusalem sets the agenda for the church in mission:

1. **A Restored Communion.** The New Jerusalem represents intimate communion with God and restored relationships among humans. Citizens of the holy city live in full loving fellowship with one another, with the triune God as the focus of their shared life. Above all, they enjoy the unhindered presence of God (Rev 21:3; 22:3-4). Such a vision energizes the church to lead others into fellowship with God. But redeemed persons don't relate to God simply as individuals. They must be brought into an authentic, loving, worshipping community, as members of God's family (Rev 21:7).

2. **A Healing Community.** Whereas wicked Babylon deceives and intoxicates the world's nations (Rev 14:8; 18:3, 23), the New Jerusalem's mission is the "healing of the nations" (Rev 22:2; cf. 21:24, 26). This suggests God's restoring work in every arena of human life—spiritual, relational, physical, social, and political. If the church has the tree of life in its midst, whose leaves are for the healing of the world's nations (22:2), then what the Christian community mediates to the nations is no less than the abundant life and wholeness promised by God.[52]

---

52. See Mangina, *Revelation*, 248.

3. A Just Community. Injustice finds no welcome mat in the New
Jerusalem. Whereas Babylon enriches itself by exploiting others (Rev
18:11-17), Jerusalem's extravagant wealth is shared by all. "The New
Jerusalem," comments J. Nelson Kraybill, "has no hoarding, no
exclusive neighborhoods, and no poverty."[53] All its citizens, without
exception, enjoy an abundance of food and water (Rev 21:6; 22:1-2;
cf. 7:16). This hope-filled vision calls God's people to prophetically
unmask the powers that exploit the powerless. The church must be a
signpost of justice and generosity, a foretaste of God's coming rule.

4. A Hospitable Community. In contrast to the exclusion and elitism
of imperial society, the New Jerusalem embodies perpetual hospitality. Its gates are always open to receive those who desire to leave
Babylon and enter the city of God (Rev 21:25).[54] What's more, the
city gates face every direction, welcoming people from all nations and
every point of the compass (Rev 21:13).[55] John's vision beckons the
church to be an instrument of blessing to all peoples, "drawing them
from the ruins of Babylon to their eternal destination in the new
Jerusalem."[56]

5. A Holy Community. At the same time, the holy city retains moral
boundaries, which separate the life of God's people from the moral
bankruptcy of Babylon (Rev 17:1-6; 18:2-5). Holiness becomes the
hallmark of God's new creation. The *whole city*, with its perfect cubic
shape, forms a sanctuary like Israel's holy of holies, sanctified by the
presence of God and the Lamb (Rev 21:15-17, 22). Only those who
wash their robes are invited to enter (Rev 22:14). Everything morally
unclean is excluded (Rev 21:27; cf. 21:8; 22:15). Only a holy people
can fulfill the mission of a holy God. In the New Jerusalem, holiness
and mission walk hand in hand.

6. A Renewed Creation. God's restoring mission is as wide as creation
itself. Instead of the church being "raptured" to heaven, the New
Jerusalem, the heavenly manifestation of the church, *comes down* to a
renewed earth (Rev 21:2). John envisions the new paradise as a lush

---

53. Kraybill, *Apocalypse and Allegiance*, 177.
54. Howard-Brook and Gwyther, *Unveiling Empire*, 188.
55. Kraybill, *Imperial Cult and Commerce*, 222.
56. Simon Woodman, *The Book of Revelation* (London: SCM, 2008), 114.

urban garden, one that seems to erupt through the city's main street (Rev 22:1-2).[57] This is a picture of ecological harmony and the *re-creation* of the world. God's loving purpose embraces the whole of his creation. If so, then what it means for the church to participate in the *missio Dei* includes *being* good news, not just to people but to all of creation.[58] We are caught up in God's transforming work of making "all things new" (Rev 21:5).

John's breathtaking vision of the New Jerusalem seeks to redraw the hearers' geography of the imagination. As Simon Woodman observes, "When the earth is seen from heaven's perspective, everything is different."[59] Catching a glimpse of the new heaven and the new earth equips the church to bear witness *now* to God's redemptive future. It challenges Christians to embody the life of New Jerusalem on the very streets of Babylon.

Conclusion

Revelation, then, both witnesses to the *missio Dei* and serves as an instrument of that mission, calling John's audience to actively participate in God's redeeming purpose for his creation. I am convinced that such a missional reading of the Apocalypse is not only *possible* but also *crucial* for grasping the theological message of this book and its pastoral implications for the people of God. It will help us steer clear of the tendency to relegate Revelation to the ancient past on the one hand or to view it as a speculative playbook for the end times on the other.

But interpreting Revelation in light of God's sweeping purpose for all of creation not only encourages a more faithful reading of the Apocalypse. It also enhances our theology and practice of mission. Too often, popular conceptions of the church's mission have focused simply on getting individuals ready for heaven, or even on making sure that they are not "left behind" when the church is suddenly whisked out of the world. In contrast, mission in Revelation is comprehensive. God's redemptive purpose is no less than the "healing of the nations" (Rev 22:2) and, beyond that, the restoring of all of creation. Revelation will not abide any narrow, squinty visions of the *missio Dei*.

What's more, if part of John's purpose is to equip his audience to embody the life of heaven on earth, then the act of reading Revelation becomes an

57. Howard-Brook and Gwyther, *Unveiling Empire*, 190–91.
58. Wright, *Mission of God's People*, 60–61.
59. Woodman, *Book of Revelation*, 236.

invitation to the church in every generation. Revelation still calls us to "come out" of Babylon (Rev 18:4). That surely starts with prayerfully discerning where modern-day "Babylon" is to be found and then actively disentangling ourselves from the systems of power, exploitation, consumption, and injustice that play Babylon's part on *our* world stage. Revelation challenges us to resist whatever beastly powers demand our ultimate allegiance. It summons us to bear prophetic witness in the face of all the present-day idols that try to usurp God's rule.

Positively, Revelation beckons God's people to mediate the healing of the nations, which involves not only evangelizing people from every tribe and nation, but also practicing and working for peace, justice, and reconciliation within and among the world's nations. And it calls us to do so, even as we reenact the drama of the slaughtered Lamb, the one who in love "emptied himself," to the very point of death on a cross (Phil 2:5-11). If we are listening, John still tells us that this story of the slaughtered Lamb is not only the source of our salvation. It is the pattern of our life and mission in the world.

Epilogue

Wat have we discovered in this missional reading of New Testament texts? To try to answer that, I will ask three further questions: First, what have we learned about the distinctive contributions of diverse New Testament voices to our understanding of mission? Second, what holds these various missional readings together? Finally, what does it matter for the church today?

Distinctive Notes

Let us begin, then, with the different emphases we found as we read seven representative New Testament writings in light of the mission of God. These themes may not appear *only* in, say, Matthew or John or 1 Peter. But they do represent what seem to be special contributions of these books to our understanding of God's mission and to how scripture energizes the church to participate in the *missio Dei*.

Regarding Matthew, our reading strategy was to "read from the back" in two senses, each of which uncovers a particular emphasis of this Gospel. First, Matthew reads the entire Old Testament narrative "backwards," through the lens of what God has done in the kingdom mission of Jesus, the Messiah of Israel. Jesus of Nazareth represents the climax of Israel's story, the fulfillment of Israel's scriptures, and the embodiment of Israel's mission.

Second, reading Matthew "from the back" means reading from the vantage point of Jesus's post-Easter commission to the church in Matthew 28:16-20. Such a backward reading enables us to see the entire Gospel as a "mission text," which calls readers of this Gospel to enter the story of God's mission.

Matthew especially spotlights the missional role of *making disciples of the nations* (Matt 28:19). The call to discipleship throughout the Gospel is a call to mission. The Great Commission passage brings out other distinctive emphases, which include the teaching ministry of the church in mission, patterned after Jesus, the Teacher of Israel, as well as the close connection between the church's loving obedience to Jesus and its mission in the world (Matt 5:13-16; 28:20).

Our missional reading of Luke and Acts shows both common themes and distinctive threads in Luke's two volumes. We traced three missional streams that highlight Luke-Acts' contribution to the New Testament understanding of mission. First, we encounter a robust, holistic understanding of mission, which pictures salvation in all of its fullness touching the whole range of human need. Luke's Gospel, in particular, teases out the social, political, and economic dimensions of Jesus's kingdom mission (see Luke 4:18-19). In Acts, the focus falls especially on the witness and progress of the *word*, which draws people to repent and believe in Jesus. Yet, that verbal witness is continually integrated with the church's identity ("You will *be* my witnesses," Acts 1:8) and practice.

Second, mission in Luke and Acts embraces outsiders and shatters boundaries. In Luke's Gospel, Jesus's ministry of inclusion sets its sights on peripheral people who dangle precariously on the margins of Jewish society. The book of Acts unfolds a universal mission that crosses cultural and ethnic barriers, ultimately including Gentiles and extending to the "end of the earth" (Acts 1:8). Acts also spotlights the inherent flexibility of the Christian mission, which seeks to contextualize the gospel for people in whatever life circumstances they find themselves. Finally, Luke and Acts together shine a spotlight on the Holy Spirit, who initiates, guides, and empowers the mission of God and the church's participation in it.

The Gospel of John drives us deep—into the source and motivation for mission. John distinctively portrays mission as the overflow of God's sending love for the world God has created. Missional love involves the whole Trinity and comes to visible expression in the sent one, Jesus, the incarnate Son. For John, the church's mission is, in the first place, not something we do, but who we *are*. It is anchored in the church's relationship with Jesus and continues his own mission in the world: "As the Father sent me, so I am sending you" (John 20:21). John underscores that mission results from the community's practice of the love and unity that characterize the triune God (John 13:34-35; 17:20-23).

130

As for Philippians, mission, in the first place, flows out of a "V-shaped" story. The crucial mission text is Philippians 2:6-11, which narrates Jesus's self-humbling and death on a cross, along with his exaltation as Lord of all. This story becomes both the message the church proclaims and the character of its mission. God's mission is cruciform, and the church is called to embody Christ's self-giving love for others. Philippians characteristically appeals to examples in order to energize the church for mission. Believers are to emulate Christ above all, but also his servants—Paul's coworkers, the Roman Christians, and not least, Paul himself (Phil 1:12-18; 3:6-14, 17; 4:9).

A second noteworthy missional emphasis in Philippians concerns the calling of God's people to live out the gospel in their public and communal life—their "citizenship" (Phil 1:27). Third, the church's participation in the gospel (Phil 1:6) may take a whole variety of forms, including financial gifts, intercessory prayer, suffering, and actively telling the gospel. Fourth, sharing in God's mission involves critically engaging the values of the culture (Phil 4:8). Christians are to recognize God's grace wherever it is to be found, while at the same time reading those values through the lens of the cruciform story of Christ.

First Peter paints the mission of God with its own distinctive colors. Peter, for example, accents that God's redeeming mission in the death and resurrection of Christ involves liberation from bondage *to* sin and *from* the powers of evil. He also spotlights Christ's redemptive suffering, which, in turn becomes a model for how believers participate in the *missio Dei* (1 Pet 2:21).

For Peter, the church engages in mission out of an identity as *exiles* and *immigrants*, a community of "misfits" in their own social world. Exiles are called to missional holiness. Peter urges them to live distinctive, Christlike lives, in the midst of exclusion and suffering. When such lives display the character of God before others, they carry the potential of magnetically drawing outsiders into the sphere of faith (1 Pet 2:11-12; 3:1-2). Exiles may be radically different, but they are also fully engaged in the public life and relationships of their culture in redemptive ways.

Finally, our missional reading of Revelation unearths a number of characteristic themes. First, mission in Revelation is creation oriented. The creator God is on a mission to restore the whole of his creation. Ultimately, that goal is realized in God's new heaven and earth, when the New Jerusalem descends to earth from heaven (Rev 3:12; 21:2). Second, the master symbol for God's redemption in Revelation is the slaughtered Lamb, who overcomes God's enemies through his sacrificial death (Rev 12:11). The church, in turn, must reenact the Lamb's story in its costly, prophetic witness. Third, the scope of

God's missional purpose in Revelation is breathtaking. It embraces all tribes and peoples, as well as the entire creation. It envisions the healing of the nations and its rulers (Rev 21:2, 24-26), with the holy city's gates flung open to people from every point of the compass (Rev 21:13, 25).

Fourth, Revelation calls God's people in mission to reimagine their world from the vantage point of God's future and God's throne. What does this mean? On the one hand, the church must distance itself from the idols, greed, and exploitation of the empire, forsaking their collusion with arrogant "Babylon." Mission in the Apocalypse is inherently "political." On the other hand, Christians are to positively live as a foretaste of God's future, embodying the life of New Jerusalem on the streets of the empire. Fifth, Revelation weds mission to worship, which both declares allegiances and calls others into the worship of the true God.

Each of these various perspectives contributes to a rich New Testament understanding of mission.

Common Threads

In addition, reading these New Testament books missionally reveals some shared emphases among different authors. Both John and 1 Peter, for example, underscore that mission is grounded in who we *are* in relation to the missional God, rather than in what we do or say (see John 17:18; 20:21; 1 Pet 2:9-11). Similarly, Philippians and Revelation share in common that God's people are called to live out the life of heaven, here and now (Phil 1:27; 3:20; Rev 21–22).

Above all, our missional readings uncover a number of themes that run like golden threads throughout the New Testament witness to God's mission and its call for churches to embrace God's mission. These include the following:

- Witness to the *missio Dei* focuses firmly on the story of what God has done in Jesus—his life, saving death, resurrection, and return, along with the gift of the Spirit.

- That story is anchored in the story of Israel. Jesus represents the fulfillment and climax of what God has been doing all along, and what was promised and prefigured in Israel's scriptures.

- God's mission is universal and inclusive. It embraces all people, all nations, and all of creation.

132

- The mission of God in Jesus confronts and ultimately triumphs over evil in all of its forms, personal as well as corporate.

- God accomplishes his redemptive mission, not through coercion and violence, but through the humble, sacrificial love and service of Jesus Christ.

- God's saving and restoring mission in Christ is oriented toward the future. What God is doing now to accomplish his redemption anticipates and bears witness to the fullness of God's salvation to come.

- The church is called to participate in God's missional purpose for the world.

- The church's mission, like the mission of Jesus, is all-embracing and integrated. It involves being, doing, and telling.

- The holiness and lifestyle witness of God's people are crucial components of mission.

- The mission of God's people is lived out in public, before a watching world. What C. Kavin Rowe concludes about Acts fits the New Testament as a whole: "There is no such thing... as being a Christian in private."[1]

- Mission is communal, not simply individual. The Christian community as a whole is called to proclaim and to embody the good news.

- The humble, self-giving love that characterizes Jesus's own ministry and death must shape the church's public missional practice. In other words, the *manner* of doing mission must be consistent with the *message* of mission.

- The goal of mission is not simply initial evangelization, but the formation of loving, obedient, worshipping communities that reflect the character of God and join in the mission of God.

1. C. Kavin Rowe, *World Upside Down: Reading Acts in the Graeco-Roman Age* (Oxford: Oxford University Press, 2009), 101.

• The church is called to engage its culture and social world. It will enter the bloodstream of its culture, and, at the same time, challenge and even subvert aspects of the culture.

• Christian mission, in our texts, is married to suffering. Christians who partake in Christ's mission must be willing to embrace Christ's suffering.

• The gospel the church proclaims and embodies must be contextualized in order to make sense to people in their various circumstances, without diluting the gospel to make it easier to imbibe. Christian witness remains both flexible and firm.

This is not an exhaustive list. But it does indicate that, across a variety of representative New Testament writings, we find a great deal of cohesion in the understanding of the mission of God and the church's participation in that mission.

So What?

This attempt to read the New Testament missionally primarily has focused on two questions: What is the New Testament witness to the mission of God? And how does the New Testament equip and energize the church to get caught up in that mission? What's more, it has remained our working assumption throughout this study that the second question not only concerns how the first-century audience of Acts or 1 Peter, for example, participated in God's mission. It also presses us to ask, how do these texts draw us, as twenty-first-century readers, into the mission of God?

At the end of the day, we can only read scripture *faithfully* as communities of people who are actively engaged in God's mission, in our various contexts and cultures, just as the original authors and readers of the New Testament were caught up in the *missio Dei*. Only as we *participate* in the mission of God can we hope to embody scripture's missional intent. The New Testament envisions no role for spectators. A missional reading of scripture, then, seeks to bring about not only a clearer understanding of scripture but also a better grasp of what it means to live as a missional people today.

This need to read scripture as communities engaged in God's mission carries two further implications, which have to do with *ecclesiology* and *appropriation*. First, ecclesiology. It has become rather fashionable in recent Christian circles to talk about the "missional church." I genuinely appreciate the intent behind the term—to recapture a more biblical and outwardly focused understanding of the church. But the very language makes me wonder: Is there such a thing as an *un*-missional church? Mission means more than a line item on a church budget. It is more than something we *do*, whether that involves sending out overseas missionaries, witnessing to a neighbor, or running a local food pantry. Mission, in the first place, is an *identity* issue. Ultimately, if there's no mission, there's no church.

Second, if we read scripture missionally, we must take up the hard work of appropriating those missional readings for our present cultures and contexts. I have tried to offer some preliminary suggestions as to how we might begin to do that in each chapter of this book. Yet it is imperative that communities of faith throughout the world contextualize the missional message of the New Testament for their own particular circumstances.

The Gospel of John, for example, emphasizes that the uncommon love and unity among Christians becomes a catalyst for mission to a watching world (John 13:34-35; 17:20-24). How, then, should this missional attitude and practice shape the use of social media in North America, in which Christians too often publicly air their differences in ways that mimic the incivility and polarization of the wider culture? When we label or belittle other believers in public forums, when we cannot learn to speak the truth *with love* (Eph 4:15), the world has little hope of witnessing the gospel of Christ crucified in his followers. Given the powerful presence of social media, Christian communities must wrestle with how this medium can be used as a channel for attracting others to the gospel, rather than building barriers to faith.

Ultimately, reading New Testament texts missionally involves not merely understanding, but embodiment. What that will look like will vary, even as the circumstances of the church vary. For example, many Christian communities around the globe can identify closely with the texts of Philippians or 1 Peter that speak of missional suffering (e.g., Phil 1:27-30; 1 Pet 2:11-12, 18-23; 3:13-18). While writing this book, I learned of a Christian leader who, some time ago, had been severely injured in an attempt on his life by those opposed to his ministry. He survived the ordeal, and, undaunted, continued his courageous service to Christ. More recently, his enemies returned. Sadly, this time their attack achieved its goal of taking his life. Following his death, followers of Jesus in that area promised that many new Christian communities would rise out of the blood of this martyr for Christ. Christians in the West have much to learn from such faithful disciples, for whom participation in God's mission is costly, even to the point of following in the suffering footsteps of Jesus (1 Pet 2:21).

In a very different context, I watched my father, in his later years, embody the mission of God in his public world. After he retired from many years of leadership ministry in the church, a local coffee shop became his "mission field." My father made it his destination every morning and, over time, he became enmeshed in the lives of the regular patrons and employees. I watched him call them by name, ask them about their families and their health concerns, and listen to their hopes, their longings, their fears. He prayed for some of them by name every day. And, when the Spirit prompted, he spoke to them of a God who loves, forgives, and reconciles.

When my father was afflicted with an aggressive brain tumor, his final outing was to visit his friends at the coffee shop. Arriving in his wheelchair, he was greeted by about fifteen patrons, who had gathered to express their farewells. Many of them made a point to tell me how his joyful, loving spirit had touched their lives, how much they would miss him. My father sought out a young man among the group, who, through his influence, had come to believe in Jesus as Lord. "I'm passing the torch on to you," my father told him. "Now this is *your* mission field."

Woven into the pages of this book is the hope that a missional reading of the New Testament, through the guidance of the Spirit, will lead God's people (including myself) into a richer and more robust understanding of the mission of God, as well as a more faithful embodiment of the *missio Dei*, in whatever field of mission they find themselves.

For Further Reading

Barram, Michael. "The Bible, Mission, and Social Location: Toward a Missional Hermeneutic." *Interpretation* 61 (2007): 42–58.

Bauckham, Richard. *The Bible and Mission: Christian Witness in a Postmodern World*. Grand Rapids: Baker, 2003.

Bosch, David J. *Transforming Mission: Paradigm Shifts in Theology of Mission*. Maryknoll, NY: Orbis, 1991.

Brownson, James V. *Speaking the Truth in Love: New Testament Resources for a Missional Hermeneutic*. Harrisburg, PA: Trinity Press International, 1998.

Flemming, Dean. *Contextualization in the New Testament: Patterns for Theology and Mission*. Downers Grove, IL: IVP Academic, 2005.

———. *Recovering the Full Mission of God: A Biblical Perspective on Being, Doing and Telling*. Downers Grove, IL: IVP Academic, 2013.

Goheen, Michael W. *A Light to the Nations: The Missional Church and the Biblical Story*. Grand Rapids: Baker Academic, 2011.

———, ed. *A Missional Reading of Scripture: Hermeneutics, Preaching, and Theological Education*. Grand Rapids: Eerdmans, forthcoming.

Gorman, Michael J. *Becoming the Gospel: Paul, Participation, and Mission*. Grand Rapids: Eerdmans, 2015.

Hunsberger, George R. "Proposals for a Missional Hermeneutic: Mapping the Conversation." *Missiology* 39 (2011): 309–21.

Köstenberger, Andreas J., and Peter T. O'Brien. *Salvation to the Ends of the Earth: A Biblical Theology of Mission*. Leicester: Apollos, 2001.

Laansma, Jon, Grant Osborne, and Ray Van Neste, eds. *New Testament Theol-*

ogy in Light of the Church's Mission: Essays in Honor of I. Howard Mar-shall. Eugene, OR: Cascade, 2011.

Wright, Christopher J. H. *The Mission of God: Unlocking the Bible's Grand Narrative.* Downers Grove, IL: IVP Academic, 2006.

———. *The Mission of God's People: A Biblical Theology of the Church's Mission.* Grand Rapids: Zondervan, 2010.

Bibliography

Achtemeier, Paul J. *1 Peter: A Commentary on First Peter*. Minneapolis: Fortress, 1996.

Arias, Mortimer, and Alan Johnson. *The Great Commission: Biblical Models for Evangelism*. Nashville: Abingdon, 1992.

Balch, David L. *Let Wives Be Submissive: The Domestic Code in 1 Peter*. Atlanta: Scholars Press, 1981.

Barram, Michael. "The Bible, Mission, and Social Location: Toward a Missional Hermeneutic." *Interpretation* 61 (2007): 42–58.

Barrett, C. K. *A Critical and Exegetical Commentary on the Acts of the Apostles*. Vol. 1, *Preliminary Introduction and Commentary on Acts I–XIV*. Edinburgh: T&T Clark, 1994.

Bauckham, Richard. *The Bible and Mission: Christian Witness in a Postmodern World*. Grand Rapids: Baker, 2003.

———. *The Climax of Prophecy: Studies on the Book of Revelation*. Edinburgh: T&T Clark, 1993.

———. *God Crucified: Monotheism and Christology in the New Testament*. Grand Rapids: Eerdmans, 1999.

———. "Mission as Hermeneutic for Scriptural Interpretation." Lecture given in Cambridge. Accessed June 26, 2015. http://richardbauckham .co.uk/uploads/Accessible/Mission%20as%20Hermeneutic.pdf.

———. *The Theology of the Book of Revelation*. Cambridge: Cambridge University Press, 1993.

Beach, Lee. *The Church in Exile: Living in Hope after Christendom*. Downers Grove, IL: IVP Academic, 2014.

Beale, Greg K. *The Book of Revelation*. Grand Rapids: Eerdmans, 1999.

Billings, J. Todd. *Union with Christ: Reframing Theology and Ministry for the Church*. Grand Rapids: Baker Academic, 2011.

Blount, Brian K. *Revelation: A Commentary.* Louisville: Westminster John Knox, 2009.

Bock, Darrell L. *A Theology of Luke and Acts: God's Revised Program, Realized for All Nations.* Grand Rapids: Zondervan, 2012.

Bockmuehl, Markus N. A. *The Epistle to the Philippians.* Peabody, MA: Hendrickson, 1998.

Boring, M. Eugene. "Narrative Christology in the Apocalypse." *Catholic Biblical Quarterly* 54 (1992): 702–23.

————. "Narrative Dynamics in 1 Peter: The Function of Narrative World." In *Reading First Peter with New Eyes: Methodological Assessments of the Letter of First Peter,* edited by Robert L. Webb and Betsy Bauman-Martin, 7–40. London: T&T Clark, 2007.

Bosch, David J. "Reflections on Biblical Models of Mission." In *Toward the Twenty-First Century in Christians Mission: Essays in Honor of Gerald H. Anderson,* edited by James M. Phillips and Robert T. Coote, 175–92. Grand Rapids: Eerdmans, 1993.

————. "The Structure of Mission: An Exposition of Matthew 28:16-21." In *The Study of Evangelism: Exploring a Missional Practice of the Church,* edited by Paul W. Chilcote and Laceye C. Warner, 73–92. Grand Rapids: Eerdmans, 2008.

————. *Transforming Mission: Paradigm Shifts in Theology of Mission.* Maryknoll, NY: Orbis, 1991.

Brown, Jeannine K. "Matthew, Gospel of." In *Dictionary of Jesus and the Gospels.* Edited by Joel B. Green, Jeannine K. Brown, and Nicholas Perrin, 570–84. 2nd ed. Downers Grove, IL: IVP Academic, 2013.

Brownson, James V. *Speaking the Truth in Love: New Testament Resources for a Missional Hermeneutic.* Harrisburg, PA: Trinity Press International, 1998.

Bruner, Frederick Dale. *Matthew: A Commentary.* Vol. 2, *The Churchbook: Matthew 13–28.* Dallas: Word, 1990.

Burridge, Richard A. *Imitating Jesus: An Inclusive Approach to New Testament Ethics.* Grand Rapids: Eerdmans, 2007.

Carey, Greg. *Elusive Apocalypses: Reading Authority in the Revelation to John.* Studies in American Biblical Hermeneutics 15. Macon, GA: Mercer University Press, 1999.

————. "Teaching and Preaching the Book of Revelation in the Church." *Review and Expositor* 98 (2001): 87–100.

Cargal, Timothy B. "'His Blood Be on Us and Our Children': A Matthean Double Entendre?" *New Testament Studies* 37 (1991): 101–12.

Carter, Warren. *What Does Revelation Reveal? Unlocking the Mystery.* Nashville: Abingdon, 2011.

Chin, Moses. "A Heavenly Home for the Homeless: Aliens and Strangers in 1 Peter." *Tyndale Bulletin* 42 (1991): 96–112.

Comblin, José. *Sent from the Father: Meditations on the Fourth Gospel.* Translated by Carl Kabat. Maryknoll, NY: Orbis, 1979.

Costas, Orlando E. *Christ outside the Gate: Mission beyond Christendom.* Maryknoll, NY: Orbis, 1982.

Crossan, John Dominic. *God and Empire: Jesus against Rome, Then and Now.* San Francisco: HarperSanFrancisco, 2007.

deSilva, David A. *Honor, Patronage, Kinship, and Purity: Unlocking New Testament Culture.* Downers Grove, IL: InterVarsity Press, 2000.

———. *Seeing Things John's Way: The Rhetoric of the Book of Revelation.* Louisville: Westminster John Knox, 2009.

Dickson, John. *The Best Kept Secret of Christian Mission: Promoting the Gospel with More Than Our Lips.* Grand Rapids: Zondervan, 2010.

Donelson, Lewis R. *1 & 2 Peter and Jude.* Louisville: Westminster John Knox, 2010.

Elliott, John H. *1 Peter: A New Translation with Introduction and Commentary.* New York: Doubleday, 2000.

———. *A Home for the Homeless: A Sociological Exegesis of 1 Peter, Its Situation and Strategy.* Philadelphia: Fortress, 1981.

Esler, Philip F. *Community and Gospel in Luke-Acts: The Social and Political Motivations of Lucan Theology.* Cambridge: Cambridge University Press, 1987.

Fee, Gordon D. *Paul's Letter to the Philippians.* Grand Rapids: Eerdmans, 1995.

Flemming, Dean. *Contextualization in the New Testament: Patterns for Theology and Mission.* Downers Grove, IL: IVP Academic, 2005.

———. "Exploring a Missional Reading of Scripture: Philippians as a Case Study." *Evangelical Quarterly* 83 (2011): 3–17.

———. "'On Earth as It Is in Heaven': Holiness and the People of God in Revelation." In *Holiness and Ecclesiology in the New Testament,* edited by Kent E. Brower and Andy Johnson, 343–62. Grand Rapids: Eerdmans, 2007.

141

———. *Philippians: A Commentary in the Wesleyan Tradition.* Kansas City, MO: Beacon Hill, 2009.

———. *Recovering the Full Mission of God: A Biblical Perspective on Being, Doing and Telling.* Downers Grove, IL: IVP Academic, 2013.

———. "Revelation and the *Missio Dei*: Toward a Missional Reading of the Apocalypse." *Journal of Theological Interpretation* 6 (2012): 161–78.

———. "'Won Over without a Word': Holiness and the Church's Missional Identity in 1 Peter." *Wesleyan Theological Journal* 49 (2014): 50–66.

Furnish, Victor Paul. *The Love Command in the New Testament.* Nashville: Abingdon, 1972.

Garland, David E. *Luke.* Grand Rapids: Zondervan, 2011.

Goheen, Michael W. "Continuing Steps Towards a Missional Hermeneutic." *Fideles* 3 (2008): 49–99.

———. *Introducing Christian Mission Today: Scripture, History, and Issues.* Downers Grove, IL: IVP Academic, 2014.

———. *A Light to the Nations: The Missional Church and the Biblical Story.* Grand Rapids: Baker Academic, 2011.

———. "A Missional Approach to Scripture for the Theological Task." In *The End of Theology: Shaping Theology for the Sake of Mission*, edited by Jason S. Sexton and Paul Weston. Minneapolis: Augsburg Fortress, forthcoming.

Gorman, Michael J. *Becoming the Gospel: Paul, Participation, and Mission.* Grand Rapids: Eerdmans, 2015.

———. *Cruciformity: Paul's Narrative Spirituality of the Cross.* Grand Rapids: Eerdmans, 2001.

———. *Inhabiting the Cruciform God: Kenosis, Justification, and Theosis in Paul's Narrative Soteriology.* Grand Rapids: Eerdmans, 2009.

———. *Reading Revelation Responsibly: Uncivil Worship and Witness: Following the Lamb into the New Creation.* Eugene, OR: Cascade, 2011.

Green, Joel B. *1 Peter.* Grand Rapids: Eerdmans, 2007.

———. *The Gospel of Luke.* Grand Rapids: Eerdmans, 1997.

———. "Living as Exiles: The Church in the Diaspora in 1 Peter." In *Holiness and Ecclesiology in the New Testament*, edited by Kent E. Brower and Andy Johnson, 311–25. Grand Rapids: Eerdmans, 2007.

———. "Luke, Gospel of." In *Dictionary of Jesus and the Gospels.* 2nd ed., edited by Joel B. Green, Jeannine K. Brown, and Nicholas Perrin, 540–52. Downers Grove, IL: IVP Academic, 2013.

142

———. "Narrating the Gospel in 1 and 2 Peter." *Interpretation* 60 (2006): 262–67.

———. *Practicing Theological Interpretation: Engaging Biblical Texts for Faith and Formation*. Grand Rapids: Baker Academic, 2011.

———. *The Theology of the Gospel of Luke*. Cambridge: Cambridge University Press, 1995.

Guder, Darrell L., ed. *Missional Church: A Vision for the Sending of the Church in North America*. Grand Rapids: Eerdmans, 1998.

———. "Missional Hermeneutics: The Missional Authority of Scripture—Interpreting Scripture as Missional Formation." *Mission Focus: Annual Review* 15 (2007): 106–24.

Hagner, Donald A. "Holiness and Ecclesiology: The Church in Matthew." In *Holiness and Ecclesiology in the New Testament*, edited by K. E. Brower and Andy Johnson, 40–56. Grand Rapids: Eerdmans, 2007.

Harink, Douglas K. *1 & 2 Peter*. Grand Rapids: Brazos, 2009.

Harris, R. Geoffrey. *Mission in the Gospels*. London: Epworth, 2004.

Hastings, Ross. *Missional God, Missional Church: Hope for Re-evangelizing the West*. Downers Grove, IL: IVP Academic, 2012.

Hays, Richard B. *The Moral Vision of the New Testament: Community, Cross, New Creation; A Contemporary Introduction to New Testament Ethics*. San Francisco: HarperSanFrancisco, 1996.

———. *Reading Backwards: Figural Christology and the Fourfold Gospel Witness*. Waco, TX: Baylor University Press, 2014.

Hellerman, Joseph H. *Reconstructing Honor in Roman Philippi*: Carmen Christi *as* Cursus Pudorum. Society of New Testament Studies Monograph Series 132. Cambridge: Cambridge University Press, 2005.

Hertig, Paul. "The Jubilee Mission of Jesus in the Gospel of Luke: Reversal of Fortunes." *Missiology* 26 (1998): 167–79.

Hesselgrave, David J. *Paradigms in Conflict: Ten Key Questions in Christian Missions Today*. Grand Rapids: Kregel, 2005.

Howard-Brook, Wes, and Anthony Gwyther. *Unveiling Empire: Reading Revelation Then and Now*. Maryknoll, NY: Orbis, 1999.

Hunsberger, George R. "Proposals for a Missional Hermeneutic: Mapping the Conversation." *Missiology* 39 (2011): 309–21.

Jenkins, Philip. *The Next Christendom: The Coming of Global Christianity*. Oxford: Oxford University Press, 2002.

Jobes, Karen H. *1 Peter*. Grand Rapids: Baker Academic, 2005.

Johnson, Luke Timothy. *Prophetic Jesus, Prophetic Church: The Challenge of Luke-Acts to Contemporary Christians*. Grand Rapids: Eerdmans, 2011.

Joseph, Abson Prédestin. *A Narratological Reading of 1 Peter*. Library of New Testament Studies 440. London: T&T Clark, 2012.

Keener, Craig S. *A Commentary on the Gospel of Matthew*. Grand Rapids: Eerdmans, 1999.

———. "Sent Like Jesus: Johannine Missiology (John 20:21-22)." *Asian Journal of Pentecostal Studies* 12 (2009): 21–45.

Keown, Mark J. *Congregational Evangelism in Philippians: The Centrality of an Appeal for Gospel Proclamation to the Fabric of Philippians*. Paternoster Biblical Monographs. Milton Keynes: Paternoster, 2008.

Koester, Craig R. *Revelation and the End of All Things*. Grand Rapids: Eerdmans, 2001.

———. "Revelation's Challenge to Ordinary Empire." *Interpretation* 63 (2009): 5–18.

———. *The Word of Life: A Theology of John's Gospel*. Grand Rapids: Eerdmans, 2008.

Köstenberger, Andreas J. *The Missions of Jesus and His Disciples according to the Fourth Gospel*. Grand Rapids: Eerdmans, 1998.

Köstenberger, Andreas J., and Peter T. O'Brien. *Salvation to the Ends of the Earth: A Biblical Theology of Mission*. Leicester: Apollos, 2001.

Kraybill, J. Nelson. *Apocalypse and Allegiance: Worship, Politics, and Devotion in the Book of Revelation*. Grand Rapids: Brazos, 2010.

———. *Imperial Cult and Commerce in John's Apocalypse*. Journal for the Study of the New Testament Supplement Series 132. Sheffield: Sheffield Academic Press, 1996.

———. "The New Jerusalem as Paradigm for Mission." *Mission Focus Annual Review* 2 (1994): 129.

Kruse, Colin G. *John*. Grand Rapids: Eerdmans, 2003.

Lambrecht, Jan. *Collected Studies on Pauline Literature and on the Book of Revelation*. Analecta Biblica 147. Rome: Pontifical Biblical Institute, 2001.

Lincoln, Andrew T. *The Gospel according to Saint John*. Peabody, MA: Hendrickson, 2005.

Mangina, Joseph L. *Revelation*. Grand Rapids: Brazos, 2010.

Marshall, I. Howard. *New Testament Theology: Many Witnesses, One Gospel*. Downers Grove, IL: IVP Academic, 2004.

144

———. *Philippians*. London: Epworth, 1991.

Maynard-Reid, P. U. "Samaria." In *Dictionary of the Later New Testament and Its Developments*, edited by Ralph P. Martin and Peter H. Davids, 1075–77. Downers Grove, IL: InterVarsity Press, 1997.

Michaels, J. Ramsey. *1 Peter*. Waco, TX: Word, 1988.

Moore, Stephen D. "The Revelation to John." In *A Postcolonial Commentary on the New Testament Writings*, edited by Fernando F. Segovia and R. S. Sugirtharajah, 436–54. London: T&T Clark, 2009.

Nolland, John. *The Gospel of Matthew*. Grand Rapids: Eerdmans, 2005.

Oakes, Peter. *Philippians: From People to Letter*. Society for New Testament Studies Monograph Series 110. Cambridge: Cambridge University Press, 2001.

O'Brien, Peter T. *The Epistle to the Philippians: A Commentary on the Greek Text*. Grand Rapids: Eerdmans, 1991.

Osborne, Grant R. *Matthew*. Grand Rapids: Zondervan, 2010.

———. "The Mission to the Nations in the Book of Revelation." In *New Testament Theology in Light of the Church's Mission: Essays in Honor of I. Howard Marshall*, edited by Jon C. Laansma, Grant Osborne, and Ray Van Neste, 347–68. Eugene, OR: Cascade, 2011.

Ott, Craig, and Harold A. Netland. *Globalizing Theology: Belief and Practice in an Era of World Christianity*. Grand Rapids: Baker Academic, 2006.

Pervo, Richard J. *Acts: A Commentary*. Minneapolis: Fortress, 2009.

Peskett, Howard, and Vinoth Ramachandra. *The Message of Mission: The Glory of Christ in All Time and Space*. Downers Grove, IL: InterVarsity Press, 2003.

Peters, Olutola K. *The Mandate of the Church in the Apocalypse of John*. Studies in Biblical Literature 77. New York: Peter Lang, 2005.

Peterson, Brian K. "Being the Church in Philippi." *Horizons in Biblical Theology* 30 (2008): 163–78.

Peterson, David G. "Maturity: The Goal of Mission." In *The Gospel to the Nations: Perspectives on Paul's Mission*, edited by Peter Bolt, Mark Thompson, and Peter T. O'Brien, 185–204. Downers Grove, IL: InterVarsity Press, 2000.

Plummer, Robert L. *Paul's Understanding of the Church's Mission: Did the Apostle Paul Expect the Early Christian Communities to Evangelize?* Paternoster Biblical Monographs. Milton Keynes: Paternoster, 2006.

145

Plutarch. *Moralia*. Translated by Frank Cole Babbitt. Loeb Classical Library. Cambridge: Harvard University Press, 1928.

Rapske, Brian. "Opposition to the Plan of God and Persecution." In *Witness to the Gospel: The Theology of Acts*, edited by I. Howard Marshall and David Peterson, 235–56. Grand Rapids: Eerdmans, 1998.

Rodriguez, Darío López. *The Liberating Mission of Jesus: The Message of the Gospel of Luke*. Translated by Stephanie E. Israel and Richard E. Waldrop. Eugene, OR: Pickwick, 2012.

Rowe, C. Kavin. *World Upside Down: Reading Acts in the Graeco-Roman Age*. Oxford: Oxford University Press, 2009.

Scheffler, E. H. "Reading Luke from the Perspective of Liberation Theology." In *Text and Interpretation: New Approaches in the Criticism of the New Testament*, edited by P. J. Hartin and J. H. Petzer, 281–98. Leiden: Brill, 1991.

Schnabel, Eckhard J. *Acts*. Grand Rapids: Zondervan, 2012.

———. *Early Christian Mission*. 2 vols. Downers Grove, IL: IVP Academic 2004.

———. "John and the Future of the Nations." *Bulletin for Biblical Research* 12 (2002): 243–71.

Seccombe, David. "The New People of God." In *Witness to the Gospel: The Theology of Acts*, edited by I. Howard Marshall and David Peterson, 349–72. Grand Rapids: Eerdmans, 1998.

Seland, Torrey. "Resident Aliens in Mission: Missional Practices in the Emerging Church of 1 Peter." *Bulletin for Biblical Research* 19 (2009): 565–89.

Senior, Donald P. "1 Peter." In *1 Peter, Jude, and 2 Peter*, edited by Donald P. Senior and Daniel J. Harrington, 4–160. Collegeville, MN: Liturgical Press, 2008.

Senior, Donald, and Carroll Stuhlmueller. *The Biblical Foundations for Mission*. Maryknoll, NY: Orbis, 1983.

Smalley, Stephen S. *The Revelation to John: A Commentary on the Greek Text of the Apocalypse*. Downers Grove, IL: IVP Academic, 2005.

Smith, D. Moody, Jr. *John*. Nashville: Abingdon, 1999.

Steinmetz, David C. "Uncovering a Second Narrative: Detective Fiction and the Construction of the Historical Method." In *The Art of Reading Scripture*, edited by Ellen F. Davis and Richard B. Hays, 54–68. Grand Rapids: Eerdmans, 2003.

Strauss, Mark L. "The Purpose of Luke-Acts: Reaching a Consensus." In *New Testament Theology in Light of the Church's Mission: Essays in Honor of I. Howard Marshall*, edited by Jon C. Laansma, Grant Osborne, and Ray Van Neste, 135–50. Eugene, OR: Cascade, 2011.

Swift, Robert C. "The Theme and Structure of Philippians." *Bibliotecha Sacra* 141 (1984): 234–54.

Tennent, Timothy C. *Theology in the Context of World Christianity: How the Global Church Is Influencing the Way We Think About and Discuss Theology*. Grand Rapids: Zondervan, 2007.

Thomas, John Christopher. "New Jerusalem and the Conversion of the Nations: An Exercise in Pneumatic Discernment—Revelation 21.1–22.5." Paper presented at the Annual Meeting of the Society of Biblical Literature, Atlanta, GA, November 22, 2010.

Thomas, John Christopher, and Frank Macchia. *Revelation*. Grand Rapids: Eerdmans, forthcoming.

Thompson, Alan J. *The Acts of the Risen Lord Jesus: Luke's Account of God's Unfolding Plan*. Downers Grove, IL: IVP Academic, 2011.

Thompson, Marianne Meye. "John, Gospel of." In *Dictionary of Jesus and the Gospels*, edited by Joel B. Green, Scot McKnight, and I. Howard Marshall, 368–83. Downers Grove, IL: InterVarsity Press, 1992.

Trites, Allison A. *The New Testament Concept of Witness*. Society for New Testament Studies Monograph Series 31. Cambridge: Cambridge University Press, 1977.

Twelftree, Graham H. *People of the Spirit: Exploring Luke's View of the Church*. Grand Rapids: Baker Academic, 2009.

Volf, Miroslav. *Exclusion and Embrace: A Theological Exploration of Identity, Otherness, and Reconciliation*. Nashville: Abingdon, 1996.

_____. "Soft Difference: Theological Reflections on the Relation between Church and Culture in 1 Peter." *Ex Auditu* 10 (1994): 15–30.

Wagner, J. Ross. "*Missio Dei*: Envisioning an Apostolic Reading of Scripture." *Missiology* 37 (2009): 19–32.

Wall, Robert W. *Revelation*. Peabody, MA: Hendrickson, 1991.

Ware, James P. *Paul and the Mission of the Church: Philippians in Ancient Jewish Context*. Grand Rapids: Baker Academic, 2011.

Wilson, Alistair I. "An Ideal Missionary Prayer Letter: Reflections on Paul's Missionary Theology." In *New Testament Theology in Light of the Church's Mission: Essays in Honor of I. Howard Marshall*, edited by Jon Laansma,

Grant R. Osborne, and Ray Van Neste, 245–64. Eugene, OR: Cascade, 2011.

Winter, Bruce W. *Seek the Welfare of the City: Christians as Benefactors and Citizens.* Grand Rapids: Eerdmans, 1994.

Witherington, Ben, III. *John's Wisdom: A Commentary on the Fourth Gospel.* Louisville: Westminster John Knox, 1995.

Woodman, Simon. *The Book of Revelation.* London: SCM, 2008.

Wright, Christopher J. H. *The Mission of God: Unlocking the Bible's Grand Narrative.* Downers Grove, IL: IVP Academic, 2006.

———. *The Mission of God's People: A Biblical Theology of the Church's Mission.* Grand Rapids: Zondervan, 2010.

———. "Reading the Old Testament Missionally." In *A Missional Reading of Scripture: Hermeneutics, Preaching, and Theological Education*, edited by Michael W. Goheen. Grand Rapids: Eerdmans, forthcoming.

Wright, N. T. *John for Everyone, Part 2: Chapters 11–21.* London: SPCK, 2002.

———. *Matthew for Everyone, Part 1: Chapters 1–15.* London: SPCK, 2002.

———. *The New Testament and the People of God.* Minneapolis: Fortress, 1996.

Index of Scriptures

150

157

158

161

Index of
Modern Authors

Index of Subjects

167

of the nations, 111, 114, 116,
124, 126–27, 132
heaven, 13–14, 19, 22, 29, 44,
77, 80, 86, 88, 110–12, 118,
121–26, 131–32
hermeneutics
missional (*see under* scripture)
theological, xvi
holiness, missional, 63, 68–69,
81–82, 87, 98–99, 103–5,
107, 120, 125, 131, 133
Holy Spirit, the
anointing of, 26, 28, 45–46, 51
baptism with, 47, 59–60
boldness and, 48–49
filling of, 35, 48–49, 51
gift of, 32, 37, 39, 46–47, 56,
59–60, 62, 71, 132
guidance of, 43, 46, 47–48, 60,
130
initiating role of, 35, 46–47, 51,
130
in Jesus's mission, 26, 28, 45–46,
51, 62, 71, 92
and mission, xix, xxiii, 9, 11, 21,
23–26, 30–32, 35, 37–40,
45–49, 50–51, 59–62, 64, 66,
71, 81, 121, 130
power of, xix, xxiii, 9, 11, 21, 23,
30–31, 38–40, 45–46, 48–49,
51, 66, 130
prophetic inspiration of, 25, 45,
49–51, 121
as prosecutor, 60–61
and unity, 81
as witness, 60, 64, 66
honor, 9, 35, 76–77, 97, 99–101
hope, 77, 91, 94–95, 105–7, 116,
125
hospitality, 11, 19, 33, 41, 125

household, 29, 40, 42, 101–3
household code, 101
humility, 4, 9–10, 27, 76–77, 81,
84, 105–6, 131, 133

identity, missional, xxiv, 19–21, 34,
41, 55–56, 71, 76, 79–80,
83–84, 89, 91, 96–99, 104–7,
116, 118, 124, 130–32, 135
idolatry, 35, 43–44, 97, 102, 105,
114, 117, 119–21, 127, 132
imagination, transformed, xxiv,
118–20, 126, 132
immigrant, 89, 96–97, 102, 131
Israel. *See* story: of Israel
as light to the nations, 3, 6, 19,
47, 54, 82
restoration of, 3–6, 14, 21, 25,
28, 46–47

Jerusalem, 6, 9, 17, 25, 31, 33–34,
39–40, 43, 45, 47–48, 50–51,
60
Jerusalem Council, 41–43
Jesus
abiding in, 62, 66–67
authority of, 7, 10–16, 22, 30
death of, xxiii, 1–2, 6, 10, 24–25,
31, 34, 46–47, 56, 58, 68–70,
73, 76–77, 84, 90, 92–93,
106, 112–13, 116, 122, 127,
131–32
earthly ministry of, 5–9, 11,
15–18, 21, 26–28, 36–38,
50–51, 56–59, 133
incarnation of, 54–56, 69–70, 76,
130
as Lord, 5, 7, 11, 13–14, 16, 22,
30–33, 35, 39, 44, 62, 65–66,
75–77, 83, 84, 87, 106, 112,
131

169

riches, 115, 119–20, 125
righteousness, 19, 21, 60–61,
    77–78, 105
Roman colony, 75, 80–81, 84–85
Roman emperor, 64, 75, 79–81,
    83–85, 97, 101, 117, 122–23
Roman Empire, 34, 75, 77, 80–81,
    83–84, 96–97, 112–13,
    117–20, 122–24, 132

sacrifice, Jesus's death as, 58, 68,
    91–92, 112–13, 116, 131
salvation, xviii, xix, 8, 24–33, 36,
    42, 46–47, 49, 52, 63, 66,
    77–78, 81, 90–91, 93–95,
    105–6, 130, 133
Samaritans, 17, 36–37, 39–40, 51,
    55, 57, 60, 63, 65, 70
Satan, conflict with, 13, 16, 27,
    29–30, 32, 35, 45, 61, 112,
    114, 121. *See also* demons,
    driving out; powers, hostile
scripture
    appropriating for today, 134–36
    missional reading of, xvii–xxiv,
    134–35
sermon
    Jesus's Nazareth synagogue,
    25–28, 33, 38, 45, 50
    Paul's in Athens, 44–45, 50
    Paul's in Lystra, 43–44, 50
    Peter's at Pentecost, 31–32, 50
Sermon on the Mount, 4, 8, 18–19,
    101
servant of Yahweh, 4, 32, 47, 49,
    54, 76, 93
shalom, 43, 63. *See also* peace
shepherding, mission as, 48, 66
signs and wonders. *See* miracles
slavery, 11, 28, 58, 75–77, 83, 85,
    93–94, 98, 100–102

social justice, 9–10, 19, 28, 34–35,
    119, 125, 127
story
    of Christ, xxiii, 3–4, 25, 30, 73,
    75–77, 83–85, 90–92, 106,
    112–13, 121–23, 127, 131–32
    entering the, xxiii, 22, 24, 45, 49,
    51–52, 83–85, 90–91, 123,
    129
    of God's mission, xviii, xix–xxiii,
    24, 26, 51–52, 90–92, 110–
    13, 123–24
    of Israel, xxiii, 1–4, 91–92, 129,
    132
    V-shaped, 73, 75–77, 83–85,
    87–88, 131
suffering, 8, 11, 21, 51, 70, 74–81,
    84, 89, 90–94, 97–98, 102,
    105–7, 120–21, 131, 134–36

table fellowship. *See* meals, mission
    and
tax collectors and sinners, 29,
    36–37, 39, 50
teaching, mission of, 7–9, 11–12,
    15–16, 18–19, 21, 30–31,
    33–34, 37, 45, 50, 56–57, 60,
    71, 130
temple, Jerusalem, 7, 9, 33, 40
theological interpretation, xvi
trinitarian mission, xxiii–xix, 18, 46,
    54, 60–61, 67–68, 130
Trinity, xxiii–xix, 18, 46, 54, 60–61,
    67–68, 130
truth, 55–56, 60, 64, 68–69, 81,
    112, 120–21
Twelve, the, 6, 10–12, 14, 30, 61

vision, xxiv, 28, 41, 110–19,
    121–26, 132

CPSIA information can be obtained at www.ICGtesting.com
Printed in the USA
LVOW07s0502180915

454582LV00006B/7/P